Sociology, work and i

CW00321571

By the same author
The Personnel Managers: a study in the sociology of work and employment

Sociology, work and industry

Tony J. Watson
Principal lecturer in Industrial Sociology, Trent Polytechnic

ROUTLEDGE & KEGAN PAUL
London, Boston, Melbourne and Henley

First published in 1980
by Routledge & Kegan Paul plc
39 Store Street, London WC1E 7DD,
9 Park Street, Boston, Mass. 02108, USA
464 St Kilda Road, Melbourne,
Victoria 3004, Australia and
Broadway House, Newtown Road,
Henley-on-Thames, Oxon RG9 1EN
Photoset in 10 on 12 Plantin by
Kelly Typesetting Ltd, Bradford-on-Avon, Wiltshire
and printed in Great Britain by
Whitstable Litho Ltd, Whitstable, Kent
Reprinted 1981, 1982 and 1983

British Library Cataloguing in Publication Data

Watson, Tony J.
Sociology, work and industry.
1. Industrial sociology
I. Title
301.5'5   HD6955   80 40232

ISBN 0 7100 0542 3
ISBN 0 7100 0543 1 Pbk

Contents

Figures

Introduction

The aim of this text is not simply to produce an account of the work done to date by sociologists in the field of work and industry. My purpose, rather, is to provide an introduction to such work in the context of putting forward a justification and a rationale for the sociological study of this, and other, areas of social life. But to make it more likely that the sociology of work may fulfil the kind of potential which I believe it to have I feel that it needs to be developed in two ways. First, it needs to overcome its current subdivision into often mutually exclusive areas of study – occupations, organisations, work, industrial relations and so on. And, second, it needs to examine the coherence of the conceptual and theoretical thinking on which it is based. The present work represents an attempt at consolidation in both of these respects.

In *Sociology, Work and Industry* I am attempting to provide a text which can be both useful to those studying industrial sociology as a specialism within their wider sociological studies and of value to those with a more direct or practical interest in the world of work who wish to learn how sociological thinking might contribute to their understanding in this area. Primarily with this latter audience in mind – but by no means exclusively – I have made the first chapter of the text an introduction to the discipline of sociology itself. In writing this, and indeed the rest of the book, I have drawn on my own experience of the industrial world as an employee, researcher and teacher and have tried to pass on some idea of the ways in which sociological thinking can be an aid to one's understanding of the problems, dilemmas, rewards and delights which arise in the world of work.

In writing this book I have striven hard to achieve a level of integration which I feel to be lacking in many works in this area. I hope that I have gone some way towards achieving my desired level of integration by my giving the book its own built-in introduction to the sociological discipline, by my making clear the assumptions on which my arguments and organisation are based, by providing a theoretical framework in which subsequent analysis and the reporting of the work of others is contained, and by the constant relating back of the issues which arise in the spheres of individual work experience, occupations, organisations, industrial conflict and the rest to the ways in which industrial capitalist society has developed and is currently organised with all its potentials, conflicts, strengths and contradictions. At first sight it may appear that my chapter organisation simply reflects the old subdivisions of the sociologies of industrial society, work, occupations, organisations and industrial relations rather than transcending them. This, however, I hope is not the case. The headings which I use are the ones I find the most useful available and the links which I make between the chapters themselves together with the basic links from the content of each chapter back to the theoretical framework and back to my characterisation of industrial capitalist society should help avoid the danger of any one aspect of the working world being regarded as fully understandable in isolation from the others.

Despite my interest in the reconsolidation of the sociological study of work and my aim of producing an integrated account of it, I do recognise that some students and readers will wish to concentrate on one aspect of the field rather than on others or may wish to approach the various areas in an order different from the one in which these chapters are set out. I am well aware that a book like this is not always read from the beginning through to the end! Consequently, I provide cross references between chapters and allusions back to earlier arguments whenever necessary so that readers primarily interested in, say, organisations or industrial conflict can take the relevant chapter as their 'way in' to the book. To help further the reader wanting to see how any particular section of the book relates to the analysis as a whole I have provided the following outline of the book.

Chapter 1: The nature and problems of sociological analysis: Sociology is seen as having developed alongside the institutions of industrial capitalism – institutions which sociologists have been concerned to understand and with which sociology might help people to come to terms. The discipline, it is claimed, can continue to fill such a role, helping people to choose whether and how they might change, preserve or adjust social institutions and ways of living. The distinctive characteristics of sociological thinking are established and the use of basic insights and typical concepts illustrated by their application to examples of the types of problem which tend to arise in the world of work and industry. The typical methods and procedures of sociological investigation are discussed with particular attention being paid to the scientific claims of the discipline, and the variety of research techniques which are used is illustrated in an imagined industrial research project. The ethical, practical and political implications of sociological research and its dissemination are then considered and, finally, the problem of the current subdividing of the areas covered by the sociology of work is described and the associated difficulty of the diversity and range of existing theoretical perspectives within sociology is explained. The scene is thus set for the attempted consolidation in the next chapter.

Chapter 2: The sociological analysis of work and industry: It is pointed out that the existing components of the sociology of work and industry range from ones intended to be practical and manipulative to ones based on a radical and critical interest. Five theoretical strands of the sociology of work, falling within this range, are then identified. First, the *managerial-psychologistic* strand which includes both 'scientific management' thinking and the partly contrasting work of the 'behavioural science entrepreneurs' is considered. Second, the *Durkheim-systems* contribution is reviewed, followed, third, by an account of the American *interactionists*. The fourth strand is that of *Weber-social action* and, fifth, the insights of *Marxian* analysis are considered. To achieve a more consolidated framework for the subsequent examination of the area of work and industry with which this book is concerned a basic theoretical scheme is developed. Here the assumptions with regard to human nature, to social organisation in general, to industrial capitalist society in particular and to the place of organisations, individuals and groups within such societies are made clear. These are the assumptions, and the conceptual apparatus derived from them, on which the organisation and presentation of material from across the existing literature of the sociology of work is to be based in the following chapters.

Chapter 3: The industrialised society: Here the basic features, both structural and ideological, of the advanced industrial capitalist society are reviewed. The necessity of rejecting popular deterministic views of the development of contemporary society in favour of an approach which recognises the importance of human initiative, politics and conflict of interest is argued and this is taken up in an attempt to distinguish the essential characteristics of the industrial capitalist type of society. The development of contemporary societies of this type is then outlined and the range of ways in which contradictions, paradoxes and conflicts run through them established. The contradictions and tensions which will later be seen to underlie so many of the problems in the sphere of work and industry are then considered by looking at four particular areas of contemporary society: class and power; government, politics and welfare; culture, values and education; sexual divisions, the home and the family.

Chapter 4: Work and the individual: Having now considered the basic theoretical issues and the structural context in which work is carried out, the level of analysis is switched to the working individual who operates in this structural context. The focus is not an individualistic psychological one but is on human beings as social individuals. The relationship between the nature of man in general and the work which people do is therefore reviewed with currently popular social psychological views being considered alongside Marxian assumptions in this area. Questions are raised about both the assumed human need for 'self-actualisation' at work and the widely discussed pathology of 'alienation'. To help understand better the relationships between the intrinsic and the extrinsic satisfactions which can be derived from work the idea of 'work orientation' is discussed and the idea developed to show how an interplay goes on between individual choice and initiative at work and the shifting structural and contextual conditions in which these occur. The processes whereby people end up in particular work settings are then examined and the dynamics of the relationship between employers and employees based on an 'implicit contract' established. The sources and conditions of the rewards and the deprivations experienced by different people in different kinds of work are then considered with particular attention being paid to the role of technology. From this the focus is then moved to the complex and two-way relationship which exists between the work which people do and the way they lead their lives outside of work.

Chapter 5: The structuring of work – occupations: The first of the two principles which underlies the structural context in which the individual works is the focus of attention here: the occupational principle of work structuring. The nature of an occupation is examined and the relationship between occupations and formal organisations discussed. The occupational structure of advanced industrial capitalist society is considered with attention being given to the relationship between occupation and class, to the division of labour in society and to suggestions that a shift is occurring in occupational structures whereby a new type of society – a 'post-industrial' one – is emerging. The intention of the second half of the chapter is to look more closely at specific occupations but, instead of simply running through and describing a list of such occupations, the strategy is followed of using specific occupations to illustrate the six headings which I believe can be generally applied in the process of analysing occupations. Consequently I give examples of how one can examine the structural location of an occupation; the recruitment and socialisation procedures of an occupation; the tendency towards occupational association and the use of strategies to increase autonomy of members; the culture and ideologies developed within occupations and, finally, the possible existence of so-called occupational communities.

Chapter 6: The structuring of work – organisations: Having earlier pointed to a problematic relationship existing between occupations and formal work organisations it is now claimed that it is the organisational, administrative or bureaucratic principle of work structuring which is the currently dominating one. This is related to the association between the spread of large employing organisations and the changing patterns of class and power which have occurred with the rise of industrial capitalism. The involvement of organis-ations in wider patterns of power and advantage has led to con-siderable problems in the field of organisation theory – a body of thought whose ideological implications are considered here prior to the setting out of what is seen as a more successfully *sociological* way of viewing work organisations. Central to this view is a conception of organisation structure as something which is not pregiven but which emerges from the relationships and behaviour of the actors who make it up and from the interplay between what I call the 'official control' aspects and the 'unofficial' aspects of organisational patterning. Also central is the idea that the structuring of organisations is based upon work design criteria which are congruent with the interests of the most advantaged groups in society. But the contradictions which exist in society as a whole are seen as also leading to a host of contradictory tendencies, conflicts and 'dysfunctions' in organisations themselves. And this fact is shown to account for much of what goes on within organisations as these tensions are played out and attempts at adaptation made. Among the adaptations to control structures which are looked at are ones which have recognised, at the lower levels, the limits to the validity of 'scientific management' principles and, at the higher levels of structure, the limits of the applicability of the administrative principles which classical organisation theory put forward as prescriptions for organisational design.

Chapter 7: Conflict, challenge and defence in work: The emphasis here turns away from controls exerted by dominant interests in work organisations to the efforts and accommodations of the subordinate, the disadvantaged and the aspiring although, once again, these are set in the wider context of the structure and dynamics of the type of society in which they occur. The conflicts which are discussed are those between people at work and their peers, customers and clients as well as their employers. The basic concern is with divergences of interest and orientation between individuals and groups in the course of their work lives and, to evaluate the variety of possible ways of looking at conflict at work, three typical approaches are examined: the unitary, the plural and the radical. Following this, what is believed to be an appropriate framework for studying conflict is set out. Attention is then given to the variety of ways in which people at work adjust to the exigencies of their situation and defend their personal and group autonomy. Attention is then turned away from the relatively spontaneous activities discussed here to the more strategic mobilisation of interest and uses of sanctions which occurs in workplaces in a variety of forms ranging from job control practices to unionisation and from 'resistance to change' to strike action.

Chapter 8: Individual, work and society – choice and possibility: Sociology is seen as a human resource which can help people consciously and rationally control social institutions. In proposing that sociology should be used to *inform* democratic political debate about means and ends, at all levels of social life, alternative possibilities of sociology's becoming either a 'servant of power' or the privatised pursuit of disengaged academics are rejected. To illustrate the ways in which sociological thinking can be applied to the possibilities, paradoxes and problems of work and society in the future, consideration is given to a range of different images of future: a professionalised society, a corporate society, an order based on the 'small is beautiful' principle, a more purely market-based economy, an economy based on principles of industrial democracy (socialist or otherwise), a service-orientated post-industrial society, and a self-service society. Following this, it is argued that sociological understanding is not only relevant to issues at this grand level of social change: it is equally helpful to the everyday practitioner who is more concerned with the problems of 'Monday morning' than with questions of the 'millennium'. However, it is then suggested that at whatever level sociological thinking is applied, its essential characteristic is its concern to relate every issue, however microscopic, back to questions about the way society is organised. And such questions are ones vital to achieving democratic control over work, industry and all other social institutions.

Complementary and further reading

Among texts which are complementary to this one and which deal with fairly broad aspects of the sociology of work are Eldridge (1971a), Fox (1971) and Parker *et al.* (1977). Useful collections of readings are Child (ed.) (1973), Esland *et al.* (eds) (1975) and Weir (ed.) (1973). To follow up chapter 1 I would recommend the introductory text in sociology by Worsley (ed.) (1977) and suggest as back-up to this Berger (1966), Bryant (1976), Mills (1970) and Bottomore and Nisbet (eds) (1979). To extend the coverage of chapter 2, Rose (1975) is invaluable and useful for chapter 3 are Brown and Harrison (1978), Giddens (1973), Kumar (1978), Lipset (1976) and various of the readings in Scase (ed.) (1977). To follow up chapter 4, I would recommend Anthony (1977), Carter (1966), Fox (1971), Parker (1971), Terkel (1977), Weir (ed.) (1976) and Willis (1977). Among the many books on the sociology of occupations, particularly helpful for chapter 5 are Dunkerley (1975a), Johnson (1972), Larson (1977), Montagna (1977), Ritzer (1972) and Watson (1977a). For chapter 6, relevant books and articles are those by Albrow (1970), Braverman (1974), Child (1972 and 1977), Elger (1975), Grusky and Miller (eds) (1970), Pettigrew (1973), Salaman and Thompson (eds) (1973), Silverman (1970) and Sofer (1972). Helpful for chapter 7 are Banks (1974), Beynon (1973), Bowen (1976), Clarke and Clements (1977), Eldridge (1975), Fox (1974), Hill and Thurley (1974), Hyman (1977a and 1977b), Hyman and Brough (1975) and Hyman and Fryer (1975). Among the many books which follow up issues discussed in chapter 8 are Cherns (1979), Fay (1975), Dickson (1974), Gershuny (1978), Kumar (1978), Rex (1974) and Vanek (ed.) (1975).

The bibliography at the end of this book gives the full references for these works and all of those cited in the body of the text. It also contains books and articles which are not cited in the text but which are felt to be of interest and value to students of the sociology of work and industry generally.

Chapter 1

The nature and problems of sociological analysis

The sociological project

Sociology is an academic discipline, but it is much more than this. It represents one of the many attempts made by modern men and women to make sense of the world in which they find themselves. It involves attempts to contribute to the understanding of people's predicaments in the world. In this it promises help with the problem of *coping*, whether coping is seen as involving attempts to change, preserve or simply adjust to given institutions or ways of living.

There is nothing new about social thought, of course. Thinkers have reflected on and made generalisations about social life since ancient times. Two things make sociology a modern phenomenon. First, it constitutes a systematic or 'scientific' attempt to analyse social relationships and patterns and, second, it tends to deal with problems which have developed in an especially acute form in recent times. These are the problems associated with all those changes which have occurred in societies which have experienced the process of industrialisation: the disruption of traditional communities, the stress placed on the individual and the smaller family unit, the development of factories, bureaucracies and large-scale urban living, and so on. Accompanying all this, if not underlying it, have been major changes in the ways that work is organised and experienced.

Whilst studying work sociologically, we must not forget that sociology itself tends to be a form of work. This means that it too has been caught up in the increasing division of labour and the growing specialisation within occupations which has occurred over the past two hundred or more years. The rise of sociology has paralleled the rise of industry and it can be seen as having within it the potential for an ongoing and critical examination of the institutions associated with industrialism. However, because it has taken its place in the modern organisational world as the province of the specialised professional academic, it is in constant danger of becoming the peculiar concern of an occupational group in whose interest it well may be to maintain their area of study as a specialism – with its esoteric language and special mystique contributing to and symbolising membership of a prestigious élite. But this is not the only possibility. Another aspect of the modern industrial society is a relatively developed education system, alongside which we tend to find expectations on the part of members of society for some kind of democratic involvement in the running of that society. It is, therefore, possible that instead of the educational system simply providing slots for sociology professors to earn a living by teaching a small number of undergraduate sociologists, it might equip a much wider range of pupils, students, trainees, as well as a more general audience, with the insights and analytical apparatus of sociology.

In the past, social thinkers were a tiny minority addressing a slightly larger minority of the population. The modern age is one of vastly increased literacy and access to schooling and communication media. This means that critical reflection on the values and institutions of society need no longer be the preserve of the privileged social philosopher or the dilettante intellectual of a leisured class. An ability to be analytical about social, economic and political issues could be developed in every citizen – this furthering the ideal of democratic *control* of society and its institutions. Whether sociologists and sociology (as well as other social sciences) are up to this is, of course, another matter, but it is a conception of the sociological project worth exploring: that sociology should address as wide an audience as possible, not watering down its substance but striving to make its inherited and developing concepts and analytical potential comprehensible to those involved in the everyday and 'practical' worlds as well as to those in the professional-academic sphere. From this one would hope that within the present area of concern – work and industry – we might see the worker, the manager, the engineer, the trade unionist, the provider and the user of goods and services able to make better-informed judgments about the world of work and perhaps contribute towards ensuring that human beings control economic institutions and not, as many feel to be the case nowadays, the other way round.

This may appear to be an ambitious project for sociology but it is conceived in the belief that sociology is not automatically owed a living by its host society. Sociology should turn a critical eye on itself as it goes about its business, and sociologists should strive to indicate just where they can make a contribution and point out just where their work might have a relevance. It is not felt here that the sociological study of work is to be justified by the manipulative potential which it might hold for the administrator. I cannot deny that such a potential exists but feel personally bound to argue for a wider conception. This is a conception in the tradition of some of the classical sociologists of the past who, as I shall now try to show, established the basic framework of the discipline – a framework which is relevant today and will be relevant in the future.

It may seem strange to the person approaching sociology for the first time to note that modern contributors to the discipline, and the present work will be no exception, are always harking back to writers of the past. Not only do we find that a high proportion of the books on the library sociology shelves are studies of sociology's 'founding fathers' but we also find that sociologists who are analysing contemporary issues frequently depend on such figures as Marx, Durkheim, Simmel, Weber, Mead or Parsons – all of whom are dead – for their insights, concepts, models or styles of investigation. Does this dependence on founding figures arise because sociologists as a type are looking for some sort of hero or a father figure or is it, rather, that in recent years the discipline has simply not produced thinkers of the calibre of these giants and that one is thus forced to look to the past for inspiration? There may be truth in both of these suggestions but they are not complete explanations. A better explanation for our continued reference to the ideas of the writers of the past and, in particular, to the big three, whom we shall meet shortly, Marx, Weber and Durkheim, is that they lived in the same *type* of society in which we find ourselves today but that they, unlike ourselves, lived in a period when the essential features of this type of society, together with its fundamental problems, were more visible and could be observed more acutely. To understand the basic features of the modern way of life we need to refer back to those who were able to observe it as it was developing. The places and period in which Marx, Weber and Durkheim lived – England, Germany and France in the nineteenth and early twentieth centuries – were such that industrial capitalism (and ideas about it) was sufficiently well developed for its basic features to be observable whilst it was, as yet, insufficiently *established* for its institutions, assumptions and values to have become as near to being taken for granted as they are today.

As an illustration of the need and the value of looking to these thinkers of the past let us take that institution whose significance is frequently seen as crucial by contemporary sociologists: social class. Those phenomena identified as class-based are so taken for granted that non-sociologists tend to deny their significance if not their very existence. The existence of social class as a basic feature of social structure was strikingly apparent to the founding sociologists and, by reading their analyses, we are sensitised to the existence of similar, albeit further developed phenomena in our own times. To read Marx and Weber on the ways in which inequalities were structured in their times, without necessarily accepting the evaluations of either man, is to gain incomparable insights into our contemporary situations and invaluable leads for our own investigations.

A generalisation which can be drawn from the above argument is that the person who can analyse a social situation most effectively is he who is in some way on the *margin* of that situation whilst, at the same time, having fairly close knowledge of it. For example, the cripple among the fit may be able to say more about 'being fit' than the fit themselves and the Scot living in England may be more observant about English customs than the Englishman. Even more prosaically, the day-shift worker doing temporary night-shift work may observe 'night-shift life' far more sharply than those who have always worked on nights can ever do. One of the first thinkers to write in what we would now see as a sociological vein, Adam Ferguson, came from a Gaelic-speaking Highland background into lowland eighteenth-century Scottish society to make his particular contribution to the important intellectual production of that time and place. The alien-within is especially well fitted to observe and to analyse. The best known sociological founding fathers were often 'marginal men' in a personal sense, whether because of *émigré* status, Jewish background, or conflicting political and religious influences within their families. More important than this is their historical marginality: their being caught up in the European transitions following from the French and Industrial Revolutions, the Enlightenment and, going back even further, the Reformation.

We can see, in psychological terms, those who created sociology as men writing partly to cope with their personal marginality but we can also, and more importantly, see their work as a social product: as a striving to make sense of the dislocations of their age. Their attempts to make sense of their situation are invaluable to us because these men, in an historical location more marginal than our own, were better able than we are to look at the industrial capitalist world in the light of *conceptions of alternatives*. This is their humanistic significance. I shall be arguing later that what makes humans essentially different from other animals is that they can make choices of a peculiar kind: choices based on abstract and evaluatively based conceptions of alternatives. The founding sociologists were perhaps more aware of alternatives on a societal level than we are because they were better placed historically to contrast the modern with the traditional, the urban with the rural, the class with the estate, the secular with the religious and so on. This, combined with the great interest of their age in primitive and ancient social orders, helped to inspire their analyses with the most basic sociological insight of all: that there is more than one way and one way only for men and women to organise their lives. To put this another way, we might say that the way society *is* is not necessarily the way society has to be. In the realm of work this means that the way we currently organise production and distribution does not possess some immutable inevitability – it is only one of a range of possibilities.

The doing of sociology, I am suggesting, is dependent on an awareness of the possibilities of alternative forms of community. Throughout the history of social thought we find people looking at their own social worlds in the light of conceptions of alternative forms of community. Sometimes these are backward-looking, where people compare their own age with a past 'golden age', a garden of Eden or an Arcadia. These conceptions may, on the other hand, be forward-looking where the present is compared to the coming Utopia, Kingdom of God or perhaps the perfect communist society. Conceptions of this type, however implicit or semi-consciously held, underlie all social thought: they are needed, if only as rough benchmarks for measuring and evaluating the present. These conceptions are informed by certain sentiments and it might be argued that whenever the social thinker speaks or writes of 'community' he is in some way involved in the pursuit of some ideal model of living together, some conception based on the ideal of the warm, close, intimate, co-operative and meaningful *family*.

Sociology can be seen as involved in some kind of pursuit of community in this sense, sometimes using as its comparative model a conception of the supposedly integrated small-scale community of the past and, at other times, images of a rational planned society of the future. Perhaps something similar can be said of all the planning and thinking which people do about how they are to organise their lives. By this 'pursuit of community' here I mean the seeking, in principle, of an ideal or authentic form of social organisation. Such conceptions are brought into play, for example, in formal politics with one party encouraging a conception of community based on a 'free' market whilst another argues for a conception based on 'rational' planning and equality. Different conceptions of community also underlie thinking at a lower level of planning. For example, different approaches to the management of work involve various conceptions of the ideal. The advocates of the variety of organisational and managerial policies and strategies to be considered later in this book – from that of industrial democracy to such things as job enrichment programmes – imply particular directions in the pursuit of community. I have suggested that all these notions of community, these ideals of meaningful and co-operative living together, are dependent at root on some analogy with an ideal of *family*, but the specific way in which the ideal is conceived is always influenced by the values and, especially, the interests of the particular individual or group articulating and advocating that conception. In a world of competing and conflicting interests we should expect competing notions of the ideal to be on offer, but this is to look ahead. Let us for the moment confine our attentions to the discipline of sociology and to the importance to it of the concept of community.

The glue which held together the fabric of European society giving it stability and a widespread taken-for-grantedness had been coming unstuck for some centuries prior to the time in which sociology emerged. The Reformation saw a questioning of the authority of the Catholic Church and with the emergence of Protestantism and dissent came a trend towards an increased emphasis in social life on the conscience, duties and rights of the individual (as opposed to the collectivity) and a developing rational (as opposed to traditional) approach to life. Later the rational and critical spirit of the eighteenth century's Enlightenment brought under close scrutiny institutions of religion, inequality, kinship, property and monarchy – institutions which were to be severely disturbed and often overturned by the two revolutions: the French and the industrial. Nisbet in *The Social Philosophers* (1976) argues that a 'quest for community' lies behind all western social philosophy, and he points to the importance of social upheaval in stimulating such thinking and in *The Sociological Tradition* (1970) he shows how the discipline of sociology can be seen as emerging as part of intellectual concern to reconsolidate and restore some of the order which had been undermined by the two revolutions. The most 'fundamental and far-reaching' concept in sociology, he argues, is that of community, this referring to 'social bonds characterised by emotional cohesion, depth, continuity and fullness'.

Nisbet emphasises the philosophically conservative aspects of the new discipline and he probably goes too far in this. Another contemporary writer, Dawe (1970), says that although some of the classical sociologists can be seen as largely in *reaction*, others were operating in a more positive Enlightenment spirit, showing less concern with the pursuit of *order* than with man's *control* over social institutions. Nevertheless, we can accept that, in broad terms, sociology emerged in response to the ways in which the traditional elements of European society had been, as Nisbet puts it, 'dislocated by revolution' and 'scrambled by industrialism and the forces of democracy' and that it was involved in 'theoretical efforts to reconsolidate' these elements of power, wealth and status; that is 'put them in perspectives having philosophic and scientific relevance to the new age'. Where the forces of modernism were stressing the importance of the *individual*, the virtue of thinking for one*self*, and the necessity of *self*-interest, sociology was partly reacting by stressing the social, and warning of the dangers accompanying the ongoing loss of community. If order was no longer to be found in tradition and the work of God it might be sought through careful and rational attention to the nature of society and its institutions. Figure 1.1, although a gross simplification of historical trends, indicates the direction of the shifts in social, political and economic life which saw the emergence of sociology.

Of all the changes occurring during the period of sociology's growth perhaps the most immediately felt and striking were those following from the industrial revolution. These changes in the organisation of work and their wider ramifications should not be seen in isolation but, for present purposes, it is useful to concentrate on the way in which the new discipline of sociology was part of the intellectual response to these major industrial changes. The stimulus to sociology provided by the industrial revolution is such that we might see a concern with work and industry as fundamental to the early growth of the discipline. The same might be said of its future.

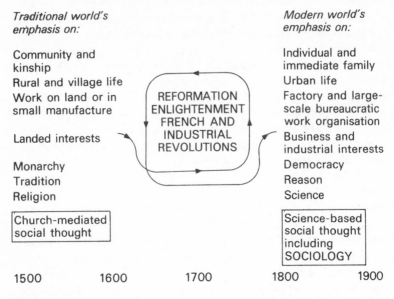

Traditional world's emphasis on:		Modern world's emphasis on:
Community and kinship		Individual and immediate family
Rural and village life	REFORMATION	Urban life
Work on land or in small manufacture	ENLIGHTENMENT FRENCH AND INDUSTRIAL	Factory and large-scale bureaucratic work organisation
Landed interests	REVOLUTIONS	Business and industrial interests
Monarchy		Democracy
Tradition		Reason
Religion		Science

Church-mediated social thought

Science-based social thought including SOCIOLOGY

1500   1600   1700   1800   1900

Fig. 1.1 Sociology in historical context

Nisbet points to five crucial aspects of the industrial revolution which were 'to prove most evocative of sociological response, most directive in the formation of sociological problem and concept'. These were: (1) *The condition of labour*, where both the radical and the conservative showed shock and concern at a new type of degradation, that of working people torn away from their traditional guild, village and family settings. (2) *The transformation of property*, in which abstract shares, stocks and the depersonalised medium of cash brought a new fluidity and calculative morality into play, replacing the social stability and set of allegiances inspired by landed wealth. What kind of social order could exist when relationships were increasingly dominated by cash payments?

(3) *The industrial city*, which saw the breaking up of the natural rhythms of the countryside and its replacement by artificial pressures, rootlessness and alienation of the urban sprawl. (4) and (5) *Technology* and *the factory system*, where the regimentation, the division of labour and machine-pacing degraded both the work and the worker.

However much these reactions, observable among radical and conservative alike, may have depended on unrealistic assumptions of an idyllic rural past, they nevertheless inspired analytical interest as well as moral fervour. Here were problems on a massive scale, problems inviting rational scientific reflection and hard analysis as well as literary comment and political protest. However, sociology, for all its scientific pretensions, was inspired, Nisbet stresses, by moral concerns which it shared with philosophers, writers and activists of a range of sentiments, from the radical to the ultra-conservative.

The ways in which some of the classical sociologists grappled with these problems, with all their inadequacies and personal biases, can give us important leads today. Durkheim's recognition of what he termed 'pathological' trends in the changing division of labour and its attendant undermining of social norms has relevance to contemporary problems of wages competition and inflation as well as to current debates about the alleged need to 'enrich' jobs; Marx's concern about alienation and his emphasis on the underlying conflict between capital and labour have a similar relevance to everyday issues ranging from workplace skirmishes to political and industrial policies of the state; whilst Weber's emphasis on the rationalising trend underlying our history is as helpful to our understanding of the deskilling experienced by such people as modern newspaper printers as it is to our appreciation of the impact of massive bureaucracies and multi-national corporations on individual freedom and the survival, let alone the growth, of democracy. Industrial sociology in the twentieth century has concerned itself largely with small-scale plant investigations and with administrative problems. This it can continue to do, but a fuller potential might be realised by the sociological study of work and industry if it sets its efforts in the wider, morally-informed tradition established by those who, in creating the discipline, demonstrated the importance of locating even the most individual or private act in the context of large-scale historical processes and in the nature and structure of society itself.

Having said this, one is bound to emphasise that the talk of a 'tradition' is not to deny the plurality of approaches existing within sociology. Although in the next section I shall try to write about the nature of sociological thinking at a general level, the subsequent sections of this chapter and the next will reveal the extent of the diversities existing within the discipline. These may be regretted, but to work through them, I suggest, is to help to understand better the diversities and indeed paradoxes existing within social life itself. Once having recognised and accounted for the existing plurality of approaches we can move towards a basic set of working assumptions and concepts which will be applied to the areas of real life to be considered in the subsequent chapters.

Thinking sociologically

Sociology is concerned with how people relate to each other. It looks at how human beings organise both themselves and each other. In looking at how people behave and think it tries to detect patterns or 'structures' which underlie social life. These patterns are seen as both the outcome of the activities of individuals and as something which, in turn, influences, encourages and constrains the individual. This is not easy to grasp, stated abstractly in this way, and before illustrating how we can apply this perspective it might be helpful to look at how human behaviour tends to be explained in everyday or 'man-in-the-street' – as opposed to sociological – thinking.

What I would suggest happens in everyday thinking in this sense is that simple explanations are often found to be sufficient and that these explanations therefore rarely do justice to the complexity of the ways in which human activity is an outcome of individual characteristics and, *at the same time*, is a result of social patterns and influences. Thus, explanations tend to be confined to either individual characteristics (*individualistic* explanations) or to social factors (*holistic* explanations). Examples of these, contrasted with a possible sociological explanation are represented schematically in Figure 1.2.

In the examples shown in Fig. 1.2 I have deliberately chosen a phenomenon which is currently topical amongst both social scientists and those participating in lounge-bar or coffee-break discussions. Despite first appearances, it is by no means a trivial issue: the nature of the explanations which ultimately prevail in this area of child upbringing will have considerable implications for how we organise ourselves socially in the future, in the family, the schools, and the workplace. This fact, whilst indicating the importance of developing sociological explanations, also raises certain problems which are inherent in such a task. Note, for instance, how the sociological statement is rather tentative and thus somewhat lacking in that quality of certainty which is so important to a sense of security in everyday life. This tentative tone ('in so far as . . .', 'not necessarily on the basis of . . .') implies the need for investigation, the collection of contemporary data and an examination of the processes of the past.

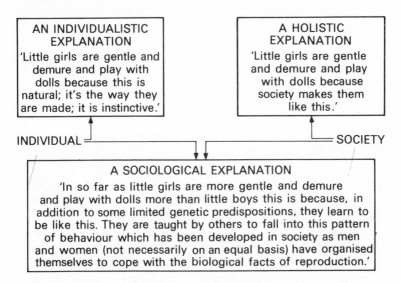

Fig. 1.2 Examples of individualistic, holistic and sociological explanation

Added to the challenge of rigorous investigation in sociology is that of coping with the very complexity of the issues which are to be taken into account. This is not simply the result of the existence of a large *number* of factors or variables to be considered but follows from the fact that we must look at the *inter-weaving* of these factors. In our example one could imagine an open-minded non-sociologist, having listened to examples of the two one-sided explanations (the individualistic and the holistic), saying, 'Ah well, neither explanation is good enough: it's really a matter of a bit of both – it's partly the physical make up of girls and it's partly society.' This may be an advance, but it does not go far enough to constitute a useful sociological analysis: the sociologist has got to confront the complexities of the *interplay* of the two elements – the individual and the social. The possible sociological explanation offered in Fig. 1.2 illustrates this. Between the individual factors of 'the biological facts of reproduction' and the social factors of girls being 'taught by others' are various distinctively sociological notions referring to patterns of behaviour, inequality, historical development and social organisation. This suggests how we might recognise sociological thinking. Sociology is not simply the study of the social. It is, rather, a study of the interrelationships between the individual and the social which makes use of a distinctive range of concepts such as structure, process, culture, norms, values and so on. To appreciate the distinctiveness of sociological analysis we must look closer at these key concepts. Appreciation of them is vital to any recognition of the nature of sociology and to any ability to examine issues of work and industry in a distinctively sociological manner.

Applying what has been called the *sociological imagination* involves switching our focus from the level of the *private problems* of, say, the steelworker faced with redundancy to various contextual *public issues* (Mills 1970). These issues range from the state of the international market in steel and managerial, governmental and trade union policies, to patterns of technological change and the different nature of involvement in that industry of technical and managerial staff on the one hand and manual workers on the other. Sociology, then, shifts the level of focus from that of the close-up to that of the 'big picture', but sociology is not simply to do with producing the broad picture: it necessarily goes beneath the surface to look for the underlying regularities or patterns. When it records these frozen in time it calls them *structures* and when it observes them in movement it calls them *processes*. The sociologist in this case of steel redundancies will want to know about the occupational structure of the industry and the industrial relations processes which go on; he will look at the managerial structures and the ongoing processes of technological change. All this will be set in its historical context and the overall structure of society, its industrial base and its capitalist or its socialist nature. In analysing these structures and processes the sociologist would try to show how they potentially both constrain people as well as enable people to further their personal wishes, noting how they both result from the initiatives of individuals and can be seen to restrain individual initiatives.

To illustrate the interplay of tendencies towards initiative and tendencies towards constraint, let us consider the implications of the threatened steelworkers considering a possible initiative. Let us assume that these men get together and decide that they would like to share out the remaining work – each becoming a part-time worker. The union structure might be used to pursue this aim and existing bargaining arrangements used to argue the case with management. These negotiations might succeed but, before they did, the con- straining aspects of social structure would soon become apparent to those involved. For example, the *norm* in that society or town of each household having a male as the main breadwinner might need to change (norms being part of the underlying pattern of social life – the standards to which people are expected to conform or the rules of conduct whose infringement may result in sanctions intended to encourage conformity). Changing these norms would involve changing *values* (definitions of what is desirable within a group or society) with regard to the place of work in people's lives. Thus the *institutions* of work and family would be affected (an institution being a regularly occurring and therefore normal pattern of actions and relationships) as, potentially, would be the overall *culture* of the society (the sum of the things which people think or do in society, things which are not purely instinctive or totally involuntary). All this may appear to stress the constraining rather than the enabling aspects of social structures and, indeed, sociology often leans this way – afflicting the mind with a pessimism about possible change in social life. Nevertheless, what a full sociological analysis would do would be to examine how these structures developed historically – this analysis in itself reminding us of the existence of social and cultural relativity and suggesting that varieties of social organisation are possible. The maintenance of the status quo, this suggests, is not inevitable. Here we are back to our *conceptions of alternatives* and to the existence of human choice – choices which sociology may be used to inform.

The foregoing arguments and examples are intended to show the distinctiveness of sociological analysis, particularly in contrast with everyday thinking. But it is clear that many of the issues raised are ones where we might expect a contribution from other social sciences. Indeed, it is sometimes argued that the study of the social aspects of work organisation or business should not be performed by a variety of different disciplines but by a general 'behavioural science'. The very rationale behind the present work suggests a rejection of this position. In the first place, the very term 'behavioural science' is to be rejected. This is not so much because of its being coined by social scientists nervous of business clients and worried that research fund donors might confuse social science and socialism but, rather, because of its inaccuracy. Sociology, for example, is not just about social *behaviour* but about socially meaningful behaviour or, in Weber's terms, *social action*. Sociology operates by considering meanings, ideas and the interpretations of human beings as much if not more than by studying their behaviour as such. The actual behaviour of a coalminer preparing for his end of shift shower could well be technically identical to that of a striptease dancer in mid-shift. To fail to take into account the different meanings, the social significance and the motives behind these acts would make sociological nonsense.

The rejection of misleading titles is not terribly important, however. I would argue that it is inappropriate to attempt to conceive of an overall 'social scientific' approach for studying any given area. Human life has too many dimensions for any one discipline to develop models, concepts and theories which do sufficient justice to this complexity whilst remaining simple enough to be manageable. What we need is a minimal division of theoretical labour with people operating within each specialism whilst taking into account the work of those in other specialisms (economists advising on incomes policy, for instance, taking into account psychological and sociological factors). Out of the multiplicity of the disciplines involved in the study of social life we can pick three which are distinguishable primarily by their particular conceptual and analytical styles: psychology, economics and sociology. These are distinguished from other disciplines in the way shown in Figure 1.3.

DISCIPLINES DISTINGUISHED PRIMARILY BY THEIR AREA OF KNOWLEDGE		DISCIPLINES DISTINGUISHED PRIMARILY BY METHODS, CONCEPTS OR STYLES OF ANALYSIS	
social history human geography political science public administration criminology social administration management and business studies organisation studies industrial relations	When these go beyond the descriptive and attempt to explain 'scientifically' they must draw on . . .		psychology economics sociology

Fig. 1.3 The relationship between the three primary social sciences and other disciplines which study the social

If we were to seek an overall social scientific explanation of, say, the case of a particular married woman who is unable to get a job, we might seek a psychological dimension (perhaps her personality and intense nervousness lead to her failing interviews), an economic dimension (maybe wages paid to women in this area would be insufficient to allow her to pay bus fares, child minder, etc.) and a sociological dimension (her husband possibly comes from a culture where working wives are frowned upon). It is conceivable that a single social scientist could give an adequate explanation here, but once we move up to the complexities of explaining, say, a case of major industrial strife, this would be unmanageable. The greatest challenge to an overall explanation would face the person left trying to weave together the contributions from the three disciplines. Any argument that the sociologist is potentially the best fitted for this task in cases of social complexity is inevitably and perhaps justifiably open to charges of sociological imperialism. Nevertheless it could be argued that the whole point of sociology is to relate the individual to the social and that this means taking into account the contributory individual and economic dimensions of the social.

The sociologist trying to explain a particular strike could usefully listen to a psychological analysis of such matters as the personalities of the individuals leading each side and would be dependent on the economist for an expert appraisal of such matters as labour market conditions, relative wage rates and local living costs. All of this has to be thrown into the much bigger picture which is the realm of the sociologist: the patterns and conflicts of interest (employer-employee, craft-semiskilled, male-female etc.), the solidarity or otherwise of local communities, the expectations of work and incomes currently prevailing in the culture both nationally and locally, and so on. Let me stress here that in no way is this to argue for the superiority of sociology in status terms: the very level of generality at which it operates, compared to economics and psychology, is as much the source of its weaknesses as its strength. Its concerns are so diffuse that it often ends up at a level of abstraction where its analyses become almost meaningless to those outside the sociological community. The psychologist's talk of people's needs, attitudes or personalities or the economist's talk of numbers of unemployed or rates of inflation or economic growth will, understandably, be more readily listened to than the sociologist's talk of cultural factors, the changing social structure, or work ideologies. The former ideas are not necessarily more simple. Somehow they are more easily grasped – their relative specificity if not their simplicity makes them manageable.

This suggestion that the level of abstraction involved in applying a sociological perspective makes it difficult to manage implies that people in the 'practical' rather than the academic worlds might be likely to prefer psychological or economic approaches to sociological ones, and, indeed, might think more happily in such terms. Particularly important in this is the fact that economic and psychological variables are often more manipulable than those of sociology or, at least they are often seen to be so. Economic variables are characteristically measurable and economic policy and much business activity is devoted to manipulating them. Psychological variables are correspondingly manageable: if a management difficulty can be put down to some individual's personality problem you can either sack the individual or send him for therapy; if managers' or employees' attitudes need to be changed you can attempt persuasion or 'improve communication'. Paradoxically, psychological thinking also has the opposite virtue. Psychological factors which are not manipulable – things like basic human needs or 'instincts' – cannot be changed and therefore simply have to be lived with. Sociology does not have a comforting potential in the same way. On the one hand, its variables of social structure, culture, patterns of expectation sound too complex to be thought of as manipulable whilst, on the other hand, the discipline's underlying assumption of social and cultural relativity suggests that, although these things may be difficult to change, we cannot expect to take comfort in their inevitability and thus ignore them.

Where social scientific thinking has penetrated the practical world of work – and this, not surprisingly, has been largely on the management side of things – it has been in the *psychologistic* form rather than the sociological. I deliberately use the word 'psychologistic' here rather than 'psychological' because the form which this thinking generally takes tends to lack the rigour associated with academic psychology and because it tends to be 'psychologically reductionist' – that is it excludes considerations of wider social, political or economic factors. This is illustrated in my own study of personnel specialists, people who, I show, tend to be the most highly qualified group within management in social science disciplines and yet who, in replies to a range of questions asked about problems of both a workplace and a wider social nature tended to be very markedly individualistic if not crudely psychologistic in style and content (Watson 1977a). Structural insights at either the organisational or the wider social-structural levels were little in evidence. This can be explained to a large extent by the fact that people in management are paid to solve short-term problems, to be pragmatic, to get the job done – in short, to be practical. To analyse structures, let alone change them in other than a piecemeal way, is generally out of the question. Even where social scientists are actually employed as such in industry they are likely to find those with whom they work highly reluctant to operate in the structural terms characteristic of the sociological perspective. As Klein (1976) found to her cost, there is a common preference for the neatly packaged and cunningly marketed psychologistic products of what I term the *behavioural science entrepreneurs* – of whom more later.

The problem with the prevalence of psychologistic thinking in the industrial world is not that it is depriving the sociologist of work or influence but that it often leads to woefully inadequate, not to say simplistic, diagnoses of problems and, following from this, a reduced chance for people to control work institutions. Explaining strikes in terms of communication breakdown or people's greed, 'poor motivation' in terms of basic human needs, payment systems or organisational structures in terms of 'human nature' is simply misleading. More adequate theories of work activity will inform better managerial, employee, social and political decision-making. A foreman's decision on how to reorganise a shopfloor layout, a union decision on whether to negotiate for increased cash or reduced hours or a social policy decision on national leisure provision, each has a sociological dimension. A simple and straightforward statement of how sociology can be applied to these issues is not possible. That is part of the problem of the discipline and is why the present work is a book and not a pamphlet!

Perhaps most usefully at this stage we can point out again that sociology looks at how people *organise* themselves and each other. Whilst recognising that individuals have different personalities, needs and attitudes, we must recognise too that work organisations and the associated institutions in the wider society have a reality over and above these factors. People in industry have tended to see the relevance of social science to their problems in terms of how it can help 'change attitudes', 'improve communications' or 'involve people better'. Without looking at the structure of the work organisation, the administrative system, technology, management and trade union structure and the relationships between these and other such factors inside and outside work, little can be achieved. The way much industrial, social or behavioural science is written and applied gives the impression that it is all based on the ludicrous proposition that you rewrite a play by changing the actors rather than by rewriting the roles. Perhaps you can – but only marginally.

Methods and procedures in sociology

It has been suggested in what has been said about sociology so far that it is in some sense a *scientific* discipline and that the developing of sociological explanations involves rigorous *investigation* of phenomena. We must now consider how it goes about investigation in the course of analysing the kinds of structure, patterns and process discussed above and in what ways it tries to formulate generalisations about the social world.

First, we must look at the notions of science and the scientific. Earlier, science was put in the context of the ways in which modes of thinking tended to move away from an emphasis on religion and tradition in the course of changes in western societies. To talk of science today inevitably brings us up against the image of the typical scientist as a cool, objective and precise white-coated laboratory investigator doggedly discovering laws of the universe (the inspired but absent-minded and half-mad scientist figure being archetypal but atypical), and this first image must be rejected, at least in part, if sociology is going to claim any scientific validity for itself. This can be achieved to some extent by pointing out just how far physical scientists have moved towards the social scientist in their new preference for talk about 'probability' rather than prediction and to their willingness even to admit that their own involvement may affect their investigations. But a more fruitful approach to deciding the distinctiveness of the scientific approach in general is to view it as merely one way of making sense of the world – a way that can be differentiated from others. It can, for instance, be contrasted with a religious approach or a literary one. Thus, to make sense of a thunderstorm we could perhaps consider what part it plays in God's (or the gods') purpose or, alternatively, we could write a poem to express our emotional reactions and describe our experience of the storm. But the third possibility is a scientific one. Here we would formulate concepts or working definitions of what a thunderstorm and its constitutive elements are, collect data on thunderstorms, make comparisons of specific aspects of thunderstorms, and draw up classifications of thunderstorms, noting antecedent conditions and apparent effects. Out of this we would propose tentative explanations (or hypotheses) which can be tested as a generalisation through collected evidence. In a similar way we could attempt to understand or account for phenomena such as strikes in the motor industry either theologically, or through novels or in a scientific manner.

A scientific approach to industrial strife can be differentiated from literary, emotional, religious or philosophical approaches, but is the approach any different in reality from the attempts made to explain this strife by workers, journalists, managers and politicians? Do not these people develop concepts, put forward explanations and even act on the basis of the theories which they develop? To this one can only respond by accepting that there is a very positive continuity between scientific thinking and everyday *practical reasoning*. The householder works out a theory of why the local dustmen are working to rule just as the baby in its pram works out for itself some notion of gravity. The differences between common sense and science, then, are not differences of essence but differences of degree – in three main respects. The scientific approach is (a) more formal, systematic and precise in its observing, classifying, conceptualising and interpreting, (b) it is more rigorous in the extent to which it submits its procedures, testing, etc. to critical examination (seeking to falsify rather than prove its tentative explanations for example) and (c) where everyday or common-sense analysis is merely interested in the short-term pragmatic practicalities of everyday life, formal science is more committed to building up a body of knowledge and a series of generalisations which go beyond immediate and practical needs. This body of knowledge is, therefore, available to be drawn upon when there is a practical issue to which it may be relevant.

Science is about generalisations, we might say. An important product of science is obviously knowledge but its more characteristic product is that part of knowledge which we call theory or *theories*, and here we have a problem with regard to the industrial scene. There is a strong tendency, at least in the British industrial world, to associate anything academic with the irrelevant and to regard theories as useless. Whilst accepting that many academics are indeed 'out of touch' and that many theories are built on sand we must necessarily recognise the nonsense of this position. What the practical man often forgets is that his actions are as much based on theories (in the sense of generalised propositions about phenomena) as are those of the scientifically informed, and his reluctance to explicitly examine and question his theories (or even accept that they are theories) can lead to his downfall. This can be illustrated with the case of a particular junior manager. This man moved from running a light engineering workshop to a job which involved his being in charge of a yard gang of labourers. He had a certain theory about employee behaviour which was based on his experience in his former job where his whole success as a manager was based on his friendly and regular chats with men and women on the shopfloor. This experience, together with what he had once been told on a supervisory training course run by management consultants, led him to follow the logic of his theory in his new job. However, he soon found himself being laughed at and disregarded as some kind of fool by the yard gang. Now, if his theory had been less simplistic, less founded on simple psychologistic assumptions about human nature and had been more attuned to the logic of the situation in human behaviour, the influence of structure, culture, tradition and the rest, he would have adjusted accordingly. He did not: his analysis was that the labour department was recruiting the 'wrong type of person' and, ultimately, he concluded that the company was not for him.

The above example illustrates a general problem with sociological theories or generalisations. This is that because sociology deals with the exceedingly complex world of human activity and relationships its general propositions can rarely take the simple form 'a causes b'. Much more typical would be something on the lines 'to understand the relationship between a and b in any given situation, we must look at the influence of c, d, e, f, g, etc'. Thus the sociologist trying to generalise about, say, employee behaviour will look at such things in any given situation as the technology, local community, union structure, general management style, etc. However, to look at things sociologically one does not start afresh in each situation: the body of knowledge and theory already existing within the discipline guides this analysis, so leading to a more informed conclusion and potential practical action.

This extreme complexity of social life and the consequent difficulty of making usable generalisations is often taken to deny the sociologists' claim that they are scientific in approach. It is because of this complexity, the fact that every individual is different and every human act unique, that it is seen as impossible for the scientific observer to systematically observe or experiment. Furthermore, since the sociologist is a human being like those he is studying, he is inevitably 'involved' and is therefore incapable of being anything like objective. To make sense of the complex human world he is forced to indulge in moral argument, to make use of imagination and insight and to succumb to the influence of his personal experience. He is thus no different, this argument would continue, from the literary observer or the journalist. Nevertheless, as long as we do not use the scientific label as some kind of fetish but regard it as providing a set of guiding principles (as opposed to concrete rules), I would argue that sociology can and should be seen as a scientific discipline.

What makes sociology a science is not a sterile value-neutrality or a concern with amassing facts uncontaminated by subjectivity. Neither is it a pursuit of final laws. Sociology does use insight, imagination and even inspiration; it is motivated by moral concern and even by political commitment, and it is characterised by internal debate and rivalries of both method and interpretation, but, in the end, it falls in the category of the sciences rather than the arts. Sociology is a scientific pursuit because it goes about detecting *regularities* and because it makes its generalisations on as *systematic* a basis as possible given its subject matter. This involves the *testing* of propositions and the basing of statements on *evidence* – this being collected, explained and interpreted in such a way that others can scrutinise that evidence and make their own judgments on the generalisations which are offered.

One of the greatest problems in the development of a science of sociology has been its inevitable entanglement in a horrible methodological paradox. This arises because sociology, to be able to proceed, has to *simplify* the vast complexities of social life whilst, in going about this and stating its assumptions, developing sets of concepts and working out models, it seems to be trying to *complicate* matters. The sociologist is often accused of making things too complicated when, in fact, he is drastically simplifying them. The paradox is resolved when we realise that sociologists are recognising the extent of the complexity in their analyses to a greater extent, typically, than does the everyday practical man and woman. I illustrate this, in a slightly tongue-in-cheek way, in Fig. 1.4.

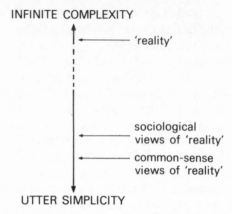

Fig. 1.4 Sociological and common-sense perceptions of the complexity of social reality

What Figure 1.4 implies is that sociology is totally incapable of ever giving a full account or any final explanation of the social world. And, indeed, there is no objectively existing ultimate social reality. Morally (and, thank God, might say the religiously inclined), this is welcome. What, it might be asked, is being suggested here other than that sociology is merely an upgraded form of common-sense under-standing? To this I would reply that this 'upgrading' is such that the sociologically informed will be better able to understand the complexities of what is the case and, just as important, will comprehend better the possible outcomes – the intended and unintended consequences – of actions which might be taken. The point of all social science investigation is to give a more *effective* rather than a *true* understanding.

We can now turn to some of the ways in which the sociologist goes about simplifying the vast buzzing confusion of the social world in order to render it amenable to analysis. The basic method is the development of some kind of *model* or overall theoretical scheme which picks out certain aspects of reality whose interconnections are felt to be important. Some kind of metaphor is often used to make the abstract more manageable: system, structure, stratification etc. The last is a good example. To study the inequalities which exist between human beings, sociologists often picture society as if it were a geological diagram and this helps give a sense of structure or pattern. People are located in 'strata'. Models like this are made up from *concepts*. In the present example of stratification for example, we often find the groups into which people fall conceptualised as 'classes' – upper, middle and working classes perhaps. The characterising of class as, say, dependent on the ownership or non-ownership of capital is not a 'definition' but a concept. By this I mean a *working* definition, if you like. I stress this because we are not saying that class exists in an objective sense when we talk of it in sociology, rather, we are suggesting that it provides a useful tool for analysing human inequality. This does not mean that 'class' is a mere linguistic plaything of the intellectual. Ultimately, sociological concepts have to relate to what people experience in their lives. Although people may believe that 'class is dead', they may well experience certain things which are best understood by being related to what the sociologist calls 'class'. Were those people to look at some sociological analysis in this area, they might well come to understand their own situation better. To put this important point another way: the sociologist is not really concerned to look at any given person and say that he *is* working class or that she *is* middle class. His concern is, rather, to decide which class it is analytically most useful to place him or her in. This is in order to understand what is happening to these persons and what they are doing in that society.

Connected with the development of both concepts and models in sociology, and fundamental to the process of simplification, is the use of types or to use Weber's term *ideal types*. Sociology universally constructs these. As the discipline is interested in generalising, it looks at the typical rather than the specific in directing its analysis. Thus if we wished to find out whether the employees of a factory were generally more interested in money rewards or job satisfaction we might envisage an ideal typical *instrumentally oriented worker* (a totally money-oriented person) and then his opposite: an ideal typical *expressively-oriented worker* (one only concerned with intrinsic satisfactions). Clearly, neither would exist in reality, but these extreme types can be held in mind whilst we construct our questionnaire, which will provide data to enable us to find what patterns exist in that factory. We might find a pattern in one workshop like that in Fig. 1.5.

It is very important to stress that all of these analytical devices – concepts, models, ideal types and theoretical schemes – are merely tools or means and are not ends in themselves. They are to be judged by their usefulness and not by any criterion of correctness. This is not to suggest any one is as good as any other and, throughout this book, I will examine various approaches to different phenomena in order to reveal their value. But this will not prevent me from utilising my own overall theoretical framework in an attempt to give one overall framework for the sociological study of work and industry.

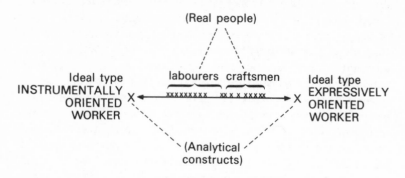

Fig. 1.5 Application of IDEAL TYPE constructs in the study of orientations to work in one industrial workshop

Having clarified these issues – generally described as being of a *methodological* nature – we can turn to look briefly at the *techniques of investigation* which are used by sociologists. There are a range of techniques available to the investigator and the particular ones chosen will depend on various factors such as the theoretical assumptions the researcher holds about social life, and more down to earth, the type of research *access* which is available. The sociologist wishing to use direct observation techniques to study boardroom behaviour, for instance, will be lucky indeed to gain such access. To give an account of the available techniques I shall use a case-study device, sketching out an imaginary research project in which practically the whole range of techniques are used.

Let us envisage a research team who take on the task of giving a sociological account of the running down of a manufacturing concern in a northern town. The owners of the company, all of whom are intending to retire shortly, have given open access to the sociologists. One member of the team is a former worker in the factory and his *personal experience* has been used to direct his colleagues towards various organisational and industrial relations issues and he will also contribute certain qualitative material to the final research reports. This man is being temporarily employed in the personnel department of the firm to help with the tasks of carrying out early retirements, redeployments and redundancies. Valuable data on both managerial and employee experiences will be collected by this *participant observation*. A second researcher is engaged in combing through company *records* and local *historical documents* to build up a picture of the firm's past and the background to the present situation in the company and in the surrounding community. The quantitatively-inclined team member is running through various *statistics* varying from figures supplied by the marketing department to ones on labour turnover and on disputes provided by the personnel department. A *survey* designed to reveal the expected impact of the firm's decline on surrounding small businesses and other parts of the community will be using *postal questionnaires* and *structured interviews* with key people in the community. Both structured and more informal *unstructured interviews* will be used to collect data from *samples* of company employees at each level in the organisation.

Here we have, then, a fairly large and no doubt expensive sociological research project which is deploying a whole battery of techniques of investigation. But to what end, we might ask, and in what way is all this material going to be brought together and interpreted? It might be the case that the style of this research team is that of pursuing what Glaser and Strauss (1967) call 'grounded theory' which means that they will hope to see concepts and hypotheses *emerging* from this mass of data, which can be applied and tested within the project. But this, let us assume, is not the case in this particular piece of research. The leader of the team, as it happens, was born in the town where the research is occurring and she is particularly interested in and worried about the problems of industrial decline in this part of the world. An early paper written for a sociological conference suggests that the academic rationale for the research is an investigation of the impact of unemployment resulting from technological change and patterns of investment on a community with a record of industrial decline. Theoretically, the concern is with how expectations in the community affect the orientations of employees and others towards job loss in such a community context. However, the foundation which is funding the research views its expenditure as an investment which will yield useful information which will give guidance to other companies and to government agencies in similar cases in the future. The company board members who agreed to give access, on the other hand, welcomed the project as a possible way in which the 'human problems' of the rundown might be reduced by the involvement of sociologists – people with special knowledge of the human aspects of work.

It is hoped that this case study, for all its brevity and its purely fictional status, reveals something of the processes by which sociological material is generated. What we see is a complex web of personal values, private and public concern, theoretical interests and research skills. Despite the range of motives and interests behind the project, a set of research reports will eventually appear and will be scrutinised by other sociologists and by lay commentators, reviewed in the literature and discussed at conferences and seminars. And at the end of this process of evaluation there should be an increased understanding of a range of issues among the academics and the practically-involved alike. But what this material will not do, as we shall see shortly, is to tell government, employers, trade unions or whoever what they *should* do in such situations.

Relevance, objectivity and bias

In the research case study discussed above we saw how a variety of motives and values underlay the work which was done. It would not be at all surprising if, in a corresponding way, the findings of this project were not taken up to argue for a range of different political ends and commercial interests after their publication. It is exceedingly important to stress this point: social scientific investigations simply cannot in themselves produce political, commercial or individual programmes for action. Yet they may well be used as if this were the case. A study indicating the overwhelming pecuniary attachment of workers to their jobs, for example, could be taken to 'prove' that the best thing to do in that industry is to forget the possibility of improving job satisfaction and simply to organise for wage maximisation. This is highly illegitimate, not to say dishonest. The type of decision about work design to be made here must ultimately be based on values – on social and political preferences. To expect to arrive at such decisions as a result of scientific investigations such as industrial surveys or perhaps 'cost benefit analyses', is to ignore the fact that the social world contains a diversity of value positions and many conflicting material interests. Science can be no substitute for political activity and is incapable of settling moral questions. Sociology, like any other science, has to be kept in its place. It is an invaluable tool. But it is only a tool: it is a means of improving understanding, informing decisions and indicating the implications of proposed alternatives.

To argue in this way that sociological investigation should be subservient in the realm of practical activity to democratic processes in the formal political sense or in the industrial and collective bargaining sense is not really enough. We have to remember that the idea of science can be a powerful legitimating symbol. The Marxist activist is likely to claim scientific validity for his actions just as is the employer who attempts to persuade his employees of the 'clear economic need' for the redundancies which have been 'recommended by highly objective consultants'. This tendency means that there are considerable ethical problems for the sociological investigator in the industrial sphere and one way in which this can be handled is to argue that the sociologist should be value-free or ethically-neutral.

The term 'value-free' has been used with various different emphases since it was taken up from the arguments of Max Weber. Weber's actual position was probably very like the one argued above about the necessary subservience of science to politics and the 'autonomy of the moral realm' (Dawe 1971) but, partly because he probably overstated his case in the course of reacting to the politically biased work of some German academics of his day, his notion has been taken up by many sociologists as part of a 'rhetoric of non-involvement' (Douglas 1970). This suggests that the sociologist's work is uncontaminated by values and moral issues and that his contribution to social life is merely a technical one. In contradiction to this it is nowadays increasingly accepted in the world of academic sociology that sociological work is value-oriented from the start. From the choice of research topic, the assumptions about social life made, the concepts applied to the problem, the investigative techniques used, the source of funding and the place of publication, value judgments and choices are ever present. The sociologist, then, cannot be value-free. This does not mean that objectivity is out of the question.

The arguments about value freedom and the possibilities for objectivity are to be understood as being about the relationship between *analysis* and *evaluation* in sociology. Whereas it is indeed impossible for the sociologists' work to be value free it is nevertheless incumbent upon them to pursue a certain *objectivity*. This does not mean that they should totally separate their analysis and evaluations. This would be impossible. What they can be expected to do is to go as far as possible towards revealing the grounds on which their interpretation is based. That is, they might reveal where their evidence came from, how it was collected, upon what assumptions these procedures were based and, as far as possible, reveal the ways in which the investigators themselves were implicated in the ways their work was done. As long as sociologists work in this way, their readers or students will be able to make their own evaluations of the generalisations made. To justify the type of acceptability indicated by the scientific label, sociology must not deny its audience the opportunity to draw its own conclusions.

The position taken here is clearly value-based in itself, and it is prescriptive: it sets criteria of judgment which students and readers are encouraged to apply in evaluating sociological material, and it also demands much of sociologists themselves in researching and writing. It is very easy to do this in the comfortable role of the writer of generalisations about sociology. In practice, things are not so simple. Both the sociologist wanting to do empirical research and the sociologist wanting to teach or write material for a 'practical' audience faces problems. And many of these come down to the question of *access*.

Sociology in the form bequeathed by the sociological tradition described earlier always tends to raise 'big questions' and go to the root of the nature and tendencies of the democratic, industrial and capitalist world which saw its birth. In this sense it can be seen as radical – probing deep down and raising potentially unsettling questions. Its equipment of concepts, which includes class, alienation, anomie, industrialism, power, capitalism, conflict etc., is often that likely to unsettle a seminar of industrial managers and, more importantly perhaps, strongly discourage the owners or managers of any work organisation (public, private or whatever) from giving access for sociological research on their territory. Not only can we expect resistance to any apparently radical analysis on the grounds that it is 'political' (the organisation of work being seen as somehow non-political) but we can also expect the retort that it is pointless going into basic issues or those relating to the structure of society since nothing can be done about these anyway. This might seem to be a good justification for keeping *macro*-sociological interests out of *micro*-scale investigations. But this is to deny the very rationale of sociology, which is to locate the specific within the general; the local within the structural; the individual within the society. This whole book is, of course, dedicated to the proposition that these large-scale matters are highly relevant to people wishing to *understand* the goings on within the smallest and least significant workplace. But where this is not recognised by those controlling access to researchers, as I suggest it rarely is, then the investigator has to look hard at how he is to present himself to these gatekeepers.

Largely as a result of these considerable problems of access, twentieth-century industrial sociology has frequently stayed at a parochial level of analysis, often using value-laden concepts such as 'worker resistance to change' and 'organisational goals' in an unreflecting way and as if these were purely scientific concepts whose assumptions did not happily resonate with those of their patrons. The double problem of access – access to do research and access to an audience – has strongly influenced the development of industrial sociology and given much of it a heavily managerial bias. As Albrow (1968) has pointed out, this means that it is 'taking sides in a struggle for power', but it is doing more than this. Ironically, managerial bias in industrial sociology may be doing the managers themselves little good in the long run: telling people what they want to hear or happily leaving their prejudices untouched is hardly the way to improve their understanding. This point is simply illustrated by the need frequently recognised in industrial relations training courses to point out that industrial conflict cannot successfully be understood or 'managed' if procedures are based on the naïve assumption that there are not really 'two sides' in employment relationships and that the plant or office is a unitary and family-like entity.

Many industrial sociologists have been wary of becoming what Loren Baritz (1960) called 'servants of power' and are frequently reluctant to work directly for organisational interests. This means that some have entered industry covertly whilst others have studied it from a distance or through interviewing participants outside of their work (Beynon's *Working For Ford*, 1973, is a good example here). However, a different strategy has been followed by other researchers. This is the 'action research' approach which involves collaboration in solving problems of a client organisation in such a way that problem-solving and knowledge-acquisition gain from one another so that advantage accrues to the action researcher, the client and the scientific community alike (Clark 1972). There are advantages and disadvantages with each of the approaches available here but, for the present, I would simply invite the student to look sceptically at all the products of sociologists, regarding them in the critically rational spirit of the scientific tradition of which most see themselves as part. In the present work, each study and theoretical contribution will be grist to the mill and the reader is asked to take what he or she can from what is presented, recognising the *insights* and *understanding* to be gained by looking at managerially-biased and Marxist-inspired analyses alike. This cannot be done easily, however, if each work is seen in isolation. Just as there are, as has been shown above, a variety of method-ological, investigative and value positions held in sociology, so there are several different substantive areas of interest *within* the sociology of work and industry and, in addition to these, there are various theoretical perspectives. These too must now be looked at.

Areas of interest and varieties of perspective

Despite the above willingness to consider material from across the range of sociological sources, we somehow have to face up to the need to bring together material relevant to the overall project of the sociological study of work and industry which is at present located in several disparate and often almost self-contained areas of existing study. If sociologists of work are going to win for themselves a bigger audience amongst those directly involved in the world of work they are going to have to break down the currently existing divisions between the specialisms (Watson 1979). At present, the person involved in industry finds that he is in a formal *organisation* which has one sociology, that he belongs to an *occupation* which has another distinct sociology, and that he becomes involved in *industrial relations* situations which have their own separate literature. Figure 1.6 indicates the existing specialist areas which the present work is concerned to bring together.

The contributions made to the issues shown in Figure 1.6 have been within several different theoretical perspectives. It often perplexes students new to sociology to learn that a supposedly well-established academic discipline lacks a single overall theoretical framework. But it is not surprising that a variety of theoretical emphases should co-exist, given the immense diversity and complexity of social life which has been so stressed in this chapter. Sociological theory has the immense task of making sense of the relationship between individuals and society. Accordingly, some theorists stress the 'society' element and make particular use of concepts like *system, structure, society* and *values*. Durkheim and his successors are examples here. Others, like the interactionists and those who follow Weber's example look more to the individual as their starting point, stressing *action, meaning, interaction* and *ideas*. In a similar way, some theorists lay emphasis on the tendency towards conflict in social life (Weber and, especially, Marx) whereas others (like Durkheim and the systems theorists) concentrate more on the tendencies towards co-operation.

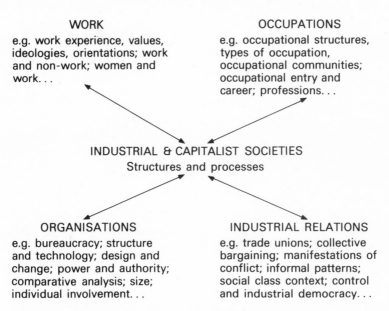

WORK
e.g. work experience, values, ideologies, orientations; work and non-work; women and work. . .

OCCUPATIONS
e.g. occupational structures, types of occupation, occupational communities; occupational entry and career; professions. . .

INDUSTRIAL & CAPITALIST SOCIETIES
Structures and processes

ORGANISATIONS
e.g. bureaucracy; structure and technology; design and change; power and authority; comparative analysis; size; individual involvement. . .

INDUSTRIAL RELATIONS
e.g. trade unions; collective bargaining; manifestations of conflict; informal patterns; social class context; control and industrial democracy. . .

Fig. 1.6 The components of the sociology of work and industry with examples of their concerns

In chapter 2 some of the major theoretical perspectives of sociology will be introduced and, by combining this with a presentation of the ways in which these perspectives have been applied to the world of work, it is intended to produce an intellectual map of the sociology of work and industry, as it has grown historically and as it is now. The most useful elements of these perspectives will then be drawn together to create a new framework for the sociology of work and industry.

This framework will be used to give structure to the explorations which will be entered in the following chapters into the areas of the industrialised society, work and the individual, occupations, organisations, conflicts and challenges and, ultimately, a discussion of human choice in the world of work and the part which sociology might play in this.

Chapter 2

The sociological analysis of work and industry

Introduction

Sociology is a scientifically oriented intellectual pursuit which is engaged in by human beings striving to make sense of the social world in which they find themselves. One basic motive of those who engage in sociological research and writing can be seen as a concern to cope better with the problems and complexities of social living. The ways in which people set about coping with these problems vary, however, with their own social position, interests and values. Many of the founding fathers of sociology were concerned to raise 'big questions' about the kind of social or community life which would be possible in a world which was industrialising and undergoing rapid structural and cultural changes. The centrality of work organisation and experience to these changes, it was suggested in chapter 1, makes consideration of industrial and other work institutions of prime importance to any sociology which hopes to stand as a resource for an ongoing and critical examination of how we organise ourselves in an industrialised society. But the materials which currently exist as the components of industrial sociology also reflect another kind of attempt to cope with problems of social organisation. These are the attempts to tackle the practical problems of organising the work of other human beings as *efficiently* as possible in the light of the goals of those doing the organising. Industrial sociology contains within it, consequently, a basic tension between a radical and critical interest and one which is practical and manipulative.

Each existing contribution to the sociology of work and industry inevitably reflects the interests, sentiments and assumptions of its author. To enable us to appreciate and evaluate the range of conceptual and empirical material which will be considered in the chapters which are to follow, I shall now draw a map which will allow us to locate these contributions within five strands. This outline, like all maps, is a simplification. It is intended not only to give an account of how the sociology of work has developed to date but to show how the several major theoretical perspectives of modern sociology tend to reflect different interests and value positions. Once these perspectives are understood and some indication given of their relative strengths and weaknesses, we can move on to construct one overall framework for the sociology of work and industry – one which will make clear its own underlying assumptions and one which might facilitate a more coherent type of industrial sociology than has existed hitherto.

Five theoretical strands in the sociology of work and industry

In Figure 2.1 are shown five major strands which can be seen as making up the sociology of work and industry. The diagram relates three of these strands to the approaches of major historical figures (Durkheim, Weber and Marx) and, it must be emphasised, it is not suggesting that these in any way constitute anything coherent enough to call 'schools of thought'. The interactionist strand is perhaps more clearly a 'school' in that its contributors have, to a greater extent, shared a theoretical position, a spiritual if not a geographical home (Chicago) and one particular mentor (E. C. Hughes). The first strand to be considered, however, contains two quite contrasting 'schools of thought': those of 'scientific management' and 'neo-Human Relations'. These are drawn together in one strand for two reasons. The first is that these approaches are quite openly managerially oriented and both tend towards the style of thought which was characterised in chapter 1 as 'psychologistic'. The second reason is that these two schools have been less a part of industrial sociology proper than catalysts helping the development of a distinctively sociological approach to work.

I The managerial–psychologistic strand
The 'scientific management' approach to work behaviour and the more recently fashionable neo-Human Relations approach, despite being diametrically opposed in underlying sentiment and assumptions about human nature, provide us with analyses to be contrasted with a more sociological or structural approach. This is because they

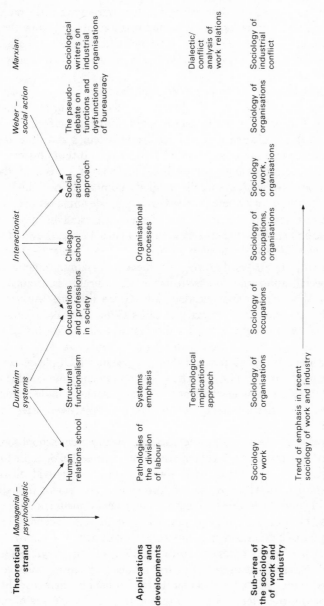

Fig. 2.1 Five theoretical strands in the sociology of work and industry

are both individualistic in emphasis, both base themselves on assumptions about 'human nature' and, as a consequence of this, both tend not to recognise the dimension of cultural variation and the range of possibilities of work organisation and orientation implied by this. Further, they both fly the banner of science to legitimate what are in effect techniques of manipulation rather than disinterested concerns with understanding.

The first and best known proponent of the scientific management approach to work is F. W. Taylor (1856–1917), an American engineer. Taylor's importance as the leader of the movement which has given the world work study, piece rate schemes and time and motion study and the like can only be understood if set in historical context. The increasingly rationalised division of tasks and the mechanisation of work eventually reached a point at the beginning of the twentieth century where the need to co-ordinate human efforts not surprisingly invited the attentions of men interested in applying scientific and engineering criteria to the human sphere as they had to the mechanical. Taylorism suggests that work tasks should be closely and scientifically analysed in order to achieve the maximum amount of task specialisation and to discover the scientifically ascertainable one-best-way of carrying out that task. Given that the worker is basically an economic animal, a self-seeking asocial economic individual who generally prefers the management to do his task-related thinking for him, one can tie the monetary rewards of the work to the level of output and thus get results which please both management and employee. There is consequently no need for conflict between management and worker (let alone trade union) as long as management follows truly objective scientific methods.

Taylor's successors within the scientific management school soon modified his refusal to accept a place for organised labour in the workplace but the approach has always retained its individualistic emphasis. Books which relate the history of management thought frequently give the impression that scientific management is a thing of the past but, in the realm of practical realities, its doctrines and techniques still dominate contemporary work design, as is shown by the study by Davis, Canter and Hoffman (1972) of 'current job design criteria'. Scientific management's techniques have clearly survived the onslaught of its intellectual critics although their use has undoubtedly been tempered by a recognition of the dangers of too crude an application. The psychologistic assumptions underlying the approach still hold great sway among practical men.

The psychologistic assumptions of scientific management are best illustrated by reference to Taylor's famous concept of 'soldiering', described in *The Principles of Scientific Management* (1911). Soldiering in Taylor's sense is 'the natural instinct and tendency of men to take it easy'. When this is combined with the men's economic interests and the failure of managers to design, allocate and reward the work on a scientific basis, it leads the men to get together and rationally conspire to hold production down. They do this to maximise their reward without tempting the incompetent management to come back and tighten the rate (which only needs tightening because it was originally guessed at and not fixed scientifically). This is 'systematic soldiering' and an inefficient evil. This systematic soldiering is not, however, seen as an inevitable phenomenon which results from the natural sociability of human beings. If the management relate directly to each individual and satisfy his or her personal self-interest then they will get full co-operation. A proper understanding of human nature, it is implied, would demonstrate that this is the case. The ultimate explanation of work behaviour, then, is a psychologistic one. It can be so labelled because scientific management is reductionist in its precluding of wider social considerations and because it is not an explanation which has stood up to more academically rigorous psychological study (see Rose (1975) on human factor industrial psychology, for instance).

When reaction to psychologistic or *individualistic* explanations occurs in social thought there is often a tendency for this reaction to take the form of a swing to the opposite extreme, that is towards *holistic* explanations. To put this another way, when we turn away from attributing something to human nature or to instincts we tend to attribute it to 'society'. Something like this happened with the appearance of the Human Relations school of thought in American industry where the famous Hawthorne experiments saw the 'discovery' of the social factors in worker behaviour and an attempt to refute the individualistic assumptions of what was labelled the 'rabble hypothesis' – the basic asocial proposition on which scientific management was now said to be based. Industrial sociology as a specialised academic discipline is often seen as beginning in the 1920s in America with the appearance of this school of thought and, because of the nature of the intellectual base which the school developed for itself, we will leave consideration of its main ideas until we come to the more holistically-inclined Durkheim–systems strand. But, despite the concern of some Human Relations writers, like Mayo, with the wider social dimension of work, we can nevertheless say that the *practical* effect of the Human Relations school within work organisations has been to encourage an approach to the organisation of work ultimately as psychologistic as that of the heirs of Taylor. It has done this through its emphasis on the development of supervisory skills at the lower levels within management and by diverting attention away from structural, technological or economic conflict issues to ones of 'communication'. How individuals relate to each other is seen as more important than the way that their economic, social and task relationships are structured.

A psychologistic concern with some notion of 'human nature' as the basis for understanding human aspects of work is clearly seen in what is proving to be one of the most influential contributions of social scientists to managerial thinking to date. This is the work of those writers frequently seen as composing a neo-Human Relations school and whom I like to label *behavioural science entrepreneurs*. These writers include some of the best known names among modern management writers, including McGregor, Likert, Argyris, Gellerman, Blake, Herzberg and Reddin. I refer to them as entrepreneurs because their work is designed to sell, whether in the form of books, management seminars, training films or consultancies. Like the task-splitting scientific managers with whom they so passionately take issue, their work is reductionist, partial, evangelistic and sociologically highly inadequate on the explanatory level, with its underplaying of structural, situational, cultural, political and economic factors. It is ultimately simplistic but by a judicious mixing of simplistic assumptions and pseudo-scientific jargon it has made itself highly marketable.

It is a commonplace among social scientists who have involved themselves with practising managers that if managers look to social science for anything it is for simple prescriptions, formulae or even panaceas. But to offer them for sale a straight-forwardly simple proposition would raise suspicions – quite justifiably. The simple proposition is therefore wrapped up in package form and stuck over with impressive sounding labels like 'hygiene factors', '3-D theory', 'managerial grid', 'management by objectives' and ' "systems four" management'. The small amount of effort (and, of course, cash) expended on unwrapping the parcel encourages the recipient to feel that he has worked his way towards something of significance. But this simple proposition is, more or less, that people in work organisations will work more efficiently if they are allowed to participate more in their own management. Klein (1976), one of the few non-entrepreneurial social scientists to write openly of their involvement as industrial employees, has commented that this participative message is often pushed in an authority-based manner – the irony of this, I suggest, illustrating how little the implications of this approach are understood or, alternatively, how pseudo-participative the intent is. But the idea has been propagated so widely that, as Klein puts it, 'whether they agree or not, this is what managers now expect from social scientists. It is therefore a brave social scientist who says social science is not necessarily about participative "leadership".'

The proposition that organisational efficiency can be achieved through participative approaches, which may take the form of subordinates taking part in setting their own objectives, the 'enriching' of jobs by reducing the extent of their supervision and monitoring and the developing of more open and authentic colleague relationships, is clearly at odds with that of scientific management. Although in some ways it is a mirror image of it. It bases its approach to human work behaviour on a theory of human nature and one of the most popular writers of this school makes quite clear the equivalence of the two opposing propositions by labelling them, alternatively, theory x and theory y (McGregor 1960). Theory x, for so long popular as a managerial assumption, sees people as naturally disliking work and therefore only doing it for its compensations or indirect rewards. Consequently, employees have to be directly and closely supervised and controlled. But theory y, which McGregor advocates and which social science research is said to support, states that people are not at all like this but would generally prefer to exercise self-control and self-discipline at work and that this would occur if they were allowed to contribute creatively to organisational problems in a way which enabled them to meet their need for self-actualisation.

It is the notion of *self-actualisation need* within the human animal which lies at the heart of most of the neo-Human Relations work. This idea is taken from the work of the American humanistic psychologist, Abraham Maslow, who suggested that once human beings have satisfied their lower order needs such as their physiological needs and their needs for safety, love and esteem, they look to satisfy a need for self-fulfilment or self-actualisation. The behavioural science management writers have tended to take up this notion as a stick with which to beat prevailing managerial approaches, these being seen as failing to obtain employee co-operation because they do not provide the intrinsic and naturally sought rewards which the employee 'needs'.

At first sight it might appear that those of us interested in scientifically investigating work behaviour have a fairly simple task here: that of testing these two propositions about work and human needs to find the validity of either scientific management's theory x or neo-Human Relations' theory y. Alas this cannot be done. If there is such a thing as 'human nature' at all it is that, to a much greater extent than is the case with other animals, humans are what they make themselves. Beyond the minimally existing instincts and some inbuilt physiologically based needs, we mould ourselves and each other to need a little simple food or a lot of rich food, to need the assurance of safety or the stimulation of danger, or to seek self-aggrandisement or self-abasement. Our socially or culturally defined nature is far more important than any 'human' or species nature: we have socially-mediated *wants* rather than built-in needs. In evaluating scientific management and neo-Human Relations ideas this leads us into a rather paradoxical muddle. In effect both are right and both are wrong! To make sense of this statement, we must add the magic words *depending on the circumstances*. By circumstances is meant the structural and cultural factors which we have seen to be central to a sociological approach to analysis. Thus, if we have a pecuniary culture and an industry structured on the basis of mechanisation and minute task-specialisation, it is possible that people will make a deliberate choice to do such work and will happily accept close supervision, etc. in return for cash. Alternatively, if the wider culture develops norms and values oriented towards 'doing your own thing' in life and if it puts work as central to that life, then we might expect the scientific managers to have to move over and allow the behavioural scientific participative managers to take over.

In practice, both scientific management and participative management approaches can 'work'. This is partly because each has the quality of a self-fulfilling prophecy. Both approaches derive from value-based assumptions (rather than scientific facts) and their very advocacy can bring about what they first claimed or pretended to be inevitable. We will see something similar later on with the Marxian approach. The reason that these approaches have to be fairly harshly examined, and their scientific validity questioned, is that our choice between work organisations which are cash-reward oriented or self-actualising is a political or value one. It is not a scientific choice. But such choices can be *informed* by social scientific understanding and the potential contribution of a sociological analysis will be looked at when we focus on work and the individual and, again, when we specifically consider the question of choice in the final chapter.

II The Durkheim–systems strand

To counter the ever present tendency in common-sense reasoning towards explaining social activity in terms of individual character-istics, sociologists are often tempted to push their analyses over into what might be called sociologism – an over-emphasis on 'society' which implies that societies have an independent and determining existence over and above the people who compose them. Ideas which suggest the primacy of the community over the individual have always existed in social thought and have frequently been propagated by those wishing to persuade people to go along with particular social orders. In the same way that Catholic thinkers of the medieval period reacted to incipient and actual peasant revolts by providing models of an organic community in which each is shown to have a part to play (rich and poor, leader and led), thinkers seeking order in industrial societies or within industrial enterprises have, not surprisingly, gravitated towards some kind of organic model for social analysis. In the present strand of the sociology of work and industry we find ideas and influence of one of the major founding sociologists, Durkheim, the human relations industrial sociology, and, more recently popular, the systems approach to work and social organisation. What all of this work has in common is its inheritance from the old *organic analogy* in social thought: the metaphor which views society or the enterprise as some kind of organism or animal which constantly seeks equilibrium or stability and is always fighting off pathological and disintegrative influences.

Emile Durkheim (1858–1917) is perhaps the sociologist *par excellence*. In this we see his importance and perhaps the major problem with his work. His position as the first senior academic sociologist (in a formal sense) meant that there was considerable pressure on him to establish the distinctiveness of the new discipline. This fact probably explains in part his over heavy stress on science (which, in contrast to the position taken here, can give moral guidance) and his overemphasis on the 'reality' of an autonomous and externally-existing 'society'. As I suggested above, ideas which stress the primacy of community over the individual have a strong ideological and conservative potential, but to picture Durkheim as an intentionally conservative thinker in this way is quite wrong. He was concerned neither to return to the past nor to justify the status quo. Yet he was strongly in reaction against certain aspects of the prevailing individualism of his age. On a methodological level he was opposed to psychological reductionism, showing that even a highly individual act like suicide has to be understood in terms of the extent of the individual's integration into a community or group rather than by simple reference to the individual's mental state. To study social life one had to isolate and examine 'social currents' and 'social facts'. These are to be seen as *things* and as existing external to the individual, exerting constraint over him. Values, customs, norms, obligations and suchlike are to be considered in this way.

Perhaps most influential in taking Durkheim towards some kind of holism in his sociology was his morally inspired reaction to the disintegrating effects of the egoism and self-interest which he saw developing in the European societies of his time. He saw the organic solidarity so necessary for a healthy society being threatened by *laissez-faire* economics and a utilitarian philosophy which encouraged an egoism strongly contrasting with the *healthy* kind of individualism which *could* exist in an industrialised society. A healthy individualism could exist as long as that society provided regulation, directing principles or norms. Without this we have the pathology of *anomie*: organic integration threatened by unrestricted individual aspirations, lack of discipline, principle or guiding norms.

Durkheim's analysis of anomie and his concern about social solidarity and integration was a major influence on the work of Elton Mayo (1880–1949) who has come to be seen as the leading spokesman of the Human Relations school of industrial sociology. Whereas Durkheim's sympathies were not with the ruling or managerial interests of capitalist society, Mayo's were. In place of Durkheim's seeking of social integration through moral communities based on occupations, Mayo put the industrial workgroup and the employing enterprise, with the industrial managers having responsibility for seeing that group affiliations and social sentiments were fostered in a creative way. Like Taylor, Mayo was anxious to develop an effective and scientifically informed managerial elite. If managements could ensure that employees' social needs were met at work by giving them the satisfactions of working together, by making them feel important in the organisation and by showing an interest in their personal problems, then both social breakdown and industrial conflict could be headed off. Managerial skills and good communications were the antidotes to the potential pathologies of an urban industrial civilisation.

The context of the growth of the Human Relations school was the problem of controlling the increasingly large-scale enterprises of the post-war period and the problem of legitimating this control in a time of growing trade union challenge. The faith of the scientific management experts in a solution which involved the achieving of optimum working conditions, the 'right' method and an appropriate incentive scheme proved to be too blind. Practical experience and psychological research alike were indicating the need to pay attention to other variables in work behaviour. Here we see the importance of the Hawthorne experiments.

The Hawthorne investigations had been started in Chicago by engineers of the Western Electric Company's Hawthorne plant. They had investigated the effects of workshop illumination on output and had found that, as their investigations proceeded, output improved in the groups investigated, regardless of what was done to the lighting. In 1927 the Department of Industrial Research of Harvard University, a group to which Mayo had been recruited, were called in. Their enquiry started in the Relay Assembly Test Room where over a five year period a wide range of changes were made in the working conditions of a specially segregated group of six women whose job was to assemble telephone relays. Changes involving incentive schemes, rest pauses, hours of work and refreshments were made but it was found that whatever changes were made – including return to original conditions – output rose. The explanation which was later to emerge has been labelled 'the Hawthorne effect'. It was inferred that the close interest shown in the workers by the investigators, the effective pattern of communication which developed and the emerging high social cohesion within the group brought together the needs of the group for rewarding interaction and co-operation with the output needs of the management. This type of explanation was also encouraged by the other stages of the investigations. The employee interviewing programme was seen as showing that many of the problems of management-worker relationships could be put down to the failure to recognise the emotions and the 'sentiments' of the employees and the study in the Bank Wiring Observation Room was taken to show the part played by informal social group needs in worker restriction of output.

The Hawthorne studies were most fully reported by Roethlisberger and Dickson (1939) and their reports and interpretations can be compared with those of Mayo (1933) and Whitehead (1938). We have already noted the relationship between Durkheim's ideas and those of Mayo but perhaps a more important influence on all of these interpreters was the classical sociologist Vilfredo Pareto (1848–1923). A key figure in the Harvard sociological circles of this time was the biologist and translator of Pareto, L. J. Henderson. He introduced the ideas of this former Italian engineer to those Harvard thinkers who, at the time, were highly receptive to ideas which might counter those of the liberals or Marxists (Gouldner 1971). The effects on this first specialised school of industrial sociology of Pareto (via Henderson) were two-fold. The first effect was the suggestion that workers' behaviour can be attributed to their 'sentiments' rather than to their reason. Apparently rational behaviour, like Taylor's 'systematic soldiering', could be better understood as deriving from irrational fears, status anxieties and the instinctive need of the individual to be loyal to his or her immediate social group. The problems did not arise from economic and rationally perceived conflicts of interest and were therefore not open to solution through skilful management. The second influence of Pareto, and this conveniently accords with the holistic tendencies of Durkheim, is his emphasis on the notion of *system*. Here we have the organic analogy again, with its stress on integration and the necessary interdependence of the parts and the whole. Only by the integration of the individual into the (management-led) plant community could systemic integration be maintained and the potential pathologies of the industrial society avoided.

Human Relations industrial sociology has been widely criticised for such things as its managerial bias, its failure to recognise the rationality of employee behaviour, its denial of underlying economic conflicts of interest, etc. (see Landsberger 1958). The investigations which were carried out have also been examined and found wanting (Carey 1967). Some of the writers in the tradition are more vulnerable to criticism than others and there is value in some of the contributions

– as is recognised by their use in appropriate places in the present work. However, one feature of the tradition which is shared by many other writers on work, organisations and industrial relations has been a dependence on the integrationist and holistic notion of *system*.

Durkheim's message to sociologists was that they should look beyond the individuals who compose society to the level of the underlying patterns of social activity. The institutions, which are part of this pattern, are to be studied not only to locate their 'genesis' but to understand their 'functioning' – that is, the contribution of the parts of the society to the continuation and survival of the whole. The idea of looking at society itself or at industrial organisations as social systems (and, later, as socio-technical systems) is rooted in the old organic analogy and has come down into contemporary sociology through the work of Durkheim, Pareto and various anthropologists working in the Durkheimian tradition. Perhaps the most influential single sociologist of the twentieth century, Talcott Parsons (1902–1979), is much taken up with biological analogies and was a member of Henderson's Harvard 'Pareto Circle' along with Elton Mayo. His influence has been enormous, establishing an intellectual ambience in which a considerable proportion of existing contributions to industrial and organisational sociology have been fashioned. Added to this has been the growing popularity of cybernetics in the industrial world and a growing interest within management thought in the so-called 'general systems theory' of von Bertalanffy (Emery 1969).

Detailed examination of the systems approach within industrial sociology will come in chapter 6 when we focus on how work is structured in the 'formal organisation' sense. To those interested in studying organisational behaviour the usefulness of considering social activities as 'things' (in Durkheim's sense) which survive and change through adapting to their environment is fairly easy to imagine, but questions have to be raised at this stage about the partiality of the approach. We must ask whether any of the integrationist approaches considered in this section live up to the sociology which was advocated in chapter 1. In making the human individual secondary or derivative of the social system of which he is a part, are we paying sufficient attention to the degree of interplay which goes on between individual initiative and social constraint in human societies? In stressing the adaptation of systems to their environments are we not restricting human choices to fairly minor changes – changes not chosen by democratic means but by the mental frame of reference with which we start? In looking at patterns, structures and interrelated institutions, are we doing sufficient justice to the extent to which the social world is the creation of interacting individuals and groups assigning *meanings* and making *interpretations* of their situations? To consider the possibilities of an approach which gives prime emphasis to meanings and to interaction rather than to systems and structures existing *outside* the individual we can now turn to a quite different strand of the sociology of work and industry.

III *The interactionist strand*

The interactionist strand has its roots firmly in the sociology department of Chicago University in America. Theoretically, the interactionist perspective, with its focus on the individual, the small group and on meanings, is almost a polar opposite of the Durkheim–systems strand described above. Yet in the contributions of interactionist sociologists to the study of work, we find important continuities with the work of Durkheim. This continuity can be seen in a common interest taken in occupations as central social institutions and also in a recognition of the importance of the division of labour in society. But before we look specifically at the interactionist approaches to work, it is necessary to give an account of the theoretical approach of the wider school of sociology of which these sociologists of work are a part – the school of symbolic interactionism.

The particular brand of sociological theory known as symbolic interactionism has developed alongside the more empirical study of work which has taken place within the same Chicago circles. Those sociologists who have performed the studies which we will look at in later chapters have drawn on and contributed to this theoretical perspective to varying degrees and, to make their generally shared theoretical orientations clear, I shall, for the present, briefly describe the main characteristics of symbolic interactionism. The origins of the approach lie in the work of C. H. Cooley (1864–1929) and G. H. Mead (1863–1931) and its basic position is that the individual and society are inseparable units: their relationship is a mutually interdependent one, not a one-sided deterministic one. As Meltzer *et al.* (1975) put it,

> The behaviour of men and women is 'caused' not so much by the
> forces within themselves (instincts, drives, needs etc) or by
> external forces impinging upon them (social forces etc) but by what

lies in between, a reflective and socially derived interpretation of the internal stimuli that are present.

Human beings construct their realities in a process of interaction with other human beings. The individual derives his very identity from his interaction with others.

According to the symbolic interactionists, all interaction and communication is dependent on the use of symbols such as words, gestures, clothes, skin colour and so on. The infant acquires an identity – a consciousness of *self* – through the *socialisation* or social learning process. This process involves the internalisation of symbols, which are organised round the concept of self to make social life meaningful. Awareness of self is acquired through 'taking on the *role* of the other'. It is through taking on the role of the other, particularly what are called 'significant others', that we learn about the expectations which others have of us. This helps us in deciding what role we will play in any given situation. Similarly, by taking the role of the other, we learn what to expect of that other. To orient us as we make our way through life we look to a variety of what are termed *reference groups* and as we move through a series of situations which bestow identity on us we are said to follow a *career*. Not surprisingly this concept of career is, as we shall see, a key contribution of this theoretical perspective to the sociology of work.

The man who established the investigative tradition of the interactionist strand was Robert Park (1864–1944), a former journalist who encouraged reseachers to make detailed ethnographic observations of both normal and deviant Chicago life in the participant observation tradition previously confined to anthropological studies of tribal life. In this and in his Durkheimian interest in what he called the 'moral order' (an ordering of expectations and moral imperatives which tend to routinise interaction) he influenced Everett Hughes who, in turn, has influenced an impressive proportion of those sociologists currently contributing to the sociology of work (see Becker *et al.* 1968). Where Durkheim tended to look to occupations as offering possible solutions to the problem of social order, Hughes tends to take the study of occupations as his starting point; his way in to learning about society.

Hughes' approach is to focus on the social drama of work – the interaction which takes place at work – taking note of the problems or tensions which are created by the work itself and by its social situation. The concern then turns to how the individual copes with or adapts to those problems. Here, I suggest, is the great fascination of this approach, a fascination which, I hope, will become apparent later in this book when we look at how policemen, prostitutes or cabdrivers *cope* with their occupational situation. Hughes encouraged his students to focus on the offbeat or deviant occupations (in the notorious Chicago 'nuts and sluts' tradition) not only for their intrinsic interest but because this would highlight factors of general relevance which we tend not to notice in more conventional settings (because of their taken-for-grantedness, we might say). To focus on the striptease dancer, for example, can alert us about things to look for when we study jobs like those of industrial managers – things which it might otherwise not occur to us to look for!

The interactionist strand of the sociology of work and industry clearly pays great attention to the individual and his role in social life and it pays very necessary heed to the human interpretative process which the holistic approaches considered earlier tend to neglect. The approach is clearly not psychologistic but we do have to ask whether, in turning from attention to social wholes, it is doing sufficient justice to the influence on human interaction of those ongoing historical processes and 'structures' of power and material interest which provide the context for the individual and his social role. To see how an interest in social meanings and individual motives can be combined with a more power-conscious and historically aware perspective we must return to the European tradition and to the work of Max Weber.

IV   The Weber–social action strand
This strand holds out great promise to those seeking a sociological approach which takes into account both the meaningful activity of the individual and the larger-scale questions of historical change and economic and political conflicts. Despite the early interest shown by interactionists in the societal 'moral order' and the overall division of labour, their interests have subsequently proved to be largely confined to the group or occupational levels. They have not successfully related meanings at the micro level to historical and cultural patterns at the macro level. A concern with such a relationship is basic to the work of the German sociologist Max Weber (1864–1920). Before we look at his ideas, however, it is necessary to note that there have been considerable problems in interpreting Weber's work. His work and ideas have often been misrepresented.

This is partly because of the incompleteness of his written works, his awkward style of writing, his own ambiguity on various issues, his tendency to separate his political writing from his sociological work and, especially, because of the fact that his work has been brought back into contemporary sociology largely via American sociologists who wished to use the name of this massively impressive European figure to legitimate their own positions or interests. Thus we find Weber interpreted at times as one who totally opposed Marx's position on the nature and rise of capitalism; one who denied the importance of class divisions in society by arguing that a plurality of interest groups counter-balanced each other; as one who 'advocated' bureaucracy as 'efficient'; as one who was an armchair thinker without interest in carrying out empirical investigations, and as one who encouraged the sociologist to be a neutral and uncommitted individual. There is some element of truth in each of these interpretations but each of them tends to be quite the opposite of what was his *essential* position.

Weber's advocacy of value-freedom and his attempts to fill out (rather than totally contradict) the one-sidedness of Marxian thinking have to be understood in the light of his social and historical context. In trying to separate scientific analysis from political interpretation and advocacy he was reacting to contemporary academics whom he saw as abusing their academic status and, as was suggested in chapter 1, he was interested in relegating sociological study to a role which was secondary to moral thinking and political activity. His reaction to the Marxist thinking of his time was not to try to demolish it but to take from it what was most useful in understanding modern capitalism whilst balancing its emphasis on material factors with fuller consideration of the role in history of ideas, individual agents and culture. It is true that, in his more political writings, he showed a clear preference for capitalism over its socialist alternative but his enthusiasm for capitalist social organisation was not much greater than that for socialism. Both of them involved the threat to individual freedom which he saw in bureaucracy. Such was the pessimism which runs through Weber's world view.

Weber defined sociology as the study of social action (discussed above on p. 14). The discipline would examine the ways in which people, through the attribution and inference of subjective meanings, would be influenced by each other and thereby oriented in their actions. Weber avoided ever talking of structures or systems and he related these social meanings to the wider society through the concept of a 'legitimate order'. This is a patterning in social life which the individual actor *believes* to exist and to which he may conform. To understand how the order becomes valid to actors it has to be seen within the human meaning-creating processes which, in turn, have to be related to the conflicts and power struggles which take place in a world where there are a variety of material interests. The interplay between ideas and interests is basic to Weber's sociology. The sociologist, as a first stage of investigation, attempts to gain an interpretative understanding (*verstehen*) of actors' behaviour. This is then followed by a second stage of analysis leading to a *causal* explanation. Since the actors who are being studied think in causal terms about what they are doing and because they base their actions on certain rationally based assumptions of regularities in the world, some causal explanation of their behaviour should be possible.

Weber's sociology is underpinned by a set of philosophical assumptions about the world which include a view of reality as infinitely diverse and leading to the existence of fundamental conflicts of value, interest and perspective. Social life is thus characterised by perpetual conflict, struggle and the exercise of power. Humans are seen as rational beings pursuing ends, but there is no direct relationship between their efforts and the resulting social order. There is a *paradox of consequences* in social life. This refers to the fact that human actions often have unintended consequences which may be quite different from or even in direct opposition to what was intended. This tendency is profoundly important for the discipline of sociology generally and is, I believe, most adequately dealt with in the Weberian perspective. To illustrate this tendency as well as the other aspects of Weber's approach described above, we can make reference to some of his most famous substantive work.

In Weber's famous study, *The Protestant Ethic and the Spirit of Capitalism*, which we will look at in detail in the next chapter, we see how the ideas developed by individuals like Luther and Calvin, men concerned with religious and spiritual ends, had the unintended consequence of helping to foster a 'spirit of capitalism' and an increasingly rationalistic world view, one of the consequences of which was the eventual undermining of religious belief. The ideas which encouraged asceticism contributed to a later materialism in western culture which would have horrified those who first set out these ideas. But Weber, in this kind of analysis, is not suggesting that ideas autonomously wing their way through history, changing their forms as they go: it is their coming together with the material *interests* of historical actors which gives *ideas* force. Weber talks of an 'elective affinity' between ideas and interests: people tend to choose, develop or adopt ideas which fit with their material interests – these interests in turn being influenced by available ideas. Weber is by no means replacing Marx's stress on material interests as a force in history with an equally one-sided stress on ideas. Instead, he is showing that the cultural or subjective aspects of social life have to be seen as equal partners in any analytical scheme.

Weber sees a process of *rationalisation* underlying western history – this is the tendency for traditional or magical criteria of action to be replaced by technical, calculative or scientific criteria. Social life is 'demystified' or disenchanted, rational pursuit of profit motivates work behaviour and efforts are increasingly co-ordinated through bureaucratic means. All this means that people more and more use calculative devices and techniques as means towards the achieving of ends (these are *formally rational* means) – the division of labour, sets of rules, accounting methods, money, technology, etc. However, because of the ever present tendency for unintended consequences to occur, these often turn out not to lead to the goals for which they were intended (thus making them *materially irrational*). In fact, the means may subvert the very ends for which they were designed. This may be difficult to understand and it is perhaps not surprising therefore that many writers on organisations have taken Weber to mean that bureaucracy is 'efficient', thus implying that he was unaware of its tendencies to develop 'dysfunctions' – tendencies towards ineffi-ciencies (Albrow 1970). Weber was in fact pointing merely to the *potential* superiority of bureaucracy as an administrative instrument (its formal rationality) whilst being fully aware that it could manifest features which rendered it materially irrational, even going so far as to threaten individual freedom in a society with an attachment to such a goal or value. But this misunderstanding of Weber (perhaps partly deriving from a failure to realise that his ideal-type construct of bureaucracy was an intentionally one-sided representation) has been such that it has led to the development of one whole area of industrial or organisational sociology, and therefore part of the present strand. This is the work in the tradition of Robert Merton's analysis of the so-called dysfunctions of bureaucracy, something we will look at in chapter 6.

The great value of Weber's sociology is that his perspective allows us to take into account the individual social actor whilst seeing ideas and actions in the context of the vast political and dynamic patterns of history, but the great sweep of Weber's interests (note that he applied his historical and comparative approach to both western and non-western societies) does not mean that he was uninterested in detailed empirical investigation. He was, in fact, closely involved in what might have become one of the classical studies of industrial sociology: factory studies which predated the Hawthorne studies by twenty years or more. For a variety of reasons (see Schmidt 1976), these uncompleted studies have only recently been brought to the attention of those interested in the sociology of work and industry. As Eldridge (1971b) shows, Weber was interested in investigating a range of issues which are very close to those which have become central to industrial sociology in practice only some fifty or sixty years later. Weber's 'Methodological Introduction' to the proposed study shows an intention to study the effects of large-scale industry on the 'individual personality, the career and the extra-occupational style of living of the workers', thus taking into account the 'ethical, social and cultural background, the tradition and the circumstances of the worker'. All this is set in the context of economic, technical and capital-investment patterns in a way which can – in some respects – show the way forward for industrial sociology today.

The Weberian strand of specialised industrial sociology could well have started early in the century had these investigations not been abandoned. But various British sociologists have recently applied a generally Weberian perspective to industrial questions and performed studies very much in the spirit of Weber's own projected work. Most outstanding here has been the 'Affluent Worker' studies of Gold-thorpe, Lockwood *et al.* (1968, 1969) which have given sociology the important concept of 'orientation to work', a notion with great potential for investigating connections between actions in the workplace and the external community and cultural life of employees. Much of the recent work which uses the Weberian 'social action frame of reference' has developed in reaction to that which emphasises the systemic aspects of social life and which puts special emphasis on the importance of technology in organisations. In the perspective to be developed here shortly, I shall endeavour to ensure that the enormously invaluable 'orientation to work' concept does not become over individualistic or too subjective in emphasis by relating it to the logic of capitalist work organisation in the tradition of Weber (and indeed Marx) through the use of the ideas of Baldamus (1961), one of the first contemporary sociologists to bring an essentially Weberian perspective to bear in industrial sociology.

I would suggest that the recent growth of interest in Max Weber's relevance to the sociology of work and industry is part of a process whereby investigations are increasingly moving away from the managerially oriented tradition which has prevailed for half a century. Connected with this is the more truly sociological concern with seeing work behaviour and patterns in the wider political, social and cultural context. The same process has led to an increased attention to the analytical potential of Marx's thinking.

V The Marxian strand

Since its first appearance on the intellectual and political scene, Marxist and Marxian thought has influenced the development of sociology. Marx and Engels created one of, if not the most, influential theories of social life ever made available to those trying to make some kind of systematic sense of the modern industrialising world (I use Marxist to mean after Marxism and Marxian to mean after Marx). Until recently, it might be said that Marxian thought provided something which sociologists reacted to whilst, at the same time, being inspired by it and wishing to provide either an alternative to it or something more subtle, objective or socially acceptable. But, in recent years, Marxian thinking has seen a revival of interest within sociology itself. This can be understood as part of a reaction to the tendency of much academic sociology to be consensus-oriented, to be non-critical at best and justifying the *status quo* at worst and also to its tendency to restrict its attention to the 'social' at the expense of the economic and political. Also much of the existing sociology was seen to be too static and tending to ignore history.

Many of these dissatisfactions, however, might have been met by turning to Weber and, as we have seen, there has indeed been a revival of interest in Weber within industrial sociology, but for many sociologists who wanted a more critical and historical perspective Weber did not fit the bill. His anxious desire to separate sociological analysis and political evaluation is partly responsible here: his arguments were seen as being used too often to justify what more critical thinkers saw as the indifference of much mainstream sociology to the persisting inequalities of the modern world and the constant tendency for the ever present underlying conflicts to manifest themselves. In addition to this we have the range of misrepresentations of Weber which prevailed and these, together with Weber's self-identification as a bourgeois and his own political nationalism and antipathy towards socialist reorganisation, led to an understandable reluctance to look behind the complexities and ambiguities of Weber's writing to find a perspective which, in analytical terms, extends rather than rejects the strengths of Marxian thinking. The extreme subtlety, ambiguity and complexity of Weber's analysis, we have to recognise, does reduce the analytical value of his perspective in some ways. The full potential thrust of a Weberian perspective in sociology is perhaps only possible when combined with some of the more immediately coherent insights which are offered by the Marxian model. Something like this will be attempted in the next section, but, for the present, we must outline the basic ideas of the Marxian perspective.

Underlying Marx's ideas is an assumption about the nature of human beings. This is the assumption that human beings achieve the fullness of their humanity through their *labour*. It is through labour – an essentially social process – that the human world is created. This is the basis of Marx's 'materialism'. However, the conditions under which that labour is performed make a crucial difference to the extent to which the human being is fulfilled. Under capitalism the worker is forced into an unequal relationship with the owner of capital, to whom he sells his labour power. The relationship is unequal, since the owner of capital always has sufficient means of subsistence whether production goes ahead or not, whilst the wage worker is dependent on work being available to him. Furthermore, the employer requires the worker to do more work than the worker himself would need to do to meet his own needs; that is, the capitalist extracts the surplus value and in this way he exploits the worker. Work within a capitalist context does not allow the worker the creative fulfilment which labour could potentially give him. Since the worker does not use tools and materials which are his own and since he neither owns nor controls the products of his labour any more than he has control over the methods which he applies in his work, he cannot achieve his potential self-realisation. He is thus *alienated*. Although this condition clearly has subjective implications, fundamentally it is an objective condition. The contented car worker is no less alienated in this sense than a frustrated one.

Marx sets the above ideas in a historical model of the way in which one form of society develops to a point where it is superseded by another (for example, feudalism is transcended by capitalism which, in turn, is transcended by socialism). These ideas are also set in a structural model of capitalist society – or, more accurately, a capitalist mode of production. This is represented in Fig. 2.2.

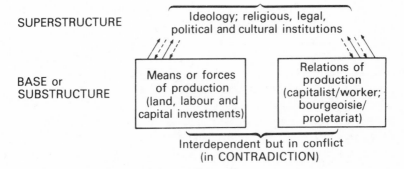

Fig. 2.2 The capitalist mode of production

According to Marx, it is the nature of the base which characterises a society. The way in which production is organised and the social relations accompanying that organisation are the more decisive factors – ideas, culture, law and politics being secondary. This again illustrates the materialist basis of Marx's work and perhaps indicates how the rather crude accusations of 'economic determinism' have come to be made against him. His approach is often described as 'dialectical materialism' and the dialectical element of the analysis can be illustrated here by pointing to the tendency of the base to contain within it conflicts and contradictions which represent the seeds of its own destruction (or, rather, supersession). The dialectic operates in history by the growth of one thing out of another in such a way that the new comes into conflict with the old, leading to its overthrow. Thus the bourgeoisie, we might say, created the proletariat but, in so doing, created the condition for its own overthrow.

Marx sees the capitalist mode of production as inherently unstable and ultimately doomed. This is because the social relations of bourgeoisie and proletariat are relations of fundamental conflict since their relationship is a one-sided and exploitative one. All of those who sell their labour power are, objectively, members of the proletariat.

They are all 'exploited'. The proletariat is thus a 'class in itself', but they will not act as a class – so releasing themselves from exploitation – until they overcome their 'false consciousness' and become aware of their common interest. Thus, class action is dependent on the growth of class-consciousness. The proletariat will become a 'class for itself' and act out its historical destiny through creating socialism. To recognise the full force of the notion of *contradiction* in Marx we have to note that the efforts of the bourgeoisie themselves, to a considerable extent, hasten their own demise. For example, the bringing together of larger and larger numbers of employees into ever larger work units will create the very conditions in which workers, through being thrown together, can become aware of shared economic and political interests. Thus class-consciousness increases and the challenge is invited.

The above is, I hope, a useful account of some of the basic ideas developed by Marx and his collaborator Frederick Engels. These ideas constitute more than simply a sociological theory. Marxism can be seen as providing a particular method of analysis – one which does not divide polity, economy and society and one which attempts to unite theory and practice. Despite the fact that Marx wanted to bring together theory and practice, sociologists can derive a great deal of analytical value from Marx and Marxian thought, without necessarily accepting a Marxist evaluation or programme for action. In doing this, however, the sociologist is clearly differentiating his enterprise from that of the Marxist and, given the central concern of Marx and Engels with human labour and their interest in relating individual experience to large-scale matters of history, economy and societal power structure, it would be surprising if there were not major insights to be gained with regard to the sociology of work.

Marx's key concepts of class and alienation play a large part in much of the sociology of work and industry, sometimes being used as simple analytical instruments and sometimes in a more Marxist way when their discussion is tied to an interest in actually affecting consciousness. In attempting to do this and combining analysis with a tendency toward self-fulfilling prophecy, there is a parallel with the managerial concerns of the neo-Human Relations writers considered earlier with 'self actualisation'. In my own analysis I shall be using a number of insights from the Marxian approach and will, in later chapters, consider various studies which form part of the Marxian strand in the existing sociology of work. The fact that many readers may not share the sentiments and the evaluations made by some of these authors need not reduce the analytical value and insight which may be gained from such studies. In saying this, however, I am not discounting the relevance to sociological theory of socialist aspirations (or vice versa). Such conceptions of alternative forms of community life are of immense relevance to any attempt to discuss the choices facing members of industrial societies.

Towards a consolidation of the sociology of work and industry

In the five strands described above as making up the present sociology of work and industry, we have seen a variety of theoretical perspectives. Each has value, but some are more likely than others to be effective in helping us to analyse and thus better understand the world of work. My present purpose is to bring together the most useful elements of what currently exists to create a theoretical scheme which might give a greater coherence to the sociology of work and industry than is seen at present. This framework is intended to make it easier to relate the various areas of interest (work, occupations, organisations, industrial relations and the societal context) and also to do fuller justice to the myriad facets of social life than do some of the more one-sided perspectives which currently exist within sociological theory. What is needed is a framework which ensures that analyses take account of both the individual and the societal, the tendency towards co-operation and that towards conflict, the tendency towards stability and that towards change, the importance of material interests and the importance of ideas and interpretations.

The motive behind what follows is not synthesis for its own sake. Both the splitting up of the world of work into watertight compartments and their being approached from often mutually exclusive theoretical points of view, tends to preclude our seeing the interconnections which exist between the different elements of people's work behaviour and experience. Some sociological diversity is inevitable and indeed welcome, but it must be controlled in order to avoid the dividing up of what might be indivisible in experiential terms. We must avoid the tendency to create divisions where, according to the very rationale of sociology, we should be seeking connections and interrelationships. It is possible that the discipline of sociology may currently be moving from its past diversity towards a state of greater maturity. There have been particularly impressive attempts at synthesis produced by Berger and Luckmann (1971) and Giddens (1976). However, it must be stressed that what follows below is merely a scheme or a model in the sense discussed in chapter 1. It is a tool kit of interrelated concepts which constitutes nothing more than an analytical device intended to aid understanding. In the form in which it appears at this stage, it is a mere skeleton. The chapters which follow are the flesh which is to hang on this structure. Inevitably, the scheme, like any other, is founded on certain values and assumptions. The emphasis on conflicts and contradictions, for example, reflects some of my own world view and philosophy. But this philosophy is an optimistic one – it assumes that history can, to a greater or lesser extent, be made by human beings through the exercise of rational choices, and the quality of understanding to which a sociology might contribute will aid or obstruct this. The scheme or model is set out at four levels, moving from the general towards the more specific.

I Assumptions about human nature

Any social scientific investigation early on has to ask the question of how much or how little it can assume about the nature of the human species. Human activity is not only limited by its environment but by the physical and mental apparatus of the species. I would argue that social scientists and other thinkers have frequently assumed too much here; making assumptions which precede investigation and which have the effect of closing off avenues of enquiry and subsequent human choice. This tends to be the case, for example, with the scientific management, human relations and Marxian approaches to work which were considered earlier. No sociologist can avoid using some model of man (my own humanistic one is fairly obvious to see) but, since such models are themselves socially constructed, the safest way to proceed is to keep our conceptions as *open* as possible. Instead of assuming that man is naturally a labouring creature, or a self-fulfilling creature, that he is inherently aggressive or 'territorial' (as some recently fashionable so-called 'ethologists' argue) we are better advised to assume that he can be any of these things – depending on his social and environmental situation. Human beings sometimes indulge in co-operative activity and sometimes in aggressive activity, depending on the various situations with which they have to cope.

There is an essential difference between human beings and other animals. This derives from the nature of their brain and their related capacities of language and abstract thought. These facilities enable the human animal to conceive of alternatives, to make value judgments and thus exercise a vast range of choices. This ability to create *conceptions of alternatives* means that even the most powerful instincts may be suppressed, channelled and overlaid with culture. Human activity therefore has to be understood in terms of an interplay between human thinking faculties and the environmental contingencies with which they are faced. It is wise, therefore, to suspend the question of what humans intrinsically *are* and to pay attention to what they *make of themselves and their situation*. To pursue the sociological path of examining how human beings organise themselves we must keep to a minimum any conception of the inherent 'needs' of the human individual and focus more on what basic problems have to be solved for social life to proceed.

II A general model of social life

For human beings to survive, certain minimal needs have to be met: first, physical needs for food, shelter and the like and, second, a mental need to be able to make sense of the world in which they find themselves. Some organisation of ideas is needed to help make order out of the potential chaos of the world; some assumption of an organised 'reality' is needed to provide what Peter Berger (1973) calls a 'shield against terror'. Thus, for society to exist, even at its very minimal level, these two needs have to be met. It is not through instinctive pre-programming but through human social organisation that we meet the problems of (a) allocating the scarce resources which people require to meet their material needs (the area of material interests) and (b) making sense of the world (the area of ideas). The procedures whereby these needs are met are closely interrelated. Since human beings are characterised by an ability to conceive of alternatives, they will tend to make evaluations about the means which are available to meet fundamental needs (preferring this food to that, this way of cooking to the other, etc.). Thus, among the resources which are available for satisfying basic needs, some will come to be *valued* more than others and these evaluations will be brought together in the *patterns of meaning* which develop in the sphere of ideas. Here, in the process of the subjective human being interacting with the objective environment, we see a dialectical interplay of the material and the mental as ideas influence interests and interests influence ideas.

Given that the physical environment is such that valued resources tend to be scarce, we find individuals forming themselves into co-operating groups or coalitions of interest, both to pursue material interests and to defend themselves against competing groups. Ideas are central to this primordial forming of groups: they give value to articles and to acts, so providing a focus for activity and, in developing the patterns of meaning which are needed to structure reality, they are tied in with *group ideologies*. These are sets of ideas which justify the group's activities ('legitimate' its interests) to both insiders and outsiders. Individuals play a major part in this process as thinkers or *group spokesmen* – people who articulate interests and aid organisation through providing legitimations of group action. Throughout history we see key individuals – leaders and thinkers – locating *objective interests* (potential interests with regard to whatever is scarce and valued in that society) which they then articulate, so converting these to *subjective interests* and mobilising the group. As time goes by, some groups win out over others in the competition for scarce resources and the pattern which they attempt to consolidate gives us the institutions and ideas which make up the *social structure* and *culture*, this including the political institutions of domination and the hierarchical pattern of social stratification. The situation in a society at any given time is the result of the currently prevailing distribution of power. By *power* is meant the capacity of any group or individual to affect the outcome of any situation in such a way that access is achieved or maintained to whatever resources are scarce and valued within a society or a part of that society. But the situation is never fully stable since the power which produces any tendency towards stability is a constant invitation to the resistance of others. In fact, all social arrangements have within them a possibility of unintended consequences arising which might threaten that arrangement or the goals which they were intended to meet (cf. Weber's 'paradox of consequences' and Marx's notion of 'contradiction'). These tendencies towards social conflict and structural contradiction are illustrated later when we look at capitalist industrial society.

Fig. 2.3 provides an outline of the model so far and I would comment that this tendency for people to form and re-form groups around interests pervades social life. It happens at the world level as nation states group and regroup into alliances and opposing camps

Two problems which have to be solved for social life to proceed

PROBLEM of allocating scarce
and valued resources
(area of INTERESTS)

PROBLEM of making
sense of the world
(area of a ideas)

Instead of each individual fighting
every other, people form into
(or are born into already existing)
SOCIAL GROUPS or co-operative
coalitions of interest (families,
tribes, classes, clubs, unions, etc.)

To create a sense of order
out of potential chaos,
people develop PATTERNS OF
MEANING or constructions
of reality (values, symbols,
norms, beliefs, etc.)

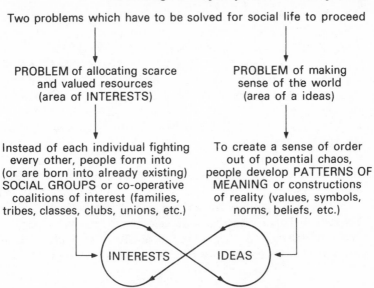

INTERESTS   IDEAS

Two processes dialectically interrelated

In the process of competition
and conflict, realities become constructed
and, in the process of reality construction, interests are articulated
and legitimated. Leaders/spokesmen assist in this articulation, so
helping group formation and the creation of GROUP IDEOLOGIES
(through the conversion of *objective* interests into *subjective* ones)

In history some
groups and ideas win out over others and in institutionalising
advantages dominant group action (and organised reactions to it)
tends to produce patterns of SOCIAL STRUCTURE and CULTURE

e.g. Political institutions
class structures
work organisations

e.g. Political ideologies
status ideas
work and managerial ideologies

Stability of social structure constantly threatened
(a) by group challenges against the dominant order (social conflict)
and (b) by the institutionalised means chosen by groups
tending to lead to unintended consequences which may subvert
the ends which they were meant to serve (structural contradictions)

Fig. 2.3 Outline of a general model of social life

and it can happen within families, tennis clubs or factory workshops. An example in the latter case might be where spray painters get together with sign writers in a vehicle body-finishing shop in a craft alliance to improve their incomes relative to those engaged in vehicle preparation and packaging operations. In the nation state example the supporting ideology might be based on some notion of 'defending democracy' whilst in the more microscopic example the core of the group ideology might be an idea of 'superior skill'. Ideological notions like these are not necessarily fictions: group spokesmen marshal existing ideas for interest-legitimating purposes as often as they create them. In processes like these, at the level of nation, work organis-ation, profession, trade union, family, workgroup, political party and so on and so on, realities are constructed and interests both fulfilled and denied. Every individual is located in a number of groups, his own advantage or otherwise in the distribution of goods being determined by his specific memberships and his particular world view influenced by the variety of reference groups so provided.

III Industrial capitalist society
Applying the general theoretical scheme to the type of society which has emerged in the west in the last two hundred years, we get a model of social organisation in which some social groups are more advan-taged than others as a result of their control over large-scale and often technologically-based means of wealth creation. This pattern came about historically as controlling landed interests were challenged by new less-advantaged groups who exploited changing historical circumstances by bringing together an *interest* in improving their own material and social position with certain *ideas* which included a 'work ethic', a utilitarian philosophy and a range of technical, economic and organisational techniques. Fundamental to the new ideas and techniques introduced by the rising industrial middle class were the rapid extension of the technical division of labour and the treatment of the labour power of an emerging working class as a commodity to be bought and sold on the market in a way which corresponds to the principle used to distribute goods and services.

Industrial capitalist society is inherently unstable, for a variety of reasons. For example, the need of those in control of work organis-ations to co-ordinate the efforts of other human beings, who tend to resist being used as means to others' ends, leads to social conflicts, but the structure (or system) of relationships itself contains inherent contradictions. Many of the techniques on which these relationships are based contain built-in tendencies towards self destruction. This can be seen, for example, in the need of employers to treat employees' pay as a cost (which must therefore be minimised) whilst the pressure of the same market economy on the employees is such that they will attempt to maximise their rewards (so tending to increase the employers' costs). This creates a fundamental and structural conflict of interests which is made manifest through employees uniting in collective action. This action, however, has itself been made possible by the employer's own actions: by his bringing together of larger and larger numbers of employees under one roof for the purpose of co-ordination and control. As a result of this contradiction, together with others, ranging from the level of national and international politics to inbuilt tendencies towards inefficiency in work organisations, adjustments and accommodations are constantly necessary for this overall mode of social organisation to survive. The tendency towards unintended consequences arising is present in every and any society and we would thus, following Weber's assumptions about social life, expect to see what we are here calling contradictions arising in any society. Marx, of course, envisaged a society free of contradictions. On the assumptions underlying the present model, however, this would be impossible. The present theoretical scheme leads us to expect that any society existing on a large scale and having a complex form of organisation would have considerable structural contradictions to cope with.

IV The organisation, the individual and the group
With the increasing application of the formally rational principles of the technical division of labour, economies of scale and centralisation and concentration of control, it has become a central feature of industrial capitalist societies that work is typically located in formal (bureaucratic) organisations. Formal organisations are conceptualised as *social and technical arrangements in which a number of people come or are brought together in a relationship where the actions of some are directed by others towards the achievement of certain specific tasks.* Employees are required to carry out these tasks by filling posts at various levels. The organisation is structured *horizontally* in terms of task specialisation and *vertically* to achieve control and co-ordination of efforts.

The individuals who approach the organisation for posts of the various types and levels come from an outside society which is itself structured on the basis of an unequal distribution of resources. Those seeking employment have (a) differing amounts of resources (such as cash, materials, skills, knowledge, physique) and (b) differing motives, interests and expectations (such as to make a living, achieve power or job satisfaction). All these factors, which are fundamentally influenced by the social groups from which the individual comes and, through these, overall structural factors of family, class, culture, education and so on, contribute to his or her *prior orientation to work*. The individual's perception of what work is available is also clearly important to this. By this prior orientation to work I refer to the significance which the prospective work has for the prospective worker – a significance which will guide the individual's 'choice' of work and his actions once work has been entered. The prior orientation of a male business graduate from a professional family seeking employment in a buoyant labour market is likely to be quite different from that of a sixteen-year-old working-class female school leaver without qualifications and who is competing with large numbers of other youths for very few jobs, and these different prior orientations to work will influence the way each of these individuals acts, once in a post. But the prior orientation will not necessarily be the prime determinant of action once work is entered. The actual *orientation to work* of the employed individual is influenced by a whole set of new job-related contingencies.

The individual approaching employment with whatever resources he has to offer and with a certain prior orientation enters into an agreement with an employer. This agreement is only made explicit in part (the official contract of employment) but, in practice, includes a range of tacitly accepted items. The individual is willing to accept certain costs – exerting a certain amount of effort, with associated fatigues and a certain surrender of personal autonomy – in return for certain rewards which may include cash, job satisfaction, security, power, status or opportunity for advancement. This agreement I term the *implicit contract* and the way in which the individual employee perceives it is central to his orientation to work. But the implicit contract is not a contract between equals: its inherent inequalities reflect those of the wider social structure, and this essential inequality contributes to its inevitable instability and to potential conflict. The employer and the employee, as buyer and seller of labour power, have inevitably conflicting basic interests. Each experiences pressure from the market context in which they have to live; pressures which encourage them, in the one case, to reduce costs (pressuring the employer to minimise the rewards given to employees) and, in the other case, to increase the same costs (pressuring the employee to maximise his reward to purchase the goods and services to be sought through the market). However, since the individual employee is relatively powerless compared to those who control the capital resources (the extent of this depending on the scarcity of his skills, knowledge or qualifications) there will be a tendency for individuals to come together with each other to defend their positions as well as to further their interests in workgroups, occupational associations or trade unions. The willingness to participate in such collective behaviour will vary with the extent to which the individual's skills are unique to him and are required by the employer. The level of consciousness of common interest will also be a major factor and to an extent this will depend on the presence of an individual who can act as a group spokesman and can articulate these interests with a supporting legitimation or group ideology.

The groups into which individuals organise themselves or are organised within work enterprises or bureaucracies are not, however, simply the result of defensive actions of employees against employers. The technology of the organisation itself requires the locating of people in groups – machinists here, accountants there; shop assistants on this floor, buyers on that – and this putting of people together to operate within the technology (in the widest sense of the term) can itself foster defensive or even offensive strategies on the part of these group members. This could be militant trade union action, a professional strategy or simple restriction of output. People's orientations to work are influenced by these group memberships in so far as the group mobilises to defend or improve the employee side of the implicit contract. The group ideology takes from and contributes to the individuals' orientations, and the fact that many of these groupings only come about as the result of the technique of work organisation chosen by those in control illustrates the existence of structural contradictions at the organisational level: chosen methods of control and co-ordination can create the conditions whereby that very control is challenged and threatened. The physical technology is of great importance in all this. Machines and working methods are no more neutral than are the more obviously social techniques of work co-ordination which are associated with them. Within the present model, technology is seen as a device used by the employer (a means to his ends), with the employee being recruited to work that technology, and it is through technical changes (deriving from investment decisions) that imbalances in the implicit contract often arise. Any such imbalance will see underlying conflict and contradictions show themselves in some overt manifestation, whether this be through strike activity, poor work performance, sackings, low morale, accidents and so on.

The individual's *orientation to work* is the link between the individual's experience within the workplace and his place in the world outside. His whole life prior to entering work is an influence on what occurs in work, as we have seen, and this prior orientation is then modified by actual contingencies within the work organisation, but the ongoing orientation to work is not only influenced by the work-related contingencies of technology, the ideologies of management and the interest groups to which the employee belongs. Outside factors still exert a major influence. Not only are societal factors like general cultural expectations of rising incomes or macro-economic tendencies towards threatened high unemployment going to influence work orientations and consequent behaviour but more individual circumstances of family life or personal attitudes can play a part. For any given individual, a change from single life to married life with children may influence the significance of a job as may something like a religious conversion or increased interest in political activity. To relate all of this we can use the concept of *career* to link the various changes of social position and associated orientation which can be seen throughout the life of the individual. Every one of us tends to view our own progress through life in some more or less coherent notion of process, from childhood interests and experiences through work and leisure activities to retirement. This succession of perceptions and orientations towards changing life situations constitutes one's *life career*, something in which the *work career* is but one component (regardless of whether that work career is one of upward progress, stability or decline in occupational prestige or status terms).

Fig. 2.4 outlines the key elements of the framework described above and is intended to help clarify the factors claimed to be important for analyses of work and employment. However, the overall theoretical scheme can only be ultimately judged in action. A model is evaluated by its utility in analysis and understanding, and not by its correctness. At this stage, I hope that it is apparent that use is being made of insights from various of the existing perspectives of

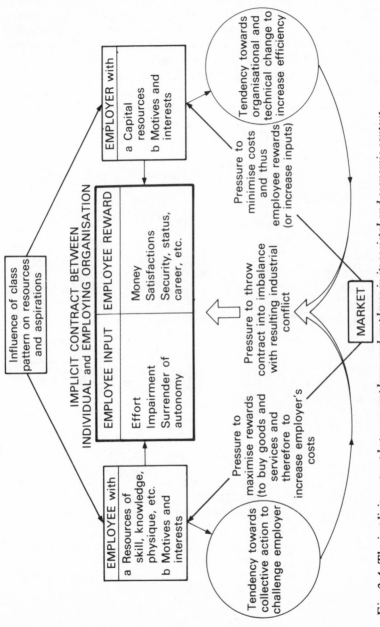

Fig. 2.4 The implicit contract between employer and employee in its societal and economic context

sociological theory and that the way in which these have been brought together might enable us to investigate the relationships and interconnections between the various aspects of working life which have until now generally been examined in isolation. We can now proceed to consider such issues as the nature of the industrial society, the meaning of work, occupational choice and individual career, work group and industrial relations behaviour, organisations, occupational strategies and the rest of the interests indicated as relevant to the sociology of work and industry in Fig. 1.6 on p. 31.

Chapter 3

The industrialised society

Introduction

To enable human beings to cope with the potentially chaotic world around them they need to develop some idea of an ordered reality. Life has to have some pattern or order to be manageable. People therefore develop sets of images and assumptions about the 'way things are'. This means that when people look at their own society they will do so with a degree of taken for grantedness. To give themselves a sense of certainty and security people tend to view their own particular social order as 'natural', if not 'inevitable'. Things are the way they are because that is the way they have to be. Yet, at the same time, people know better than this. In fairy tales heard in infancy and in fiction or political debate appreciated in adulthood people come across conceptions of alternatives.

Sociology as a form of reflection on the social world depends on the assumption that there are potentially alternative ways of life and that the 'ways things are' is not necessarily the way things have to be. It follows from this that if we are to use sociology as a means towards making more *informed* choices about our social arrangements, we must suspend those often practical and necessary everyday assumptions which we hold about our social world. One intention of this chapter is to argue that the particular type of society in which we find ourselves is by no means the inevitable outcome of some autonomous historical process. Both the structural arrangements on which our social order is based and the ideas and assumptions which we hold with regard to those arrangements are to be seen as the outcome of human efforts – outcomes which are both intended and unintended and which can only be comprehended if set in their context of human conflicts and competition.

It is an essential characteristic of a sociological view of working and industrial arrangements that this particular institutional area is set in its wider social structural setting. This chapter will examine the basic features, both structural and ideological, of the advanced industrial capitalist society and, in particular, the British case. Without an appreciation of these basic features, it is argued, one cannot fully appreciate the nature and problems of the specifics of work organisation and will therefore be less able to recognise the scope for potential choice. But at the same time as stressing the need for structural analysis, we have to remember that it has been emphasised in previous chapters that a successful sociology is one which does full justice to the *interplay* of individual and structural factors in human life. The present chapter emphasises the structural element but is very much to be seen as setting the scene into which the individual actor will walk in the next chapter and into which further structuring processes of occupation, organisation and industrial relations institutions will be introduced later. Yet the structural emphasis of the present analysis is not to be of the holistic type which was criticised earlier. The way in which the interplay of the individual and the social is to be constantly recognised even in this basically structural analysis is by remembering that structure and process in social life are closely related and that the constantly occurring process of social change involves individual and group *human initiatives*. The way our society is is not the way it was bound to be. To a vastly greater extent than is frequently assumed in both lay and social scientific thinking, our history has been made by human initiatives and group efforts, rather than by the popularly suggested forces of evolution, technical progress or physical determinism.

Determinism and choice in social change

Living in the twentieth century in a society where technological innovations are introduced daily into one area of our lives after another, it is not surprising that people should feel that they are caught up in some inevitable process. Much technical change is undoubtedly beneficial but even where individuals feel themselves being harmed by such changes they may be reluctant to be seen as standing Canute-like in an inevitably advancing tide. The machine-breakers of early industrialisation, concerned to protect their jobs, the objector to the advance of the first motor cars wishing to preserve peace and safety and the contemporary protestors against supersonic airliners wanting to defend the environment might equally well all be met with the advice not to 'stand in the way of progress'. Every form of work involves technology – universally in the sense of using some kind of technique and generally in the sense of utilising mechanical devices – and there can be few modern occupations which have been untouched by technological change (even the 'oldest profession' has adapted to the arrival of the motor car and the telephone – not to mention certain other mechanical and electrical devices!). These changes are again frequently seen as part of a historical trend which we cannot resist – as part of human evolution. 'Automation is bound to come', people are inclined to say.

Assumptions like these of the inevitability of changes in a general though not totally unspecific direction tend to permeate everyday thinking. The likelihood of technological progress, industrial advance and economic growth, even when clearly presenting problems of management, is fundamental to lay assumptions about the modern world. Both their inevitability and their desirability are frequently taken for granted, and a necessary requirement for the democratic control of industrial, technical and economic change is that this taken for grantedness be questioned. Before this is done we must examine the ways in which social scientific thinking has frequently matched lay tendencies in the ways in which it has approached the question of industrialisation and continuing social change.

Rivalling the age and persistence of the organic analogy, which was discussed earlier, as an import from biological into social thinking, has been the metaphor of *growth*. To see social change in terms of this metaphor is to imply a number of things. Growth of an entity implies change that is 'intrinsic to the entity, . . . change that is held to be as much a part of the entity's nature as any purely structural element' (Nisbet 1969). Further, it implies directionality, cumulative change, irreversibility, sequence (stages) and purpose (*ibid.*). But the metaphor of growth does not in itself imply that societies develop over generations in a direction which can be interpreted as leading to the improvement of the human lot. Yet such a notion emerged and rapidly gained ground when the novel idea of *progress* caught on in the eighteenth-century world of the European enlightenment (Pollard 1968). This, of course, was the seedbed period for both the coming social sciences and large-scale industrialisation and it is not surprising that the social sciences, from the start, took to their heart some idea of societies growing and improving *with inevitability* through history until they achieved some eventual state of industrialised peace and plenty.

Two of the very early sociologists, Saint-Simon (1760–1825), who coined the term 'industrial society', and his one-time disciple Comte (1798–1857), who invented the word 'sociology', suggested theories of change in which societies are seen as passing through stages. In both cases the final – and favoured – form is the industrial and scientifically-based social order. The ideas of the Saint-Simonians influenced later thinkers as different as Durkheim and Marx. Durkheim attempted his understanding of the industrial world by examining its evolution from less complex societies whilst in England Herbert Spencer (1820–1903) combined the biological metaphors of organicism, growth and evolutionism to show how 'militant society' develops into the more moral industrial society in which individual freedom can flourish. What all of this implies is that industrialisation is a 'natural' process. Such a suggestion gives industrialism a certain legitimacy deriving from an implied inevitability and a potential, if not always realised, benevolence. Marx, of course, stressed the capitalist nature of the industrialising society and aimed his criticism at the characteristics of capitalism rather than at industrialism itself. But Marx's analysis, despite a central recognition given to the part played by human agency and conflict (partly following Saint-Simon here) does see societies as passing through various stages. The socialist society will emerge as inevitably out of the capitalist as the capitalist did out of the feudal. Whilst it is unfair to accuse Marx of simple economic or technical determinism, there is an element of historical determinism here which brings much of Marxism into the overall category of 'historicist' thinking which we shall shortly submit to critical review.

It has been suggested that the evolutionary mode of thinking about social change, to which all the above analyses are related in one way or another, is to be understood in the light of problems faced by nineteenth-century social thought in Britain (Burrow 1966) but we can see much evidence of its survival in various forms in the twentieth century. At the centre of the twentieth-century version of evolutionary social thought is the concept of 'industrial society' and with this is associated the idea that industrial growth creates certain problems for any society and that there are only a limited range of alternative ways in which any society can respond to those problems. Any society which is industrialising is thus bound to conform more or less to a certain pattern as it follows the imperatives and indeed the *logic* of industrialism. The sociological characteristics of any society are likely to be pulled into a certain shape by the basic forces of the developing economy and its associated technology. In many ways this is reminiscent of the Marxian model of development and it is ironic that the revival of the notion of 'industrial society' by the French sociologist, Raymond Aron, in the mid-1950s was intended to help attack the Marxian position by showing that both capitalist and socialist societies had certain cultural and structural features in common. This was by virtue of their being industrially advanced and *in spite of* their different patterns of ownership and control. Yet the concept was taken over by various American writers, who were as much if not more opposed to the Marxist doctrine, in such a way that theories of industrialisation were developed which, it has been commented, seem 'to *rival* that of the Marxists in both their evolutionary cast and often too in their emphasis on the determining force of technological and economic organisation' (Goldthorpe 1971).

These theories of technological and consequential social growth are not mere neutral formulations which exist in an academic vacuum. If we are persuaded that there is only one 'correct' pattern of growth for industrial or industrialising societies, then political decision-makers can more easily be allowed to correct deviations from the proper path by treating them as pathological. The theories presented by W. W. Rostow in his *Stages of Economic Growth* (1960), for example, have been seen as influential in encouraging American policy against Vietnam in the 1960s (Frank 1971). Rostow sees the development towards the mature industrial society as a unilinear process with five stages. From a state of 'traditional society' we move to a state of 'preconditions for take-off' followed by 'take-off', the 'drive to maturity' and eventually the 'mass consumption society'. A socialist type of society is not one of the choices facing us: should a society err by moving towards communism, for example, it is to be seen as suffering a 'disease of transition'. Thus it is benevolent to act politically against any political tendency in this direction.

Rostow's theories have a clear relevance to currently 'developing' nations but other theories of this general type have equally profound implications for the degree of choice which is open to those living within the already advanced economies. Kerr *et al.* in their influential

Industrialism and Industrial Man (1973, first edition published 1960)
see a compelling *logic* underlying industrialism which means that
whatever choices are exercised by human beings they cannot avoid,
in the long run, having the technology of industrialism without a
whole set of concomitant structural and cultural features. Industrial
technology, it is argued, requires a highly skilled and professional
labour force who are controlled by a range of norms and rules. For this
labour force to exist and to be motivated there must be a certain kind
of open educational system accompanied by social mobility and
relative social equality in society at large. This society will inevitably
be a large-scale one with the consequent requirement for close
government involvement but with overall consensus being achieved
through the development of values of progress, science, mobility,
materialism, a work ethic and, especially, pluralism. No one group
dominates the world of 'pluralistic industrialism'. Various groups
compete but do so within an accepted web of rules with the
government holding the ring. Following from this is the suggestion
that in many basic respects all societies which are industrialised must,
because of the very logic of industrialism, become similar. This
notorious 'convergence thesis' will be returned to when we consider
the occupational structures of industrial societies (p. 154). However,
we will be better prepared for such a discussion when we have
developed a more detailed understanding of the characteristics of the
advanced western industrialised society and its forms of work organisation. For the present, however, we must submit to critique this
whole general approach to analysing social change, an approach which
gives a certain autonomy to historical forces and ultimately under-
emphasises both the importance of human agency and power, on the
one hand, and the degree of specificity of basic features of particular
societies and their constituent institutions on the other hand.

I would argue that to understand the nature of our particular
industrialised society we must examine how it came about as well as
characterising its essential features – these two being closely interrelated. To enable ourselves to do this effectively, we must first
exorcise the evolutionary ghost with its associated technical deter-
minist spirit which effectively haunts much of our everyday thinking
about society as well as much influential social science thought. To
achieve this aim, three areas will be examined. First, the problems
and dangers of the evolutionary type of assumption will be indicated.
Second, the more specific tendency towards technical determinism

will be questioned and, third, it will be argued, not that technology is unimportant, but that the nature of its importance lies in the part it plays in the power relations between human beings and human groups.

Most of the theories at which we have looked can be characterised as more or less *historicist* in the sense established by the philosopher Karl Popper in *The Poverty of Historicism* (1957). Popper's intention was to show the invalidity of approaches which examined the way in which history had unfolded in the past in order to predict the form which societies would take in the future. He was not saying that specific propositions of a sociological kind could not be made on the basis of historical data but that large-scale patterns of change in societies are logically unpredictable. Any major change in society is the outcome of so many different causal factors and human acts that any particular conjunction of events is to an extent adventitious. Had not certain people made particular choices at a specific time, for instance, and had not this economic development coincided with that political change in British history, then the industrial revolution might not have occurred or might have taken a quite different form. Further, if future stages of social change are capable of prediction on the basis of knowledge of past stages, why should not people act on that knowledge to contradict their own prediction? It is feasible, for example, that some advantaged and politically powerful social group might read Kerr *et al.*'s (1973) thesis of an increasing degree of equality and, as a consequence, act differently from the way they otherwise would have, choosing alternative means of meeting the problems created by industrial organisation.

These logical or methodological problems of historicism and evolutionary thinking are closely connected with that ever present tendency for social thought to utilise biological metaphors. However, metaphors can be misleading if given anything but temporary validity. To talk of societies 'growing' is to draw a parallel with the way, say, a tree grows, but the pattern of growth of a tree is genetically coded-in. Every tree, of a given species, will end up taking a form more or less identical to that of every other tree of that species. The roots cannot make any choice of the tree's future shape any more than can the leaves, the branches or the bark. Similarly, no branch is likely to engage in disagreement or enter into conflict with another branch about its share of the available moisture or sunshine. Societies are not trees and, whereas they may indeed increase in size and they may become increasingly complex over time as might such an organism, they do not have a genetic code structuring them. Social orders are *built*, we might say, to adopt a more appropriate metaphor, and in the building of the structure some people are likely to direct and some are likely to be directed and some will live in the best rooms and some in the worst. The design, for all that it is constrained by environmental and physiological factors, is likely to be the subject of choices and disputes over alternative conceptions, and disagreements, conflict and compromise will constantly threaten.

It is being suggested, then, that human understanding of the nature of life and social change is restricted by the metaphorical apparatus we tend to use. Humans must inevitably simplify the world to cope with it and we might almost say that it is 'natural' to turn to the biological notion of evolution to simplify the vast complexities of history as it is to turn to the system of organic analogy to simplify the equally complex nature of 'society'. But ideas are not neutral! It was argued in the previous chapter that human ideas tend to develop in a close relationship with the pursuit of material interests. It was also argued that the organic analogy of society has great potential for use by powerful groups to help justify the *status quo* (the *status quo* being made to appear 'natural' and inevitable). The evolutionary approach to social change is equally amenable to ideological use and political manipulation. In the same way that American politicians could use Rostow's theory of economic growth to help justify invading Vietnam, so might any politically or economically powerful group justify the building of nuclear power stations, the extension of a motorway network or the automation of a manufacturing plant. It's the way history is going, they might say. This is to act in bad faith – whether or not the proposal is generally beneficial or not. It is to speak immorally in its denial of politics, its suspension of values and its attempt to avoid contest, debate and informed choice. The ideologically suspect nature of most of the historicist theories of 'industrial society' is further suggested to us once we observe that the bulk of theorists tend to take as the future which they claim to predict the particular society in which they themselves live or, at most, some modification of their own society which they – evaluatively – favour. Is it coincidence that these generally American theorists see other societies moving towards the American pattern – albeit an often liberalised version of the present USA? We can each decide for ourselves whether this tendency is the result of ideology, an ethnocentric lack of imagination or simple defeatism: as Jean Baechler

(1975) says, 'To declare the necessity of one outcome is only to avow one's inability to explore other possibilities.'

We must now turn to the more specific role of technology in social change and note the dangers of the popular tendency to invest technical inventions with some causal power. Many of us in our early history lessons at school are encouraged, for instance, to see the scientific inventions which were made in the period of the industrial revolution as key causal factors in the occurrence of that revolution. Similarly, when asked to explain a fall in population over a given period there is a tendency to put it down to the development of more effective contraceptive techniques. Now it is true that technical changes in both of these cases might constitute *necessary* conditions for the social changes with which they are associated. What we have to avoid is assuming that they are *sufficient* conditions for change. Contraceptive techniques have, in several historical and contemporary situations, been available but have not been *chosen* by people willing to use them to limit their fertility. With regard to the major economic advances which occurred in Europe, we have to ask why the level of technical sophistication achieved by the Chinese in ancient times did not lead to industrialisation. The answer must be in terms of human initiative: the Chinese did not choose to apply their knowledge to economic ends. Eric Hobsbawm (1969) points out that the early industrial revolution was technically rather primitive. He suggests that what was novel was not technical innovation but 'the readiness of practical men to put their minds to using the science and technology which had long been available and within reach'. The motor of change was not the machinery itself but the motivation of these practical men: the novelty was 'not in the flowering of individual inventive genius, but in the practical situation which turned men's thoughts to soluble problems'. Technology is only a *means*, it is a piece of machinery or equipment with an associated technique which is used for carrying out certain tasks. Developments in technology may have massive implications for individuals and for society at large. Those implications only arise when people choose to adopt them and apply them to achieving human ends. Technology is no force in its own right. To talk of the 'iron hand of technology' as do Kerr *et al.* (1973) is to avoid the important and necessary question of who is applying technology and *to what ends*.

Although technology is in itself only a means, a mere device, there is nevertheless an important sense in which it is a mistake to see it as neutral. Technology may be a means towards certain ends, but the meeting of ends implies the fulfilling of human material interests, and all human material interests do not coincide. One man's airfield takes another man's land and one woman's capital requires another woman's labour. Thus the importance of technology in human life can only be appreciated once it is set in the context of social, economic and political relationships. Machinery itself can do neither good nor harm to human beings – it is what human beings do to themselves and to each other with machinery that is crucial. Any argument about the logic of industrialism, the inevitability of technological change or the automatic unfolding of 'progress' has to be treated with suspicion. All these notions have ideological power. They frequently justify the self-interested actions of some people which are as likely to threaten the interests of others as they are, indeed, to further them.

Having rejected evolutionary type approaches to the process of industrialisation and noted the dangers of technical determinism does not mean that we cannot examine the specific development of western capitalist industrial types of society in a sociological way. This will shortly be attempted and the analysis will be one which stresses the importance of human agency in social change and which emphasises the part played by power relationships in the emergence and ongoing development of the particular social form with which we are concerned. First, however, we must clarify this particular characterisation.

The nature of industrial capitalist society

It has been suggested that sociology proceeds in its analyses by having in mind some conception of forms of social organisation which stand as alternatives to those being studied. These conceptions may be more or less idealistic and more or less explicitly revealed. The type of society with which the present work is primarily concerned is only one kind of possible human social form. To differentiate it from other possible forms we need to characterise it. To understand how any social order differs from preceding contemporary or projected alternatives it is necessary to conceptualise it and identify its essential features. However, any such conceptualisation, model or ideal type is not to be judged in terms of whether it is right or wrong but in terms of how useful it is in helping us understand the nature of what is being studied. It is felt here that it is most useful to characterise societies like those of western Europe, North America and Japan as *industrial capitalist*. The importance of paying close attention to such an ideal type is further indicated once we realise that it was a conjunction of capitalist forms of activity and industrial methods of production which led to many of the most significant social changes which have occurred in recent world history. What goes on in the so-called developing countries of the world as well as in the more advanced 'socialist' states can only be appreciated if put in the context of what has occurred and is happening in the industrial capitalist sphere. Socialism itself, the most significant of alternatives to capitalism, which has inspired so much of the modern world, has arisen in very large part as a *critique* of industrial capitalist developments.

In a study of the sociology of work and industry it might well be expected that the focus would be on 'industrial society'. However, to choose this focus would be to neglect the extent to which industrialised societies are the way they are as a result of the growth of capitalism. It is reasonable to argue that industrialism, in anything like the sense in which we know it either in the West or the East, would never have come about but for capitalism. In addition to this, there are major objections to the concept of 'industrial society' which derive from the way this term has tended to be used ever since its first appearance. As was indicated above, the term is very much associated with an evolutionary perspective and with a basic assumption that the industrial nature of production in any society is the prime determining feature of social structure and culture. It may well be that technology does have certain imperatives with regard to social organisation but it would be a mistake to prejudge the existence of these at this stage as a result of the way in which we choose to conceptualise the social form with which we are concerned. We have to decide on the basis of analysis which features of our society are essentially concomitants of industrial technology and which relate more to the capitalistic aspects of social activity. Where we wish to allude to the basic industrial features of certain societies, we can adopt the usage 'industrialised society'. This has less implication of determinism, is less of a reification and can apply to any society in which large scale or complex technology plays a major part.

When we turn to the concept of 'capitalism' we come up against a series of problems. Not least of these is the pejorative loading which the word carries. This is largely a result of the fact that it has been the critics of capitalism who have used the term, whilst its defenders have preferred such expressions as 'free enterprise' (Williams 1976). However, there is no reason why the concept cannot be used analytically. Both the major theorists of capitalism, Marx and Weber, recognised that capitalist activity has occurred in various forms and settings historically, but both of these men became centrally concerned, as we are here, with the relatively modern phenomenon in which capitalistic activity becomes a predominant factor underlying the way in which whole societies are organised. Marx's characterisation of the capitalist mode of production was described in the previous chapter and central to it is his emphasis on the way in which the property owning *bourgeois* class buy the labour-power of a propertyless proletariat to meet their own ends. Weber fills out this picture. Whilst placing less central emphasis on the importance of property interests he nevertheless recognises their importance but he stresses the way in which, under modern capitalism, *formally free* labour is organised on a *rational* basis. By this he refers to the way it is administered on a routinised and calculative basis not known in any other kind of economic system.

From the work of these two major thinkers, Marx and Weber – one the arch antagonist and the other a partial defender of capitalism – we can draw out for our own purposes several key features which are basic to modern capitalist societies. These are: (1) a basic inequality in the distribution of resources with certain social groups controlling the means whereby wealth is produced whilst, (2) the other social groups merely possess 'labour-power' or a capacity to work under the direction of others, this being their only means of earning a living and being subject to, (3) the systematic and calculatively rational pursuit of return on capital by those who own or control that capital and buy the labour-power. The predominance of these features could not have occurred, however, without their conjunction with industrialisation. Thus we get the following working conceptualisation of the form of society with which we are concerned: *the industrial capitalist society is one in which large-scale or complex machinery and associated technique is widely applied to the pursuit of economic efficiency on a basis whereby the labour-power of the members of some groups is sold to others who control and organise it in such a way that the latter groups maintain relative advantage with regard to those resources which are scarce and generally valued.* We can follow Baechler (1975) who, after his detailed examination of the analysis of capitalism by both Marx and Weber, comes to the conclusion that the specific and defining feature that belongs only to the capitalist system is 'the privileged position accorded the search for economic efficiency'. We must note that 'efficiency' can only be understood in terms of specific goals and that the privileged significance given to the pursuit of economic ends over other values such as religious, military or political ones, is privilege given to the fulfilling of goals which may not be shared equally by all members of society. For example, it is quite common to see employees – at various occupational levels – becoming unemployed as a result of their employers' honest and conscientious pursuit of efficiency. Reducing manning levels or deskilling work is clearly in the interests of efficiency, but it is not necessarily 'efficiency' from the point of view of those experiencing job or skill loss. Whether or not such actions are to be judged efficient or otherwise at the level of whatever goals are widely shared within a society is a judgment which, ultimately, can be informed by, but not made by, social scientists.

Having now established the basic features of the *type* of society with which we are concerned, we are in a position to examine the range of social institutions and cultural forms which are associated with such a society. Instead of assuming that this range of values, like individualism, materialism and democracy, or institutions like those of the family, education and the state, are *determined* by these material or technical features, we will examine their relationship with basic structural features by looking at the intimately interrelated processes of development which have occurred historically. Instead of showing that any one institution necessarily relates to the logic of another we will see that industrial capitalist society contains major structural tensions and contradictions which both render it unstable and which give it an essential dynamic. Many of the problems faced in the organisation of work and the management of the modern economy can only be understood in the light of these structural problems. Analysis of what can, in many ways, be seen as the *peculiar* rise of industrial capitalism has to be examined to fully appreciate the nature of the fundamental problems.

Interests and ideas in the rise of industrial capitalism

The above characterisation of industrial capitalist society is incorporated in the basic theoretical scheme which is used in this book and which was set out in chapter 2. To understand the dynamics behind the rise of this specific societal form we must remind ourselves of the more general set of factors which that model brings to our attention. It was suggested that social life and social change be seen in terms of conflict and competition which occurs between social groups throughout history. These groups are formed around common interests and the formation and activities of groups are closely involved with processes whereby ideas are developed and expressed. Advantages with regard to scarce and valued resources are sought and, once achieved, attempts are made to regularise, legitimate and hence maintain advantage in the face of potential and actual attempts to challenge that advantage. This we can see happening across that period of European history between the feudalism of the Middle Ages and the vastly different social order of today.

It has been a traditional and indeed valuable method used by sociologists to accentuate the characteristic features of industrial capitalist societies to compare these with some model of a feudal type of society. The most famous attempt to do this is perhaps that of Ferdinand Tönnies (1855–1936) who contrasts the modern form of *society (gesellschaft)* with the older, traditional, small-scale *community (gemeinschaft)*. Reduced to the simplest possible model of transition we can see European society as changing its major features from a basis of small-scale, intimate, stable, rural, religious and traditional *gemeinschaft* to a basis of large-scale, individualised, rapidly changing, urban scientific and rational *gesellschaft*. Indeed, sociology is itself part of that transition (see Fig. 1.1 on p. 8). To fill out this simple image of transition we will now look back to the pre-industrial and pre-capitalist world, remembering that we are not dealing here with irrelevant and purely academic matters but are considering a world which has left us images of life which still underlie many of our contemporary ideas about how human lives could be lived.

People undoubtedly worked very hard to exist in the medieval period but this work was performed on a basis which fundamentally differs from that which we take as normal today. One's work was seen more as an inevitable burden than as a way of developing oneself. It was not a duty to work hard nor was hard work a way of improving oneself. Hard work was done because survival demanded it. Further, there was little separation of home and workplace and a quite alien notion would have been that of working *for* somebody else. This does not mean that the rich did not exploit the poor but that even the poorest and most exploited serf tended to have his own land to work – even if he was forced to supplement the income derived from this with some wage labour. However exploitative relationships were between social groups, the hierarchical relationship existing between people was one based on a certain recognised mutual dependence and some sense of reciprocity. There was a commitment from both sides of the master-servant relationship of a diffuseness quite lacking in the modern employment relationship. The essential feature of work was that it was performed to meet clearly and generally recognised needs and its rhythms, or lack of them, were given by natural and immediate human needs themselves, like the need for food, shelter and clothing, or by the rhythms of nature itself in the shape of the changing seasons, the needs of animals to be milked or crops to be harvested.

The most advantaged groups of this period not only had the greatest share of wealth, which was predominantly in the form of land and the comforts which accrued from that land, but they were also served by a church which provided ideologies helping to stabilise order. Christianity itself contained much which might encourage challenge to the feudal order and such challenges indeed did arise in combination with Christian 'heresies' and millennarian hopes on a number of occasions. However, the Roman Catholic Church and its doctrines, which put its priests as intermediaries between individuals and their destinies, was able to counteract challenges with organic models of society like that developed by Aquinas in which each person plays his natural part in the wider scheme of things. Each person serves or contributes to this scheme for the sake of the whole community. Those who rule are merely doing so for the benefit of the community. Given a largely illiterate society with the insecurities resulting from dependence on agricultural production, dangers of war and disease, it is easy to see how the church, with its near monopoly on literacy, could maintain a stabilising affinity between ruling interests and the realm of ideas.

Our theoretical scheme would suggest that we look for social groups developing to challenge this order and, indeed, we can see peasant revolts providing such a challenge, but the peasant challenge was not the one which prevailed. The one part of the feudal society which was not fully incorporated into the feudal order was the urban trading element which contained a class whose interests did not fit with a stable, landed and *rural* social order. It was amongst this growing *bourgeoisie* that we find an economically motivated group with interests which potentially challenge the *status quo*. This was a group lacking social legitimacy and which needed to find appropriate ideas to give force to its motives and thus power to its pursuits of economic ends, as well as to give itself legitimacy in its own eyes and those of others. It is in relationship to these problems that we turn to Weber's famous analysis of the influence of the Reformation and its Protestant ethic on the rise of capitalism.

Weber's study *The Protestant Ethic and the Spirit of Capitalism* (1965) has aroused fierce controversy but like so much of his writing (see above, pp. 49) it has been treated out of the context of his larger body of work and thus been subject to criticisms which are beside the point (Moore 1971, Baechler 1975). Weber is often seen as suggesting that Protestantism *caused* capitalism whereas, in fact, he was merely investigating one aspect of the chain of events which led to the specific phenomenon of modern capitalism. If one looks at his *General Economic History* (1927) and at *Economy and Society* (1968), especially his chapter on 'the city', it is clear that he sees the influence of Protestantism as just one factor to be put alongside the type of change in city life alluded to above, the growing separation of home and workplace and many other technical and commercial factors. Weber was concerned to counter the one-sided materialism and the determinism of Marxian accounts of the rise of capitalism and he chose to examine the part played by *ideas* in social change. This was by no means an alternative to concern with material *interests* but an attempt to demonstrate the necessity of examining how the congruence of certain interests and particular ideas produces forces leading to change. His analysis brings into historical analysis the variable of human agency, countering any tendency towards determinism with an emphasis on human motivation. As Reinhard Bendix (1965) points out, Weber did stress that it is interests and not ideas which govern men's conduct. Nevertheless he sees world-views created by ideas frequently acting 'like switchmen indicating the lines along which action has been propelled by the dynamics of interest'. In his famous and very useful concept of *elective affinity* Weber suggests that people *adopt* ideas to *fit in with* their interests.

The spirit of capitalism, aided by the Protestant ethic, brought a new force and a legitimation to the proto-capitalists of the cities. What it did was to encourage hard work not just in order to meet basic needs or to produce short-term capital gain but as a virtue or duty in its own right. A religious doctrine which suggests that one is serving God by

following one's mundane tasks in a self-disciplined and efficient way
and which combines this with a demand for an ascetic or frugal form
of existence has obvious potential for fostering such a spirit and
indeed encouraging the accumulation of capital. One makes money by
hard work and application but confidence of membership of the *elect* is
risked if one slacks in one's efforts or if the fruits of one's labours are
indulged in. The fruits of labour are not now hedonistic ones but
confidence of salvation. Under Catholicism a 'calling' from God
involved transcendence of the mundane but the novel Calvinist notion
of seeing one's mundane work itself as a 'vocation' overturned this.
The almost revolutionary change in religious thought brought about
by the Reformation was its removal of the church and its priests as
intermediaries between the individual and God. In a sense, every man
was to be his own priest and the demand was now less that one should
be guided in one's actions by the church hierarchy than that one
should look to one's own conscience in deciding how one should act.
As Christopher Hill (1974) points out, there had been earlier
tendencies in Christianity which looked to motives of the heart in this
way but such ideas were only able to take root once there were social
groups well placed to sustain opposition to prevailing values and 'in a
society where custom and tradition counted for so much, this
insistence that a well-considered strong conviction overrode everything else had a great liberating force'. The account given by this
contemporary historian fits well with a reading of Weber's analysis,
which sees Protestantism not causing capitalism but giving force and
legitimacy to the pursuit of economic interests by already emerging
social groups:

> the protestant revolt melted down the iron ideological framework
> which held society in its ancient mould. Where capitalism already
> existed, it had henceforth freer scope. . . . In a society already
> becoming capitalist, protestantism facilitated the triumph of the
> new values (*ibid.*).

At this stage it is worthwhile to pause and consider just why looking
back so many centuries to changes in theological thinking should be
relevant to a study concerned with work and industry today.
Attention to these matters is justified, I believe, by the need to locate
the roots of norms and values which underlie the culture of industrial
capitalist society. Protestantism played a major part in liberating

people from the forces of tradition – forces which ensured that by and large one played one's allotted role in a drama scripted elsewhere. This laid a massive stress on the individual, on a striving for individual achievement, on human competitiveness, and on the acquisition of goods for their own sake. Alongside all this was the unleashing of what Weber sees as a major process which runs through all subsequent social change in western Europe: a process of *rationalisation*. This process involves a replacement of the criterion of tradition (we do this because it is the way it has always been done) with a criterion of rationality (we must work out the most efficient means of achieving this end). The criterion of rationality, in this sense, involves submitting actions to constant calculative scrutiny and produces a continuous drive towards change. The essence of rationality is *calculation*, and, historically, this process led to the undermining of the primacy of religious or magical thought (including, ironically, those forms which gave impetus to this process) and is a force pushing forward the growth of science and technology together with an accompanying expansion of the technical division of labour and the bureaucratic organisation of work. It is interesting to note that many of the changes made in contemporary work organisations, especially changes which lead to the replacement of human skills or even basic human involvement at all, by technology and advanced techniques of control, are frequently described by those implementing such changes as part of a 'rationalisation programme'. The disturbance to human lives caused by these programmes can be seen as part of the long-running tendency of Weber's process of rationalisation and its accompanying individualism, materialism and acquisitiveness given such impetus by the Protestant Reformation to *threaten social solidarity*. The modern 'work ethic' – a secularised form of the old Protestant ethic – has long been seen as posing a threat to social cohesion or solidarity as David Rubenstein (1978) has shown. This is a tendency which, as we shall see shortly, creates basic tensions within the contemporary industrial capitalist society.

We have to be careful in looking at the importance of changing ideas not to underestimate that their force only becomes manifest when they interact with changing material and political conditions. If we turn our attention towards England, where the industrial revolution was later to occur, we see a rising *bourgeoisie* challenging the old order in such a way that by 1688, their political action and parliamentary triumph had brought about a *bourgeois* revolution. The wealth of this rising class was made possible in part by other aspects of the decay of feudalism. Massive rural changes were displacing increasing numbers from the land (as many as half a million by the mid-seventeenth century) and from traditional crafts. People were thus made available as wage labour for employment or as domestic manufacturers to be exploited by merchants. These commercial groups were not unopposed in their ascendancy, of course, and it was the very opposition of established groups to their interests which helped mould them into what can be viewed as a coalition of interest (in terms of our theoretical scheme). H. Israel (1966) suggests that England had a relatively permeable class structure by general European standards and that this encouraged aspirations towards advancement. The crown, however, pursued a policy of suppressing middlemen and the 'proto-industrialists' in ways which increased the revolutionary challenge to the established order. This threat was increased by the driving of various proto-industrial cliques into a united front, their consolidation being 'promoted by this clear perception of a common foe, the Establishment' and they were helped in their new solidarity by Puritanism – 'the only available ideology that could effectively legitimise opposition to church and state simultaneously'. Here again we see the dialectical interplay of interests and ideas brought out in our theoretical scheme.

Opposition to the rising groups had also helped foster the scientific spirit. The effective forbidding of non-conformists entering Oxford and Cambridge after 1660 encouraged the application of minds away from traditional academic pursuits towards pursuits of a more rationalising spirit, but to see the resulting scientific developments leading to the industrial revolution would be mistaken, as was suggested earlier. However, the conditions were set for yet new groups of men to emerge and apply the rationalising spirit with a vengeance to employment and to manufacture. Studies of the early industrial entrepreneurs like those of the Hammonds (1966) and Bendix (1963) suggest that a large proportion of these men were from relatively low origins and, like their merchant predecessors, they too, Bendix argues, found the opposition of ruling groups 'an important stimulus to the formation of this social class' (*ibid.*). Yet the detailed historical investigations of John Foster (1974) in Oldham indicate the importance of money made in the previous century of capital accumulation in the establishing of new manufacturing concerns. What clearly did occur in the latter part of the eighteenth century in

Britain was the beginning of a great leap forward of the capitalist spirit, a revolutionary advance facilitated by the new processes of industrialisation. In what is probably best seen as an alliance between the established capitalist groups and some of the new thrusting industrial men who managed to establish themselves with these groups, a massive initiative was taken with fundamental structural and cultural implications.

The specifically novel development of the industrial revolution was the bringing together of the now available wage labour in special premises to work under the supervision of the employer (or his agents), using the employer's tools and machinery and his raw materials. The impression is frequently given, following the lead of Adam Smith's *Wealth of Nations*, that the splitting down of work tasks among the employees in these factories simply follows some 'logic of efficiency'. Marglin (1971) has produced a useful corrective to such a view in arguing that this division of labour was not the result of a search for a 'technologically superior organisation of work but for an organisation which guaranteed to the entrepreneur an essential role in the production process'. There is thus no determining force making the appearance of the factory inevitable. There is, rather, a choice on the part of certain people to provide themselves with a niche in society – one which involved the control and co-ordination of the labour of others in the pursuit of capital accumulation and their own material advantage. It was no technological imperative that brought people into factories and set under way new methods of work organisation.

The increasing bureaucratisation and growing scale of work organisations which later occurred is central to the concerns of chapter 6 but what we will do at this stage is to look at the ways in which the new forms of work organisation, the accompanying societal changes and the emerging legitimations of both, contain within them inconsistencies, conflicts and contradictions which gave industrial capitalism a basic instability requiring it to be continually adapted.

Contradictions, adaptation and change

The preceding analysis has strongly opposed the popular tendency to view history or social change as something which operates auto-nomously and pulls human beings along with it. Instead, the importance of human agency and the pursuit of material interests have been stressed in our outline of the rise of industrial capitalism. Nevertheless, my sociological analysis is bound to show that social structures are by no means the simple result of conscious human design. What Weber calls the *paradox of consequences* is constantly operating: the pursuit of any human goal can set in motion tendencies which may not only create unforeseen and incidental effects but may in fact completely undermine the original human purpose. A large part of that which we call social structure is the result of these *unintended consequences* of purposive human action. The most basic example that we can give of this tendency is that of social class. We can see modern class systems as an outcome of the historical actions of industrial capitalist entrepreneurs, but these men never intended to create a class of human beings with all the potential which such a thing might have for the growth of opposition to industrial interests. They *did* want a pool of landless wage-labourers, of course, but this is not the same thing as a potentially self-organising social class.

Tendencies of elements within social structures to undermine those structures are conceptualised in our theoretical scheme as *structural contradictions*. Here the Marxian concept of contradiction is being used. Whereas Marxian usage emphasises the ways in which contradictions lead to the collapse of particular 'modes of production' (see above p. 55), the usage here is more open – it accepts that constant adaptation is as likely a possibility as collapse or revolutionary supersession. If the early industrial employers created a class which might well have brought them down they equally readily adopted policies which would cope with such a challenge, giving us, for example, the dynamic behind shifting employment policies over the years.

Weber's thesis of an increasing rationalisation of life in the West might be interpreted as suggesting that what this notion implies – an increasing tendency to calculate the most appropriate means to achieve a given goal – would mean that contradictory tendencies in the resulting social organisation would be less than those to be found in less 'rational' times. However, precisely the opposite is the case. The increasing concentration on *means* (rules, techniques, money, machines, accounts, etc) which the rationalisation trend involves can mean that the original human goal or purpose for which the means was chosen becomes lost or subverted. Formal rationality (applying technically appropriate means) paradoxically does not necessarily lead to material rationality (advancing the originally inspiring goal). For example, it is formally rational for a society to use money as a means towards the efficient exchange of goods which people want and need. As long as the medium of money enables people to gain the fulfilment and satisfactions which led them to adopt the device in the first place, its use is also materially rational. Should money-making become an *end in itself*, with the consequences that the originally motivating desire for comfort, pleasure or whatever is not fulfilled, then the use of money is materially irrational. Its use is still formally rational, however.

What is to be argued here is that the rise of industrial capitalist societies has occurred in such a way that these societies contain a range of structural contradictions. This means that they are in constant need of adaptation (to avoid collapse or chaos). The various contradictions which arise can be related to two major trends which underlie the processes whereby industrial capitalist societies have developed. The first trend is the rationalisation one: that of the increased application of formally rational criteria of action. This has involved an ever present instability to arise as chosen means tend to subvert the ends for which they were designed. The tendency for *means* to be a more central focus of concern than *ends* is important here. The second trend is that of the increased cultural emphasis on the individual, on his or her needs, wants and fulfilment, as opposed to the collectivity. This raises problems for social cohesion and is another potential source of instability.

Examples and implications of specific contradictions will be examined throughout the present work. However, it is useful at the present stage to simply list various of these potential sources of instability existing in industrial capitalist societies and having ramifications for life within those societies as well as for the organisation and experience of work in particular:

(1) In bringing people together under the roof of one factory (or office) employers not only act to further their own ends but also create conditions in which opposition to those interests may arise in the form of trade unions or even class-based political action.

(2) To achieve the degree of mobility of labour needed in a market economy, people have to be formally freed from any type of feudal, geographical or kinship ties. Such 'freedoms' tend to influence demands for political freedoms and interest in democratic participation, which again enables labour to challenge employing interests.

(3) Employers need a workforce willing to be controlled and

co-ordinated yet, at the same time, the complexity of industrial work techniques requires employees to use a certain degree of *initiative*, thereby encouraging possible demands for independence from control.

(4) The formally rational bureaucratic method of work organisation, whilst having great potential for efficiency in task performance, at the same time contains tendencies towards rigidity, formalism and the like, which can make it inefficient.

(5) The formally rational technical division of labour (whereby tasks are split down into small components which a specialised operator can perform more ably and more cheaply than a generalist) can lead to efficiency. At the same time it can, in its tendency to bore, tire or contribute to the alienation of the operator, encourage inefficiency.

(6) In reducing traditional social attachments and putting the emphasis on individualism, calculation, self interest, achievement and competition, dangers of *anomie* (normlessness) and social relations based on *low trust* and their consequences are risked.

(7) The increase in general wealth provided by industrial capitalism has a motivating effect. Yet at a certain level the expectations for self-development encouraged by many of the leisure forms made possible by this wealth may lead to a questioning of the tendency for there to be a lack of self-development in the work performance which creates this wealth. This may be 'demotivating'.

(8) The economic growth made possible by industrial capitalism may not only reach physical limits (as fossil fuels run out or pollution increases its destructiveness, for example) but it may itself create *social limits* to that growth as members of society realise that many of the widely pursued goals of economic activity (top jobs, the best education, the fastest transport, the most secluded home or holiday place) are, by their very nature, only ever achievable by a narrow majority.

The sources of instability introduced above briefly, and rather simplistically, are those inherent in industrial capitalist society and those most intimately connected with work organisation and experience itself (bureaucratic inefficiencies, work alienation, unionisation, workplace and occupational opposition strategies) will be central to the analyses of subsequent chapters. Others will be considered now as part of our establishing the societal context of work activities. An understanding of the problems arising in the workplace is impossible without seeing work in its overall societal, historical and political context.

The notion of structural contradiction may not be a simple one to grasp but an appreciation of it is vital to the type of insight which *sociology* offers. In arguing that industrial capitalism has created unintended consequences and fundamental instabilities, it is not being suggested that such a society necessarily creates an 'unnatural' way of life for human beings. It was suggested in the previous chapter that humans are relatively flexible and are not forever confined by an unchanging 'human nature'. Indeed I suggested (on p. 40) that people might well live happily in a pecuniary culture (as opposed to a 'self-fulfilling' one). Yet I might appear to be arguing in the present chapter that a pecuniary culture has self-destructive tendencies, but this is not the point being made. The tendency towards a materialistic or pecuniary culture in the historically specific industrial capitalist societies being considered here does indeed have self-destructive tendencies. This is not to do with the nature of man, however. It is, rather, a result of the fact that the same culture which encourages material advances or financial advantage contains within it and *at the same time* the quite contradictory encouragement towards the seeking of self-development, fulfilment and expression. The critical problem is a sociological one and not a psychological one.

Class, power and control

The model of social life set out in chapter 2 suggests that the competition which goes on between social groups for access to scarce and valued resources becomes consolidated over time as some groups win out over others. Patterns of advantage emerge and these are frequently represented by sociologists as *social stratification*. Different types of social structure have different characteristic forms of stratification or structured social inequality. Feudalism has its estates, for example, whilst other societies may have groups stratified into castes or into slave and non-slave categories. The form of structured inequality in the industrial capitalist societies, however, is generally regarded as a mixture of class and status stratification, with social class predominating.

The use of the term class in anything like its modern sense only came about during the period of the industrial revolution (Williams

1976). Prior to this terms like rank, degree and station had been used. The term 'working class' (and its contrasting to a 'middle class') is closely associated from the start with the emergence of a category of landless wage labourers. Given that one of the key defining features of a capitalist society is the existence of such a group, it is clear that social class is, sociologically, a centrally significant feature of the social structure of such societies.

The standard starting point for consideration of social class is Karl Marx's analysis. Justification can be found for his taking a labouring class of people, dependent on selling their labour power on the market, to be a central feature of the developing industrial capitalism if we consider just how radical a change in society was constituted by the growth of a large class of such persons. Economic historians have engaged in fierce debates over the alleged improvement or decline in the standard of living over the period of the industrial revolution. In many ways this misses the point, however. Christopher Hill (1974) has shown the strength of the 'ideological' hostility which many men and women felt towards wage labour at this time: 'To accept a merely wage status in the factories was a surrender of one's birthright, a loss of independence, security, liberty.' Two centuries of experience of what dispossessed wage-labour could mean had created a hostility which could only be relieved by a gradual development of a self-respecting place for the wage labourer in the community.

The Marxian model of class is one of capitalism relentlessly pushing towards what would eventually be just two classes: the property-owning *bourgeoisie* and the proletariat. The proletariat could only subsist, given their lack of sufficient property, through selling their labour power to those with property or capital. Marx recognised the existence of various other classes but saw their status as a transitional one. Sociologists have tended to follow this basically economic approach to conceptualising class although many have refused to accept the basic two-class model. Marx stressed that it was one's property situation which defined one's class – this relating to one's relationship to the means of production. This is a useful way of viewing contemporary stratification. It stresses that one's position in society is not so much defined by one's income as by *the part which one plays in the way wealth is created in society*. Max Weber took over this basic approach in so far as he regarded property or the lack of it as a basic feature, but he did recognise the possible existence of a variety of different classes.

Weber sees a class arising when a number of people share similar *life-chances* in the market. By life-chances is meant the ability to gain access to scarce and valued goods and services (home, food, education, etc). This ability derives from the 'amount and kind of power, or lack of such, to dispose of goods or skills for the sake of income in a given economic order'. The Weberian approach thus encourages us to differentiate between, say, a class of people who basically live off capital, a senior and junior class which manages, administers or provides professional services, a clerical and a shopkeeper class and a manual working class (see p. 15 for a model along these lines). A person's occupation, we can see from this, is a useful *indicator* of class position and in chapters 5 and 6 we will take up this analysis in more detail, examining how one's occupational, organisational and class positions relate. The importance of this is considerable because any perusal of a vast bulk of research materials emanating from sociologists, economists, government statisticians or market researchers will indicate that one's occupation (and the class position indicated by it) bears very significantly on so many aspects of one's life: the chances of one's infants dying, the quality of one's education, the disease from which one may die, the size of one's house, the holidays one has, the leisure one has and the food one eats, but these are all factors external to the work situation. One's class position is of equal importance, however, to the experience which one has of work itself. Not only is a higher social class position likely to give one better access to generally desirable goods and services but it will influence the physical working conditions and, especially important, the extent to which one has autonomy and discretion at work. These latter issues will be considered in the next chapter when we look at the individual's experience of work and again in chapter 6.

Social class is basically an economic category, it is argued, but Weber's best known contribution to the study of social stratification is his placing of what he calls 'status groups' alongside class grouping. Whereas class deals with the objective aspects of the way people are ranked in society, status refers to the subjective elements. A status group is a group, membership of which gives a certain amount of socially estimated honour or prestige. It is thus conceivable that certain groups in society, despite a class situation deriving from a lack of property, may nevertheless be highly regarded because of some special prestigious life style, religious affiliation, racial characteristic or whatever. Here is another basis of stratification. What is immediately noticeable is the difficulty, in actually existing industrial capitalist societies, of giving examples of groups whose class position is a subordinate one but who are a group of high status. The reason for this is that, as Weber noted, class and status stratification tend to coincide in practice, but this is what happens to have occurred, for a variety of reasons, and is not inevitably the case. High status groups tend to be in superordinate class positions because in a social order where economic criteria predominate it is very likely (though not inevitable) that high prestige will be related to life styles dependent on economic success. Where we do tend to see status groups possibly cross-cutting class stratification is in cases where the *negative* estimation of prestige is more relevant. Racial characteristics are an important example here and religious affiliations may be important in some cases (Ulster providing a British example). A successful entrepreneur of visibly different racial origins from the main population may not be generally placed in the same subjective or status ranking as a member of the majority population with an identical objective or class position, for example. These are issues to which we will return when we consider occupational structures and labour markets in chapter 5.

In Max Weber's elaboration of Marx's two-class model of structured inequality there is the suggestion of a *plural* society: one in which there are a number of different class positions and a variety of status groups. Many contemporary sociologists, especially American ones, have taken this, together with Weber's emphasis on the importance of parties and interest groups in the social structure, to locate a source of stability in industrial societies. This 'neo-Weberian' approach replaces the more Marxian class model of two basic groups of the relatively advantaged and the relatively disadvantaged who face each other in a fundamentally conflicting relationship, with a model recognising a plurality of counter-balancing interest and status groups.

The pluralist model of industrial society implies that democratic politics and government render social conflict relatively manageable since government merely has to hold the ring as the relatively equal groupings; employers and organised labour, for example, merely manoeuvre and adjust within a widely accepted consensus. However, the use of Weberian concepts of class, status and party to suggest such a stable situation is quite contrary to the emphasis on power and its implications for the access which is gained to scarce and valued goods which is basic to the position of Weber himself. The TUC and the CBI, in the British case, may indeed sit down as apparent equals to debate economic issues with governments, but once one considers the *effective* access to scarce goods and services, on the one hand, and the quality of work experience, on the other hand, of the bulk of the individuals represented by these two organisations, one gets a picture which powerfully belies the pluralist image. If one simply takes the distribution of personal wealth as an indicator of the effective power of different groups, it becomes clear that there is considerable resilience amongst the most advantaged groups, despite so-called redistributive policies of reforming governments. Material gathered for the Royal Commission on the Distribution of Income and Wealth (HMSO 1977), for instance, shows that the richest 20 per cent of the British population owned 89.8 per cent of personal wealth in 1960 – a figure which had fallen only to 85.5 per cent by 1974. This distribution of resources can still be closely related to the way in which work is organised and controlled, despite claims of a so-called 'managerial revolution', as we shall see in chapters 5 and 6.

The unequal distribution of resources, the life-chances following from this and the variations between work experiences provide a basic instability in contemporary industrial capitalist societies – not simply because inequality is in itself necessarily unacceptable but because, in these societies, there is an official rhetoric of equality and a cultural creation of expectations which is not matched by the objectively existing situation. The creation of a working class with interests objectively at odds with those of a controlling superordinate class provided industrial capitalism from the start with an internal potential challenge which it has always had to contain.

Government, politics and welfare

Success for the rising *bourgeois* groups who challenged the dominance of the landed interests in order to bring about a capitalist and later an industrial order in Britain was, as I argued earlier, partly dependent on the success of a new stress on the individual whose freedom and rights were increasingly given primacy over more collective or apparently collective values. This new liberalism did not neglect the need for social order, of course, but the utilitarian philosophy and the *laissez-faire* economics which developed to accompany it were used to argue that, by freeing individuals to pursue their 'enlightened' self interest, the greatest good of the greatest number could be achieved. These arguments were central to what our theoretical scheme calls the 'group ideology' of the newly dominant groups of the nineteenth century. Such ideologies justified the removal of long-standing governmental fetters on trade and they were also congruent with the growth of a formally free labour force. There was a great drawback in this ideology for any ruling interest which might have wished to exclude the new working class from a part in government, however. The new ruling groups had achieved their position on the basis of a philosophy which opposed exclusion on an ascriptive basis. This raised the question of how long members of the lower-middle classes, the manual workers and women generally could be excluded from democratic participation.

A great deal of nineteenth-century British political history can be understood, sociologically, as including a process whereby members of a potentially challenging collectivity – the working class – were gradually granted participation in a democratic order. The gradual spread of the franchise and of education, the growth of industrial and welfare legislation, the part played by Disraeli's idea of Empire in building 'one nation', and the national mobilisation for two World Wars, all contributed to the incorporation of what had often been seen early on as a potentially threatening *mass*. Instead of taking over society as an organised, coherent and class-conscious collectivity which Marx wanted to see, working people gained participation as *individual citizens* in a society developed by and to a large extent for the middle classes. The implications of this are enormous: the replacement of an individual achievement ethic by a more collective or socialist approach to the organisation of industrialised society was never again a serious possibility once the challenge of Chartism had been met in the mid-nineteenth century. The trade unions and the Labour Party can be seen as playing a largely defensive role on the part of working people. The tendency of trade unions to pursue largely economic ends for their particular members through free collective bargaining has presented little challenge to the basic assumptions of industrial capitalism. And the Labour Party's Fabian roots and early close relationship with liberalism set it on the tracks of liberal reformism rather than those of any *class* challenge to capitalism. The Protestant ethic has played a clear part in this with Methodism contributing significantly, as Robert Moore's (1974) study in a

Durham mining community illustrates so well, in pushing the Labour Party along liberal and reformist lines rather than towards the more collectivist alternative.

The growth of government involvement in welfare measures and the provision of 'social security' by no means represents a turning away from capitalism – it is an essential part of the way it has grown. *Laissez-faire* market economics of a pure type were never likely to have to cope with the sick, the unemployed, the young and the old in an acceptable way. Without denying the genuine philanthropic motives of many reformers and politicians, we can easily recognise that the apparatus of the so-called welfare state has, in effect, played a major part in contributing to the efficiency of industrial capitalism. Different commentators have seen welfare innovations as serving to 'regulate the poor' (Piven and Cloward 1974), 'invest in human capital' (Rimlinger 1971) or manage the 'disposal and control of the useless' (Gouldner 1971). John Saville (1975), in his historical review of the contemporary welfare state has suggested that it came about as a result of the interaction of three main factors:

(1) the struggle of the working class against their exploitation;
(2) the requirements of industrial capitalism . . . for a more efficient environment in which to operate and in particular the need for a highly productive labour force; (3) recognition by the property owners of a price that has to be paid for political security.

The *laissez-faire* model of the economy is more an ideological device than a representation of an early or 'pure' form of capitalism. As Polanyi (1945) showed, governments of quite different political complexions and in a range of industrialising countries have involved themselves in industrial matters and social services from an early stage in the industrialisation process. Such involvement (or 'intervention' as it is often pejoratively called) has undoubtedly increased over the two centuries since the beginning of the industrial revolution and governments can be seen as not only acting to deal, in effect, with what have been conceptualised here as structural contradictions but also to help manage what has become an increasingly complex type of overall economic organisation.

The difficulties which governments face in the economic sphere at the present time are considerable but there is one goal which governments appear completely unwilling to abandon. This is the goal of economic growth. It raises the question of the extent to which the possibility created by a growing gross national product over recent decades of giving most groups a rising *absolute* standard of living has deflected attention away from *relative* standards and life chances between groups in industrial capitalist societies. In other words we need to ask how far economic growth has been a major factor in the containment of the potential challenge which might otherwise have grown amongst those of the population with little wealth, low incomes and little opportunity of autonomy or self-fulfilment at work. How dependent is general acquiescence to the social order on continuing economic growth? This question can only be considered if we look more closely at the ideas and values related to the material interests which are met by such growth.

Culture, values and education

The interest of governments of officially differing doctrines in pursuing economic growth as a major goal can be partly understood, as is implied above, as a means of gaining acquiescence to an order in which goods are unevenly distributed. But this tendency has to be set in the wider context of the rationalisation process which is so intimately connected with the rise of industrial capitalist society. The process of rationalisation involves the calculated choosing of efficient means of achieving human goals or purposes. Accompanying this has been a major tendency towards a culture in which the attention paid to *means* comes to predominate over consideration given to *ends*. Formal rationality becomes more important than material rationality, in Weber's terms. This was a source of great concern to Max Weber himself and is a theme taken up by a variety of contemporary thinkers.

The French sociologist and theologian Jacques Ellul (1964) writes of a civilisation in which *technique* dominates. Merton (Introduction to Ellul 1964) describes Ellul's view as one of 'a civilisation committed to the quest for continually improved means to carelessly examined ends'. Values are not widely debated, the effect of this being that politics merely becomes an 'arena for contention among rival techniques'. Thus, governments do not ask, or put to the electorate, the question of 'why economic growth?' In the world of technique, 'technical economic analysis is substituted for the older political economy included in which was a major concern with the moral structure of economic activity. Thus doctrine is converted into procedure.' (*ibid.*)

Ellul concentrates on the centrality of *technique* (in this wide sense) as characterising the 'technological society', with machine technology merely presenting one facet of technique. Members of the Frankfurt school of 'Critical Theory' have taken a not dissimilar line, but they concentrate on the ideological role played by what Jurgen Habermas (1971) calls *technical-instrumental* thinking. This analysis suggests an important link between contemporary culture and ideas and the *interests* which are served by the maintenance of the industrial capitalist social order. Critical analysis of the social order is diverted towards attention paid to administrative devices like the size of the Gross National Product, the level of inflation or the state of the retail price index. The trade unions negotiate with employers over primarily instrumental matters such as the percentage wage rise to be achieved. What tend not to be debated or negotiated over are the ends served by economic or employment policy. Attention is paid more to the *quantity* of money or goods rather than to the *quality* of life towards which these might be means.

Concentrating attention in the ways illustrated here on the more procedural aspects of life helps avoid threats arising to the overall structure (and the interests and priorities underlying it) of which these procedures are merely constituent devices. As Fred Hirsch (1977) points out, a market economy only provides choices between 'alternative piecemeal, discrete, marginal adjustments, but no facility for selection between alternative states'. A political system basically engaged in the management of such an economy will be similarly restricted in the scale of the choices which it can consider. Democracy becomes a contest over marginal adjustments in the way people live rather than a way of disputing what purpose, value or basic human fulfilment is to be achieved by any specific form of social organisation. Again in the 'critical theory' tradition, Herbert Marcuse (1968) sees people failing to use their critical faculties and thus failing to follow 'reason'. They live with a 'one-dimensional' consciousness and in a state of 'a comfortable, smooth, reasonable, democratic unfreedom'.

There is clearly a considerable degree of moral fervour behind the arguments on which I have drawn here. I have deliberately used writers from a range of ideological positions to indicate that a concern over the tendency for contemporary policy-thinking to avoid basic values or moral questions is not peculiar to any one political position.

Indeed, I would suggest that such a concern goes back to a basic problem with which sociology has frequently been concerned: that of what it is that holds a society together. This was a major concern of Emile Durkheim. Social cohesion was dependent on some form of *conscience collective* and, traditionally, religion had provided the necessary framework of values, beliefs and principles. But in the form which industrial capitalist society was taking in his time, Durkheim saw a growing emphasis on individual success, material wealth and sectional interest which severely threatened social solidarity. There was a potential state of *anomie* – a purposelessness and moral confusion which undermined stability. This fits well with the analysis which sees concern with *means* excluding attention to values and ends.

Durkheim's analysis draws attention to the importance of *contract* in modern human relationships and a contemporary sociologist, Alan Fox (1974), has paid particular attention to this aspect of relationships. Contracts have long played a part in human social arrangements but the typical contract which is made in the industrial capitalist society is not the relatively diffuse one in which people commit themselves to each other in a very general way (master-servant, husband-wife) but the highly specific, more detailed, arrangement which Weber called the *purposive contract*. This type of arrangement is found in its most basic and typical form in the employment contract – an increasingly instrumental calculative and specific form of arrangement.

Fox's analysis of low trust dynamics is clearly going to be important in our closer examination of work relationships at a later stage but its relevance to our present discussion of the wider culture is considerable, particularly because of its suggestion of a consequential 'low-trust syndrome' which can spread through society. The low trust dynamics institutionalised in the rules, roles and relationships of hierarchical work organisations in which discretion (and hence trust) is denied to those at the lower levels can readily spill over into the non-work sphere. And what quality of social cohesion is possible where norms of distrust on the one hand and personal calculated self-interest, on the other, prevail? The citizen's fear of walking alone at night, the felt need to lock and double lock every door and other such insecurities are often seen as problems which exist in some kind of isolation and which are amenable to various repressive judicial measures. Where Fox's notion of institutionalised trust relations is invaluable is that it relates such matters not only to the form in which work itself is organised but to the even more basic question of the principles on which industrial capitalism itself is founded.

The basic principles of capitalist society are frequently taken to be those put forward in Adam Smith's *Wealth of Nations*. But what is often forgotten is that this eighteenth-century moral philosopher was not suggesting that the greatest good *necessarily* arises through the pursuit of economic self-interest by individuals. Self-interest, he recognised, could become selfishness, and checks against such destructive egoism had to be found not only in law but also in family ties, religion, education and a system of morals (see Kempner *et al.* 1976). Nineteenth-century figures as politically diverse as Carlyle, Mill and Marx saw social relationships based on 'pecuniary interests' or the 'cash nexus' as not only inadequate but as morally repulsive. Yet, by the mid-twentieth century, political legitimacy could be claimed with an electioneering slogan 'You've never had it so good', resulting in only marginal moral disapprobation. Our concern here is not to make moral judgments about moral judgments – or the lack of them! The sociological question of the continuing efficacy of the appeal to affluence as a source of social cohesion is more our present concern.

Acquiescence to the present organisation of work and economy can be seen in large part as dependent on the promise in terms of individual self-advantage which is held by the fruits of the economic growth to which such acquiescence is expected to lead. Many of the goods promised by affluence – speedy motor travel, secluded homes and access to 'good' jobs, for example – can only ever be available to a minority. As Hirsch argues in his powerful book, *The Social Limits to Growth* (1977): 'What the wealthy have today can no longer be delivered to the rest of us tomorrow; yet as we individually grow richer, that is what we expect.' Again a structural contradiction confronts us: 'The locus of instability is the divergence between what is possible for the individual and what is possible for all individuals.' (*ibid.*) However, there is a source of contradiction which probably goes deeper than this. This lies in the fact that the cultural element of *materialistic* individualism which has been a motivating force in industrial capitalist society is only one side of the larger trend towards a more individualistic ethos, and the other side, as we shall now see, may come into conflict with it.

Kerr *et al.* in their reappraisal of their influential *Industrialism and Industrial Man* (1973) recognise a developing contradiction or a 'central problem' in industrialism. They note a humanist reaction arising towards industrial discipline, as a more educated labour force seeks 'more freedom for spontaneous individual action within the work environment, as well as outside it'. They recognise that this could be the seeds of technological society's own destruction. Here, they consciously echo the language of Marx which was used to describe the contradictions of capitalism. However, they are, as ever, optimistic about the adjustments which can be made to work organisations to cope with this problem. Another American writer with equally non-Marxist sentiments has been even more ready to borrow Marxian terminology to examine the type of problem with which we are concerned here. Daniel Bell in his *Cultural Contradictions of Capitalism* (1976) suggests that in the West 'the principles of the economic realm and those of the culture now lead people in contrary directions'. The individualism released and encouraged by the Reformation and the Protestant ethic created both the form of *bourgeois* economic individualism which brought about the 'techno-economic' social structure and the opposing cultural impulse transmitted by artists and writers which encourages the enhancement and fulfilment of the individual as a whole person. To describe this 'structural source of tension' another way, we might say that industrial capitalist society has developed a culture which invites people to be free to develop themselves and to 'do their own thing', whilst the economic production of goods and services on which such aspirations partly depend involves many of them in relatively stultifying closely prescribed tasks in which the technically necessary control and co-ordination frequently creates an atmosphere of low trust and social hostility.

What we might term a conflict between the economic liberalism and the cultural liberalism of industrial capitalism inevitably draws our attention to the part played by educational institutions. These can be seen as playing a role which is supportive of the industrial capitalist social structure. Yet the situation is not as simple as this.

Examination of the recommendations of the Taunton Commission of 1868, through to the various reports on education of Hadow, Spens and Norwood, and the way the Education Act of 1944 was implemented (on the tripartite basis of grammar, technical and secondary modern secondary schools) shows the ways in which both the organisation of institutions and the thinking of educators have concentrated on the 'process of sorting and grading' people rather than on developing and reinterpreting culture (Williams 1965). Educational structures have been stratified in ways which match the class and occupational grades which they feed and, to a large degree, reproduce, but the relationship between education and work does not stop at this external level of structure. Bowles and Gintis (1976), with their 'correspondence principle', point to the ways in which the internal structuring of educational institutions facilitates 'a smooth integration of youth into the labor force'. It is not claimed that teachers, lecturers and administrators consciously and specifically prepare pupils and students for occupational roles (they are often criticised for doing too little in this direction in fact) but that the structuring of relations within education closely corresponds to those of work organisations. Pupils lack control over their curriculum to a degree which matches the control they will lack at work and, overall, the relationships of authority and control 'replicate the hierarchical division of labour which dominates the workplace'.

The problem with analyses of the above kind is that they might be taken to suggest that education acts as some kind of handmaiden to industry. Yet it is a common theme of criticism of the education system in Britain that it does not sufficiently serve the needs of industry – especially at the higher levels. The point is that industrial occupations, although they may be typical work settings in indus-trialised societies, are not the only ones available in such a society. In fact there has been a tradition in Britain that men who were successful in the industrial or commercial fields should seek a 'gentlemanly' type of education for their sons, something which would fit them better for a prestigious professional or non-commercial administrative career rather than an industrial one (see below, pp. 149). Even in a recent study of managers we see a marked tendency for those in industry to put 'an emphasis on ensuring that offspring should either marry or train to be a *professional*' (Pahl and Pahl 1972). This compares with the common complaint whereby the 'best brains' are said to choose the civil service or the higher professions in preference to business, and it is widely observed that greater status appears to be granted to higher education institutions which come nearer to the *traditional* ideal of Oxford and Cambridge than to the technological universities and polytechnics.

What we see in the educational system is a situation where, on the one hand, there is a close relationship between the structuring of institutions and the structures of employment but where, on the other hand, many non-capitalist values still pertain. The educational system is, in effect, caught up in the contradictions of the society of which it is a part. It operates with the liberal ideals of individual self-development and the pursuit of intrinsically worthwhile knowledge. However, whilst the occupational structure into which pupils move on completing their education is not so much based on such ideals as on individual-instrumental and technical criteria, there is going to be considerable tension between the two sectors. The more the educational sector were to encourage individuals generally to seek fulfilment and self-development in their lives, the more potential dissatisfaction with present forms of work design there would be. The meritocratic principle and its supporting ideology of 'equality of opportunity' has played a large part in coping with this difficulty. As Frank Parkin (1972a) argues, the mobility afforded by this aspect of education (particularly where there is an expanding proportion of higher status occupations) 'provides an escape route for large numbers of the most able and ambitious members of the under-class, thereby easing some of the tensions generated by in-equality'.

Sexual divisions, home and family

To complete our survey of some of the major aspects of the way industrialised societies are structured, we now come to consider the non-work realm of the home and the family and we will also look at that fundamentally important structuring principle which is closely related to this sphere: that by which a person's sex basically affects his social and economic life chances. The opportunities which are available in both the work and the non-work sphere are quite different for men and women and my consideration of women's situation under a common heading here with the home and the family by no means indicates a willingness on my part to 'relegate' women to the domestic sphere. It is, rather, that the structural and cultural identity of women with this sphere in the type of society which we are considering means that the role of the home and the family lies at the roots of the sexual divisions which exist here. However many women may, in statistical terms, play a part in the sphere of paid employment, such a role still carries a general cultural evaluation of deviance. This can only be understood in the light of the way in which the family, the home and the 'role of women' have developed together within the rise of industrial capitalism.

Sociologists have often debated whether the presumed emergence of the nuclear or conjugal family (man, wife and their children) as the major domestic unit in the place of a larger extended-kin family unit was more a causal factor in the industrialisation process or more one of the results of the spread of industrialism. However, of more importance than the nuclear versus extended-kin issue in reaching an understanding of the contemporary family is the historical tendency towards the separation of home life and working life – with its consequential effects on gender roles. This separation has its roots not so much in the appearance of industrialism as in the emergence of capitalism a century and a half earlier.

In the feudal period the home and the work sphere were generally one, with both men and women contributing to furtherance of the family's economic interests, whether these were simply a matter of economic survival in the case of the peasantry or one of the maintenance of superiority and honour among the nobility. But this unity of home and work and of production and consumption was eroded as the economic basis of social life changed. The steady conversion of the peasantry into wage labour meant that female tasks of bearing and suckling children could less easily be combined with the productive work which was increasingly performed in a setting away from the home. Where women could obtain work, their vulnerability to exploitation was greater than that of men, who were, in effect, biologically 'freer'. Women became more dependent on men in this way and, where wages were too low to support them and their children they became a charge on the community. A corresponding change occurred in the growing middle class where the women were not being left at home as domestic drudges as were working-class women, but as useless domestic decorations or bearers of male property-inheritors. In the more recent stages of industrial capitalist development where middle-class homes have largely lost their ability to employ servants and where working-class wages have made it more possible for males to support non-employed wives and children, it has more or less become the cultural norm for women to play the domestic role whilst men go out to work and to earn.

To talk of 'cultural norms' in this respect raises the question of socially developed ideas or ideologies which support family forms and gender divisions. Roberta Hamilton (1978), whose valuable study has done much to inform the present analysis, argues that attention has to be paid not only to the economically and biologically material factors discussed so far, but also to the part played by supporting 'patriarchal ideologies'. Once again in our considering of the interplay which takes place between interests and ideas, the influence of Protestantism on the culture becomes relevant. The effects of Protestant thinking, subtly traced by Hamilton, were that the home and the family were given an elevated and 'unprecedented ideological importance' and the ideal established for women was that of the faithful and supportive 'proper wife'. To recognise that this cultural ideal exists is not to suggest that women have not and do not make a major economic contribution in work outside the home, but such work is only fully culturally acceptable where it is marginal or it is temporary (prior to child-rearing, for example), a point illustrated by the common tendency for 'working women' to be treated as a social problem category. This tendency can be understood as connected with a perceived threat to social stability felt to arise when women 'neglect their domestic duties'. Why should this be?

Looking back to the early stages of industrial capitalist society it is possible to see the growing economic individualism as a potential threat to the institution of the family. However, the Protestant-originated image of the close family unit offered too much as a potential source for general social stability for this to be allowed to happen. Family life could be a source of affection and sentiment in an increasingly rational calculatively economic world – a place where the tensions of manual drudgery or *bourgeois* competitiveness could be relieved. It also provides an excellent market for family cars, family holidays, television sets and many other consumer and leisure goods. In this scheme of things women become (economically necessary) consumers of products, comforters of their economically active husbands and producers of the next generation of economic actors and passive consumers. Where the domestic taming of women interfered with their provision to men of sexual *excitement*, the nineteenth-century male could resort to the brothel or the bottle whilst the contemporary male has the culturally prevalent dream of the nubile (sic) female sex object – available not just in pornographic fantasies but conjured up by a range of 'respectable' entertainment forms and advertising materials. The net effect of these cultural images, both the domestic and the fantasy, is to discourage potential recognition of women as equal contributors to paid economic activity. A female labour force has indeed grown up but the cultural image of female work as part of a *secondary* role has tended to keep women within a secondary labour market. This labour market, one which pays lower wages, offers less security and opportunities for advancement than the primary labour market, is one whose general importance we will consider later (p. 171).

Within the structure of advantage existing between the sexes, the secondary labour market functions in three ways. First, it provides employers with a relatively cheap source of labour. Second, it reduces the number of potential competitors which aspiring males confront in their work careers and, third, it avoids attracting too many women away from the domestic setting. Yet, within a predominantly economically-oriented culture, the highest status roles and the high intrinsic rewards involved with these are ones associated with economic activity and occupational success. Women are, to a large extent, denied access to these prestigious roles. Consequently, we might say that the price which is paid for the social cohesiveness provided by the family unit is one largely borne by the female half of the population – people who are denied access to certain important social goals. This is not to say that these work career goals are necessarily intrinsically superior to traditional feminine or domestic ones. It is to point out that these are goals with which the wider culture associates the highest prestige and thus defines as desirable.

Sociologically, we can see the privatised nuclear family as a source of stability in industrial capitalist society: it provides *affective* support to the economically active; it counters anomie and compensates for work alienation; it provides markets for goods and, historically, has probably played its part in reducing political challenge by fostering a family consciousness instead of a class consciousness. In this way adjustments have occurred to cope with various structural contradictions underlying the basic societal form, but the paradox of consequences is never solved. For every tension reduced within any social structure another is likely to arise, and this is apparently turning out to be the case with the family.

Women are beginning to demand the kind of wider social participation which, in many ways, the democratising aspects of the way industrial capitalism has developed was always likely to encourage – sooner or later. Further structural adjustments will inevitably be made, with considerable implications for both home and working life. It may well be that the institution of the family, as it currently exists, is not only being brought into question by changing aspirations among women. Sociologists have increasingly wondered whether the strain being put upon the isolated, privatised small family unit has simply been becoming too much. Can a small unit of persons (with a short-term size of three, four or five and a long-term size of two) stand the pressure of being relied upon as the main source of emotional, expressive, intimate and cultural fulfilment? This question raises further questions about the way work is organised: if the domestic setting proves not to be able to take the massive strain of being looked to as the main source of human self-development and essential social fulfilment, the work sphere may have to play a greater part. Given contemporary trends of job design and work organisation, as we shall see later, such a development may by no means be taken for granted. The organisation of work itself may have to be looked to as a source of social cohesion and less as a simple source of instrumental involvement for many – providing cash to be spent within the family.

Chapter 4

Work and the individual

Introduction

All living creatures expend some kind of effort in the process of acting upon and taking from their environment whatever they need for survival. Human beings are no different from any other animal in this general respect. However, they are distinctive in the degree to which, as a species, they have devised a vast range of different ways of dealing with their material situation. They are unique in the extent to which they have divided up and allocated particular tasks to individuals and groups within the overall and general task of subsisting. The methods of work which humans adopt and the social organisation which accompanies it cannot be explained by reference to any clearly definable set of instincts. Human agency, choice, values and inter-pretations are essential factors to be appreciated in any understanding of work forms.

Work is basic to the ways in which human beings deal with the problems arising from the scarcity of resources available in the environment. The scarcity of resources, it was argued earlier, influences the patterns of conflict and competition which arise between social groups. It follows from this that the social organisation of work will reflect the basic power relationship of any particular society. However, as our basic theoretical model suggests, power relationships involve not only the pursuit of material interests but the development of ideas congruent with particular interests. The part played by ideas, values, ideology and culture in the growth of industrial capitalist society was discussed in the previous chapter. The concern of the present chapter is to look further at the relationship between the structural and contextual aspects of the work situation and some of its subjective aspects. This means that we will consider the ways in which the structural aspects of work are interpreted and experienced.

To concentrate on experience and interpretation in social life tends to mean that the individual rather than the social structure becomes central to the analysis. In making the individual central to our focus here, however, it must be stressed that we are not turning to a psychological level of analysis. Sociology is required to give an account of the *interplay* between individual and structural factors in social life. The emphasis in the previous chapter tended to be on the structural level and this is now to be complemented by an approach which takes the individual as the starting point. To put it simply, we will now focus on the individual as a *social individual*. My purpose is to indicate that the nature of work experience and the meaning of work vary from individual to individual, but, following the essential rationale of the sociological perspective, I will try to show that this is not a random matter. There is a patterning to be seen in the ways in which work is experienced and interpreted and both the social and cultural context of work and the work situation itself play a part in this.

Work and the nature of man

At a basic level work can be seen as the carrying out of tasks which enable people to make a living within the environment in which they find themselves. This, of course, is far too simple. A living is not simply extracted from the environment. In many ways work effectively transforms environments and, in the process, creates for many a level of living far in excess of basic subsistence. Not only this but the work which we do becomes closely bound up with our very conception of *self*.

The transformations of the western world which have resulted from the rise of capitalism and industrialism have already been shown to be dependent, in part, on a new meaning given to work by those values associated with the Protestant ethic. The work ethic, which has been such a motivating force in the growth of modern societies, defines work as having *intrinsic* value to the person carrying it out. It is something more than a means to other ends. The connection between conscientious labour, disciplined application and hope of salvation may have been severed but the cultural force of that once-existing connection lives on. As Max Weber (1965) recognised, the appeal of material goods may have replaced aspirations towards salvation or grace, but this is not the whole story: 'The idea of duty in one's calling prowls about in our lives like the ghost of dead religious beliefs.' This may be seen reflected in everyday life in the ambivalence with which those who are unable to work in our society are often regarded. It is also a major factor underlying some of the most influential ideas about work prevailing amongst thinkers and writers whether they cater for a managerial audience or a more politically radical one.

In our review of the various theoretical strands which make up industrial sociology, we came across two traditions which are fundamentally opposed in many respects but which nevertheless share an assumption about the necessary centrality of work to human fulfilment. These are the neo-human relations part of what I called the managerial–psychologistic strand and the Marxian strand.

The behavioural-science entrepreneurs of the neo-human relations tradition, people like McGregor, Argyris, Herzberg and Likert, urge the providers of work to adopt job and organisational designs which will enable people to fulfil their 'self-actualisation' needs. The implications behind many of these writers' arguments is that to be fully human or 'mature' we need to engage in a form of work which gives us autonomy, discretion and the fullest opportunity to use whatever talents we have – in order to advance self-growth. Although some writers of this school recognise a degree of cultural specificity, their work as a whole is such that it has been labelled the 'psychological universalistic approach'. As Daniel (1973) has put it:

> They are universalistic in the sense that they suggest that there are certain needs shared by workers of all types and levels and their response to the work situation can be explained in terms of the extent to which these needs are satisfied.

The problem with this is that it suggests that explanations of the meanings of work can be derived from a conception of human nature rather than their being recognised as socio-cultural *variables*. The position closes off the possible human option of treating work as a necessary form of drudgery to be quickly got out of the way in order to enable fulfilment to be found in some more central non-work sphere of life. The neo-human relations approach to the meaning of work, then, may function as a conservative ideology, for all its image of progressiveness and its reforming zeal within industry.

The Marxist approach to work may also be attacked as functioning as a conservative work ideology in this way. Peter Anthony (1977), for example, suggests that the radical critique of society which points to the *alienation* of man within capitalist society tends to entrench rather than expose or replace the values of economic society:

> the essential paradox of alienation is that it emerges with any meaning only as a result of an overemphasis on a work ethic and work-based values. Man can be regarded as alienated from his work only when he has been subjected to an ideology of work which requires him to be devoted to it.

Anthony's suggestion that the concept of alienation is a 'managerial conception' – a useful way of formulating what managers identify as a problem – may seem eccentric. But it does encourage an important insight: that even seemingly radical views of the meaning of work to human beings may be caught up in assumptions about human nature which, like those of the progressive managerial writers, may restrict the human imagination when it comes to deciding what part work *might* play in a society of the future. This does not mean that we should not look closely at the very important and much used concept of alienation, however.

The concept of alienation is used in different ways both within and outside sociology. It is appropriate to concentrate on Marx's use of the term at this stage because most sociologists who have looked at alienation in the work setting have taken Marx's ideas as their starting point – even though they often abandon or modify the main thrust of his analysis (Horton 1964). The most basic notion suggested by the word alienation is that of *separation* (Schacht 1970) and, in Marx's usage, various forms of separation within human experience under capitalism are pointed to. It must be stressed here that these are the result of the capitalist organisation of work activity and are not an inevitable outcome of the use of any particular kind of machinery or work method. Individuals may be alienated or estranged from *other people* as relationships become merely calculative, self-interested and untrusting. They are alienated from the *product* of their efforts since what is produced is expropriated from them and was not, anyway, conceived by the workers themselves to meet their own ends or needs.

Individuals are also alienated or separated from their own *labour*: they do not derive the satisfactions or the delight that is possible in labour since that labour is forced upon them as a means of meeting other needs and because they put themselves under the control of other people in the work situation. In all this, the work of individuals becomes an alien thing which oppresses them. Yet, *potentially*, it could be a source of basic human fulfilment, and here we come to the essential element of the Marxian notion of alienation: man can be alienated *from himself*.

Marx's conception of the nature of man is one in which it is assumed that people realise their essential nature, as a species, through productive work which is carried out for their own purposes and not under the control and exploitation of others. What this implies – and very many users of the concept of alienation forget this, despite an assumed debt to Marx – is that alienation is basically an objective state. Alienation is not *necessarily* reflected in felt job dissatisfaction or in frustration. A person may be very happy sitting at a desk in someone else's factory five days per week sorting pieces of paper which mean little to them in return for a wage. Yet in the Marxian conception of alienation such people are alienated: they are not fulfilling themselves in the way they might be were they working under different conditions. People are alienated when they are not being what they possibly could be, and for people to become what they could be – to fulfil themselves or achieve 'self-actualisation' – they must create a society which, although taking a basically different form, is, nevertheless, one in which work, as a source of fulfilment in its own right, is central.

It is the Marxian belief in the necessary centrality of work activity to human self-fulfilment which suggests that even the radically critical Marxist view of work is one which still operates within a basic cultural assumption which ties people to their work. Anthony's discussion in *The Ideology of Work* (1977) suggests that any ideology of work, whether it be a capitalist or a communist one, tends, in effect, to be a defence of subordination. Ideologies which stress the importance of work beyond the necessary part which it must play in meeting other needs are only required when some human groups require the labour of others to meet economic ends which might not be those of the people in whose minds the required work has to be legitimated. Anthony's aim is to severely question our cultural assumptions about work and this is something to which we are bound to return in our final chapter when we consider whether activities other than work might be made centrally significant to our lives, with work taking an appropriately secondary and instrumental role. The choice may or may not be there. But for the present analysis we have to recognise that although the approaches to the meaning of work considered above may tend to close off options for the future, they nevertheless suggest to us some useful and important criteria for examining work in the contemporary world. Work does take up a large proportion of many people's lives and the satisfactions and deprivations which it involves are not equally shared across the social structure. To understand the ways in which these experiences and meanings are patterned we must necessarily use notions which are informed by the various traditions considered here.

Intrinsic and extrinsic satisfactions

Basic to many of the debates about the meaning of work has been a distinction, implicit in the traditions discussed above, between the *intrinsic* satisfactions which work can give individuals and the *extrinsic* satisfactions which may be derived from it. What we have to be careful to do is to separate the question of whether work *ought* to give intrinsic satisfactions from more sociological questions about the ways in which human groups vary in the extent to which they are able to gain satisfactions of either type. We can use the ideas of intrinsic and extrinsic satisfactions to develop two ideal-type meanings which work can have for people. The range of possible meanings can be located on a continuum between these ideal types as shown in Fig. 4.1.

Much discussion of what is often termed 'attitudes to work' or 'work motivation' centres on whether people generally go to work to seek either extrinsic satisfaction (do people go to work 'just for the money', 'just for the company'?) or intrinsic ones (do people want jobs which are 'inherently satisfying'?). Before we can investigate just what work does mean to people in industrial capitalist society we have to go beyond this type of simplistic question to recognise that different people attach different meanings to work and that for any given individual this meaning may change over time. We must also recognise that frustrations and deprivations play as big a part as potential 'satisfactions'. Individuals' personalities will be a factor influencing the meaning of work to them but so also will such factors as their age, upbringing, sex, education, job, employing organisation, and social class. What we must now do is to develop a conceptual apparatus which will enable us to take account of the multiplicity of factors influencing the meanings and experiences of work. To do this we can turn to the ideas developed in recent decades by sociologists working in the Weberian tradition and, in particular, make use of the idea of *orientations to work.*

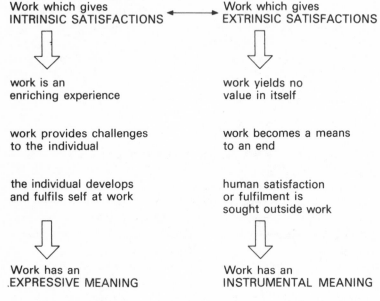

Fig. 4.1 Meanings of work: a continuum

Orientations to work

Historically, a large proportion of the ideas developed about attitudes and behaviour at work have derived from concern with manual workers. Two major reasons can be suggested to explain this. The first is that such groups have been more accessible to investigation; having less to keep to themselves than do their bosses, it might be argued. But more important than this is the tendency to regard manual workers as a particularly problematic group. This applies in an immediately managerial sense: managements are always interested in ideas which might give them insight into the motivations and activities of those whose efforts they have to direct. A corresponding concern exists at the socio-political level: the 'working class', its loyalties, aspirations and accommodations has been a focus of concern ever since its creation. Sociologists have been at the forefront of those showing this concern. In looking at the development of theoretical perspectives on the relationship between work and the individual, therefore, we inevitably find ourselves examining the changing ways in which sociologists have attempted to explain *shopfloor* attitudes and behaviour. My intention now is to look at the progress which has been made in this field and then attempt to build on what has been achieved in such a way that we can use one theoretical apparatus to look at work as it is experienced at various levels and in various spheres.

Traditional thinking about industrial behaviour tended to focus on the assumed 'needs' of workers, concentrating sometimes on the economic needs of the employees, as with the scientific managers, and sometimes on their so-called social needs, as with the human relations tradition. A major breakthrough in distinctively sociological analysis was made, however, once closer attention was given to the influence of technology in the workplace. It began to be realised that workers applying different types of technology were likely to both think and act differently. What has come to be called the 'technological implications' approach to industrial behaviour suggested that the technology being used will determine, or at least closely constrain, the way in which tasks are organised and that this will be a major influence on the attitudes and behaviour of workers. We will look more closely at the research which was done by investigators like Woodward (1965), Blauner (1964) and Sayles (1958) later on but the type of proposition which was emerging from their work was that workers' social relationships with each other, the quality of their work experience and their propensity to engage in conflict with management would be heavily dependent on technology. To make this clearer, let us compare a situation where the technology is a craft-based one like printing with the very different technology of the car assembly line. The printer will be closely bound up with his workmates through the craft group which he will have joined as a youth and, because of the nature of the tasks which he carries out, he will be relatively free to interact with his colleagues. The social aspect of the carworkers' life, however, is quite different. The lack of skill required by the work will mean that there is not the craft tradition and resulting cohesiveness and the fact that the worker is paced by the machines, rather than the other way round, will mean that he is less free to interact with others even if he wishes to. These differences both affect the social satisfactions which can be derived from work and will have implications for the type of industrial conflict engaged in, if not the amount of such activity generally. The nature of the tasks themselves – potentially interesting and fulfilling in the craft case and typically boring and frustrating in the assembly-line case – will strongly influence the feelings, thoughts and hence preparedness to act in certain ways on the part of the two groups. Other technological situations will each have their own particular determining influence. More advanced technologies, like automated process production for example, could be expected to bring about attitudes and behaviour more in line with those of the traditional craft worker and away from those of the alienated and resentful mass-production operative.

The importance of the insights provided by the above type of argument should not be underestimated. But where reservations have to be stated is with regard to the implied existence of some relatively direct *causal* link between the technology being applied and the attitudes and behaviour of those applying it. In practice we often find that there are differences in attitudes and behaviour between organisations which have similar technologies and that even within a given organisation changes may occur which are the result of adjustments other than ones in the technology itself. This can be illustrated by looking at two studies of the car industry. Turner *et al.* (1967) in their investigation of industrial relations in the car industry pointed out that the differences in strike records of different car manufacturers could not be put down to variations in technology and Guest's (1962) American case study demonstrates the possibilities of changes in conflict and general interpersonal behaviour which can be achieved by changes in managerial policy and staff.

The research study which first introduced the notion of 'orientation to work' also looked at workers in the car industry. As part of their wider study of social class in Britain in the 1960s, Goldthorpe, Lockwood *et al.* (1968) examined the attitudes and behaviour of assembly line workers in the Vauxhall plant in Luton. These workers did not appear to be deriving either intrinsic or social satisfactions from their work experience. Yet they did not express dissatisfaction with the jobs which they were doing. The possible paradox here was removed by the authors' explanation that these workers had knowingly chosen work with these deprivations, regarding such work as a means to a relatively good standard of living which could be achieved with the income made on the assembly line. The workers were said to have an *instrumental orientation to work*. The sources of this orientation were in the class, community and family backgrounds of the employees and not in the workplace itself. The technological implications approach was strongly questioned by the finding that workers in other technological situations investigated (a chemical plant and a batch-production engineering plant) had similar work orientations with consequently corresponding patterns of behaviour and attitude. Technology thus appears to be less important a variable than had been suggested. The motives, interests and extra-work background of the worker had to be taken into account if not given central emphasis. These authors accepted that the technology does have an influence but argued that to put that influence into context it is necessary to take the employee's own definition of the situation as an 'initial basis for the explanation of their social behaviour and relationships' (*ibid.*). Such an approach has the great strength of encouraging us to recognise the *variety of meaning* that work can have for industrial employees.

Whilst accepting that all work in industrial societies has an instrumental basis, Goldthorpe, Lockwood *et al.* suggest that a typology of work orientations can nevertheless be offered. These are indicated in Fig. 4.2. The *instrumental* orientation reflects that found among the study's affluent manual workers, the *bureaucratic* orientation reflects patterns found among white-collar employees whilst the *solidaristic* orientation is inferred from the authors' understanding of more 'traditional' working class employment situations like coalmining and shipbuilding.

In the same way that the technological implications approach represented a move towards an approach which was more sociological than those approaches which had emphasised universal human needs, so this move towards an analysis in the social-action tradition, can be seen as progressing towards an even more fully sociological understanding. It recognises the importance to any appreciation of what goes on within work of both the individual and his social context. This had not been totally ignored previously, however. Dalton (1948), for instance, showed that the way individuals react to incentive schemes in the workplace can be influenced by the values which they bring to work and by their social background. Such an approach only became central to industrial sociology with the appearance of Goldthorpe, Lockwood *et al.*'s *Affluent Worker* study, despite the fact that Weber himself foreshadowed such developments early in the century. Yet the analysis provided by Goldthorpe, Lockwood *et al.* can be criticised for going too far in stressing the factors which influence workers' initial choice of their job and for failing to recognise that the individual's work orientation, once in that job, is constantly liable to change both as a result of factors operating within and factors located outside the workplace. What subsequent work in this area has suggested is that attention to 'prior orientation' to work has to be balanced by a greater recognition of the *structural conditions* in which these orientations then operate and a recognition that orientations or definitions of the situation are not necessarily fixed but are *dynamic*.

ORIENTATION TO WORK	PRIMARY MEANING OF WORK	INVOLVEMENT IN EMPLOYING ORGANISATION	EGO-INVOLVEMENT	WORK AND NON-WORK RELATIONSHIP
INSTRUMENTAL	Means to an end. A way of earning income	Calculative	Weak. Work not a central life interest or source of self-realisation	Spheres sharply dichotomised. Work relationships not carried over into non-work activities
BUREAUCRATIC	Service to an organisation in return for career progress	'Moral' elements: some sense of obligation	Individual's position and prospects are sources of social identity	Not sharply dichotomised. Work identity and organisational status carried over
SOLIDARISTIC	Economic but with this limited by group loyalties to either mates or firm	'Moral' when identification is with firm. 'Alienative' when this is more with workmates than with employer	Strong social relationships at work are rewarding	Intimately related. High participation in work-linked formal or informal associations
PROFESSIONAL	No details given			

Fig. 4.2 Four possible orientations to work (based on Goldthorpe, Lockwood et al. *1968, pp. 38–41)*

Dynamic orientations and structural conditions

By showing that the workers which Goldthorpe and Lockwood studied in Luton acted at work and thought about their work in a particular way which was most strongly influenced by their deliberate choice to move into the car industry for extrinsic rather than intrinsic rewards, the authors tended to underplay the potential degree of influence which factors within work itself might have on work attitudes and behaviour generally. To apply the notion of orientation to work to a wider range of work situations we have to take into account several arguments which have been made by researchers subsequent to the publication of the Luton study.

Beynon and Blackburn (1972), as a consequence of their detailed study of a factory involved in the manufacture of luxury foods, argue that although employees tend, as far as possible, to select employment in keeping with their priorities in what they want from work they nevertheless make important accommodations and adjustments once in work, as their experience is influenced by such workplace factors as work processes, pay levels and power structures. Orientations are also shown to be influenced by biographical factors in the worker's life outside the factory. The authors argue that the rejection of the adequacy of explanations based on technological determinacy and systems needs should not lead us to adopt one which replaces an analysis of the work situation with one based on prior orientations (*ibid.*). They felt that the Luton study came 'dangerously near to being stuck the other side of the factory gates'. Wedderburn and Crompton (1972) who studied three chemical plants, make a similar point. These authors found that the workers whom they studied generally displayed the instrumental orientations to work described in the Luton study. However, they found that *within specific work settings* different workers displayed different attitudes and behaviour which 'emerged in response to the specific constraints imposed by the technology and the control setting' (*ibid.*).

W. W. Daniel, a major critic of the approach of Goldthorpe, Lockwood *et al.*, has accused those authors of failing to recognise the complexities of what it is workers look for in their jobs. He suggests that they paid too much attention to the job choice situation and thus failed to recognise that, once in work, employees display varying priorities, attitudes and interests – depending on the context in which we look at them. Daniel (1973) suggests that different attitudes will prevail, for instance, in what he calls the *bargaining context* from those which are indicated in the *work context*. In the bargaining context priority is given to the material rewards accruing from the job. The negative aspects of the job are stressed (these justify appropriate compensation) and the management are seen as being the 'opposite side'. However, if we examine worker attitudes where the work content itself is the focus of interest we find that there is more concern with the quality of work experience and with the social rewards of contact and communication with others and we find that the relationship with management is 'more characterised by a sense of common interests' (*ibid.*).

The importance of what Daniel is saying is considerable. It suggests that every employee is likely to have different priorities at different times and in different contexts. Definitions of the situation vary with the aspect of the situation which is of major concern at any particular time. The employee acting to improve his or her pay packet or salary is not likely to show much interest in job satisfaction *at that point in time*. However, once the individual returns to the machine or desk, the intrinsic satisfactions to be gained *in that specific context* may come to the fore. The study of ICI's attempt to introduce 'participation' among a semi-skilled work-force in a nylon-spinning plant illustrates this tendency. The improved quality of working experience was recognised and appreciated by the workforce yet, as the authors comment: 'this does not extend to any radical change when it comes to pay and effort-bargain. On this there are still two sides facing each other over a table in collective bargaining' (Cotgrove *et al.* 1971).

What is becoming clear is that to understand work behaviour we must recognise the importance of dynamic orientations and that, instead of relating work attitudes and behaviour in a direct way to either fixed psychological needs or technological constraints, we must recognise that individuals see things differently and act accordingly in different situations and at different times. This may seem fairly obvious but, as with so many generalisations which emerge from sociological study, this insight is not always present in our everyday thinking. We can illustrate this by looking at the common practice in industry of labelling individuals in specific ways, pointing perhaps to a certain apprentice as a 'poor worker', a foremen as a 'loyal company man', a graduate trainee as 'having no interest in the firm' and a shop steward as being 'very militant'. These characterisations or labels are important matters since they influence the way such individuals are treated by other people. The tendency is to assume that these characterisations are *fixed qualities* of the individuals. But in these four cases it is quite possible that significant changes might occur as the circumstance of each individual changes. The apprentice's girlfriend becomes pregnant, they marry and he not only settles to his training but applies himself to his work in a way which he hopes will help him achieve eventual promotion. The foreman, like many other 'loyal company men' among his colleagues, becomes increasingly angry at the erosion of supervisory authority in a period of rapid organisational and technical change and he encourages his colleagues to unionise and present a militant opposition to the management, the ferocity of which had previously been unimaginable. The graduate trainee finds himself in a training placement which he sees giving him access to the type of advancement he had previously felt unlikely to occur and the 'highly militant' shop steward, having effectively defeated a set of managerial proposals to which his shop were strongly opposed, becomes, in the eyes of the management, one of the most 'reasonable' of all the stewards.

In the above accounts can be seen illustrations of the way the individual employee's attitudes and behaviour can shift as a result of contextual changes which occur both outside the workplace and within it. If we were to attempt to understand more fully what was happening in each of these cases it would undoubtedly be valuable to examine how it was and why each individual came into his job in the first place. The workplace orientations and the way they changed has partly to be understood in terms of the prior orientations of each individual – the particular wants and expectations brought into work in the first place by each individual with his own particular social class and family background, his particular education, his community affiliations and so on. One of the junior authors of the *Affluent Worker* studies, Frank Bechhofer (1973), has subsequently accepted that in that study 'the dynamic nature of the orientation was perhaps insufficiently emphasised'. He suggests that we should not ignore the influence of such factors as technology but that these have to be regarded as non-social *conditions* of action rather than actual *sources* of action. It is to the actor's definition of the situation, his or her wants, expectations and priorities that we must initially look.

One problem which emerges from our analysis so far is that we are in danger of losing sight of the individual as an entity with some internal consistency. Each individual may, through his life, modify his attitudes and behaviour but it does not do justice to the integrity of individuals to view them as mere chameleon-like beings changing with each backcloth on which they are to be viewed. To help us here, we can turn to the ideas of the interactionist strand of industrial sociology and make use of the concept of *self* as it is used in that tradition.

The concept of self (see p. 47) refers to the felt identity which each of us has – an identity which develops an interaction with other human beings. As we move through different situations and circumstances and interact with different 'others' so we adjust ourselves to achieve what Alan Dawe (1973) has called 'self-integrative purposes'. The life of the individual can be seen as a *process*: it has a certain pattern, whether this is one viewed by the observer or by the actor himself. This process is referred to in the interactionist tradition as *career* – a vital concept in linking the subjective aspects of life with its objective circumstances. Looking at the individual's work life objectively, for instance, we see him moving through various structural 'statuses' which may be viewed as making up *occupational careers* (each occupation involves various typical stages through which a member may pass) or *organisational careers* (each organisation has series of positions through which individuals may move in typical sequences). But the individual also has his own view of the process which his life is following. This *subjective career* is what we concentrate on here.

The individual, it is suggested, makes coherent for himself what I have called his 'dynamic orientations': he is, as Silverman (1970) puts it, 'always in the act of "becoming", as successive experiences shape and reshape a subjective definition of self and of society'. My suggestion is that to understand the work experience of individuals, we have to look at their whole life-career. We have to trace through their upbringing and education to appreciate what might happen to them in their later work-career. Their work experience is likely to be fundamentally influenced by the wants and expectations of work which they derive from their upbringing as well as by the skills and abilities with which their physique, intellect and social milieu has endowed them. In the following section we will look at the factors which influence the individual's life career up to the point at which they enter work. We will then look at the work experience itself and the influences on this both internal and external to the workplace.

Approach, prior orientations and entry to work

I have suggested that a successful sociology is one which does full
justice to the interplay between individual characteristics and
initiatives on the one hand and structural factors and contingencies on
the other. In the large existing literature on the processes leading to
people's entry to work there has been a tendency for authors to argue
in such a way that either the individual's *choice* of occupation is
stressed or the *determining* influence of external influences is
emphasised. Much of the literature on the so-called process of
occupational choice is psychologically based and examines the way in
which the individual develops and passes through a series of stages
during which the self-concept grows as abilities, aptitudes and
interests develop. Two very influential theories of this type are those
of Ginzberg *et al.* (1951) and that of Super (1957), the latter giving
relatively more attention to the situational factors which condition the
eventual occupation which is chosen. Musgrave (1967) attempts to be
more sociological by concentrating on the series of roles through
which the individual passes at home, in education and early work
experience. These roles provide the settings in which the individual is
socialised and learns to select the work role in which he eventually
settles. However, the problem which arises with this kind of approach
is that the structural *limitations* on choice are underplayed.

An approach which does full justice to the limitations imposed by
the individual's structural context is that of Kenneth Roberts (1968,
1975). Here it is stressed that for many individuals entry to work is a
matter of fitting oneself into whatever jobs are available given
the qualifications which one's class and educational background
has enabled one to attain. In contrast to those theories which see
the work career which a person takes up as an outcome of that
person's ambitions, Roberts' (1975) emphasis on the 'opportunity
structure' suggests that it is careers which tend to determine
ambition:

> careers can be regarded as developing into patterns dictated by the
> opportunity structures to which individuals are exposed, first in
> education and subsequently in employment, whilst individuals'
> ambitions, in turn, can be treated as reflecting the influence of the
> structures through which they pass.

Although Roberts' approach is a great advance on much that preceded it, it can be criticised for its pessimism. Timperley (1974) points out that Roberts' model concentrates on initial entry into employment at the expense of considering subsequent job choices and I have, elsewhere, pointed to the extent to which individuals strive to improve the work situation by making job changes (Watson 1977a). The car workers studied by Goldthorpe, Lockwood *et al.* (1968), we may note, had often entered that particular work as part of a consciously chosen change in their work careers; leaving more intrinsically satisfying work for greater monetary reward.

Choice and structural constraint are best seen as two sides of a coin. Every choice is made within certain structural constraints. Some individuals, however, may find themselves in a structural context where the range of choices is greater than that existing for others, however. A white male with a middle-class accent and good educational qualifications and living in the south-east of England, for example, will have a greater scope for choice than a working-class black female unqualified Liverpudlian.

To find a model into which cases can be fitted we can turn back to the general theoretical scheme developed in chapter 2. It was suggested there that the individual's approach to work is influenced by both objective and subjective factors. Objectively, the individual has certain resources such as cash, skills, knowledge or physique. Subjectively, the individual has certain motives, interests and expectations, such as to make a living, achieve power or gain job satisfaction. Both of these sets of factors are, in turn, strongly influenced by structural factors. These are, on the one side, the structural settings of the individual's family, class, ethnic and educational background and, on the other side, the occupational structure and the prevailing job market. And all these factors are interlinked as indicated in Fig. 4.3; the structure of opportunities itself acting as an influence alongside the various non-work influences on the individual's approach to work.

The life career of the individual is influenced to a major extent by the class-family-education cluster of structural factors. The occupations of the individual's parents are a major indicator of the individual's probable life-chances. This may be direct, in so far as the parents' own experience of work either leads to the encouraging or discouraging of their children from entering work similar to their own. Alternatively, the parent may well wish the child to succeed in a sphere they themselves would have liked to have entered. The experience and knowledge of work of brothers and sisters and more distant relatives may also influence the knowledge and orientations towards an eventual work career of the child (Carter 1966). But the influence may also be less direct. Using the evidence of a large amount of interview material collected by researchers of Leicester University over several years, Ashton and Field (1976) show how the work situation of the father influences the family situation which, in turn, gives the child a certain *perspective* on the occupational world which will later be entered. However, the mechanism which links the family situation to the entry to work in the individual's life career is, of course, the education which is received.

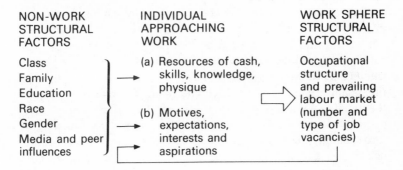

Fig. 4.3 Work and non-work structural factors influencing the individual's approach to work

There is a massive literature linking the child's social class background and his or her level of achievement at school (see Banks 1976), and the qualifications gained at school or in further and higher education affect access to certain jobs. The discussion of education in the previous chapter indicates some of the more subtle factors which may operate here but these are complemented by some very simple ones. It is quite possible, for instance, that liking or disliking a certain teacher may influence which school subjects a fourteen-year-old opts for and this, in various ways, can both open up or close off whole spheres of possible work at a later stage. A rejection of scientific subjects in mid-adolescence, for instance, switches the individual out of one whole channel or educational career area. This process has to be set within the type of school which the child is attending and the stream to which he is allocated and these factors, together with the perceptions which the teachers develop of the child, all influence the way the child perceives himself. This perception will not only influence the work aspirations which develop but also the degree of school performance which the child is thereby encouraged to achieve – thus the teaching will be matched to whatever the child sees as a realistic level of work aspiration. This aspiration will tend, also, to be influenced by the jobs known about and thought by that child to be available (the lower arrow of Fig. 4.3 operating here). Family and peer group influences are relevant to the child's access to this knowledge but so also is the nature of the counselling ('careers guidance') which is received and the facts and images encountered in the communication media.

These family and educational factors are not only relevant to the initial work career entry of the individual. The decision to change a job or, in the case of women with children, to re-enter paid employment, is influenced by husbands, wives, the media and newly gained qualifications (gained by part-time study perhaps) as well as by the qualifications gained in earlier education. The race and the sex of the individual are also likely to be major factors influencing the prior orientations and work-entry opportunities. As will be argued in the next chapter, there is a connection between certain types or level of occupation and the gender and race of its typical entrants. Both recruitment into work and the willingness to put oneself forward to the recruiters are influenced by the ethnic and gender factors operating in the social structure and culture. The socialisation of girls has a considerable influence on their work career aspirations, these influences ranging from those of the games played in infancy to the cultural models provided by the media and by actual contacts (see Sharpe 1976, for instance). Girls tend to be given nurses' uniforms rather than doctors' garb to play with as small children, they see more male than female doctors in televised fiction and they are likely to meet more male doctors than women in their own life experience, for instance. Existing patterns are in these ways reinforced.

The individual's race, like his sex, has a significance wider than simply that of a personal characteristic. The skills and language ability of an immigrant may directly affect the work he is able to do but studies indicate that when disadvantages relating to *immigrant* status are not present, the opportunities open to people of West Indian or Asian background are less than those for whites of similar apparent ability. Smith (1977) reports research which indicates the range of disadvantage experienced by blacks in the employment sphere and his investigations show the considerable part which clear acts of discrimination play in these.

Having considered a number of the structural factors influencing the life career of the individual approaching work, we have to note that the personality as well as the mental abilities and physique of the individual play their own limiting roles, albeit within the structural context described. Various work careers, especially in the manual sphere, require certain physical characteristics, and many of those occupations to which children may be encouraged to aspire by the cultural media also require specific individual characteristics, whether these be footballing skills or the physical beauty or presence expected of the model or entertainer.

The values which the individual has will also play a part in whatever occupational choice is open in his or her milieu. Students in higher education tend to have a relatively wide scope for choice and certain values have been noted by researchers as affecting choices of types of career by students. Rosenberg (1975), for example, showed that students indicating 'people-oriented' values were more strongly oriented towards careers in medicine, social work or personnel management. Students who valued pay and status to a higher degree, on the other hand, looked towards business whilst those putting values of self-expression foremost were more inclined towards careers in journalism, art or architecture.

There is a danger which we should note with analyses like that of Rosenberg, whereby it might be inferred that personal 'values' are *determinants* of choice. It is equally likely that the values which one would indicate by completing the social scientist's questionnaire would be those which one felt to be congruent with the career towards which the structure of opportunities and the influences of family, education and the rest were pushing or pulling one. Again, we have to be aware of the interplay between individual and structural factors, and values are very much influenced by the overall culture of a society and by groups within it. If, for example, the non-work culture stresses values which do not coincide with those central to certain areas within the work sphere there may be considerable problems of recruitment within that sphere. We thus often hear complaints that in Britain 'brightest youngsters' are avoiding industrial careers.

As the individual gets nearer to the point where he or she is to enter work so can we see a 'prior orientation' to work beginning to crystallise as values, wants and preferences are matched against the jobs which are available and for which the individual is qualified. Typically, the individual will enter an employing organisation, although the decision to set up one's own business or enter a partnership will involve very similar considerations. Central to the orientation to work which will influence subsequent attitudes and behaviour will be the way the individual perceives the *implicit contract* which is made between the employee and the employer. This is the largely tacit agreement made between the two parties with regard to what will be given by each and what each will take from the relationship. The employee's priorities, the resources which he takes to the labour market and his personal circumstances all influence what kind of bargain he can make. All those structural and personal factors discussed above influence this – as suggested in Fig. 4.3 above. In Fig. 4.4 we see the major elements which make up the implicit contract which is at the core of every employment relationship.

Within the individual's personal priorities – conditioned as these are by personal resources brought to the labour market and by the knowledge and the reality of the jobs available – a certain degree of calculation will be involved in the taking of any job. The individual will balance the likely personal *costs* in the shape of the amount of physical and mental effort to be expended, together with the likely deprivations of fatigue and the loss of freedom involved in accepting the instructions of others, against the available *rewards*. For certain employees cash may be a priority, for others there may be more concern with the career advancement possible in the future, whereas yet another person may be more interested in intrinsic job satisfaction, the status of a given job, the chance to control other people or simply the opportunity to fulfil personal values afforded by a job which, say, involves 'helping people'. Whatever the priority is, however, the various factors indicated in Fig. 4.4 will have to be balanced one against the other. The schoolteacher giving up the satisfaction to be gained in the classroom to earn a higher level of income in a factory, for example, will make particular calculations as will the individual entering a theological college to train for a calling which is likely to involve little by way of future material advantage. In each case the calculations made prior to the decision to enter into a particular type of implicit contract will orient the subsequent attitudes and behaviour of the individual once engaged in a work career within that organisation. As Enid Mumford (1972) has put it, the degree of *fit* that is achieved between the individual's needs and those of the organisation in what she sees as five contractual areas (the knowledge, psychological, efficiency, ethical and task structure contracts) will determine the employer's satisfaction with that employee and the employee's own *job satisfaction*.

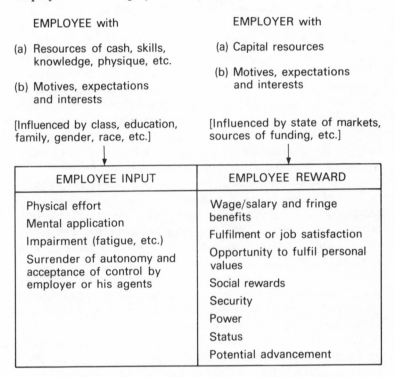

EMPLOYEE with

(a) Resources of cash, skills, knowledge, physique, etc.

(b) Motives, expectations and interests

[Influenced by class, education, family, gender, race, etc.]

EMPLOYER with

(a) Capital resources

(b) Motives, expectations and interests

[Influenced by state of markets, sources of funding, etc.]

EMPLOYEE INPUT	EMPLOYEE REWARD
Physical effort	Wage/salary and fringe benefits
Mental application	
Impairment (fatigue, etc.)	Fulfilment or job satisfaction
Surrender of autonomy and acceptance of control by employer or his agents	Opportunity to fulfil personal values
	Social rewards
	Security
	Power
	Status
	Potential advancement

Fig. 4.4 The implicit contract existing between employer and employee

The implicit contract is never fixed, nor is it ever fully stable and two of the major factors which tend to threaten its stability – the push towards increased efficiency on the part of the employer and the tendency towards collective action and challenge on the part of the employee are central to the concerns of later chapters (but see chapter 2, p. 64 for an outline). What is important to us at present is the way in which different implicit contracts are made in different types of work and, especially, at different levels within work settings. Each individual will be willing to make certain inputs and accept certain deprivations and rewards. These are basic to the way work is experienced. Certain patterns can be perceived in these experiences as we shall now see.

Rewards, satisfactions and deprivations at work

Our present analysis suggests that the work which people enter is viewed in a basically rational and generally instrumental manner. People tend to know the limitations to which they are likely to have to adjust as they weigh up the possible satisfactions and the likely deprivations offered by the particular jobs available to them. Given this tendency, it is not surprising that surveys which involve asking people about work satisfaction frequently report a large proportion of people registering satisfaction. However, satisfaction is not a totally individualistic notion: in any given society there will be certain basic notions of what is desirable and we can expect people with different degrees of access to the means of these satisfactions at work to recognise this. Some indication of the distribution of these satisfactions can be derived if only in a very general way, by looking at the variations in response to questions about 'satisfaction' between people working in different settings.

Robert Blauner (1960) reviewed a number of work satisfaction studies and found that professionals and businessmen claimed relatively high levels of satisfaction, that clerical workers claimed higher levels than manual workers, whilst skilled manual workers appeared more satisfied than unskilled workers or assembly-line operators, etc. We may well observe that these accounts fall into a pattern closely relating to the social class hierarchy – itself a patterning of the way those resources most valued in society at large are distributed. But this does not invalidate our seeking factors in the work itself which appear to relate to these differences. Blauner offers four major areas. First, he notes the importance of the relative *prestige* of the occupation and, second, the degree of *independence and control* over the conditions of work. This category covers the freedom from hierarchical control, the freedom to move about, the opportunity to vary the pace of work and allocate one's time. Third, the extent to which social satisfactions to be gained from working within an *integrated group* are noted and, fourth, the degree to which people who work together *share non-work activities* (in something approaching an occupational community). Parker (1971), on the basis of his own review of work satisfaction surveys, mentions, in addition to factors like this, such things as opportunities to 'create something', 'use skill', 'work wholeheartedly' and work together with people who 'know their job'. Dissatisfactions are likely to involve formulations which simply oppose these but Parker also usefully locates specific factors like doing repetitive work, making only a small part of something, doing useless tasks, feeling a sense of insecurity and being too closely supervised.

All the factors emerging in these studies are ones characterised earlier on as intrinsic satisfactions – that is, those relating to factors inherent in the work itself rather than the extrinsic rewards which may be obtained. However, if we look at the type of implicit contract which people at various levels in the class structure of society are able to make with employers, we may note that those likely to gain the highest intrinsic satisfactions of the type listed above are also often those most able to gain higher material or other extrinsic rewards. Let us therefore look at the patterning of work rewards and satisfactions by work *level*. Having done this, we will then return to look at the patterning which may be connected with a factor not unrelated to that of level: technology.

Different researchers have used different methods to elicit information about the nature of people's involvement in their work and hence the rewards and satisfactions which are sought or expected. Morse and Weiss (1955), for example, asked respondents whether they would continue to work if they had sufficient money to live comfortably. People in middle-class occupations pointed to the loss which would result with regard to the interest which they found in their jobs and the sense of accomplishment to which they were used. The type of loss mentioned by those in working-class jobs, however, was typically more in terms of the lack of activity with which to keep themselves occupied. Another classic study in this area is that of Friedmann and Havighurst (1954). Here the lower status workers were those most likely to stress the importance of money as the major reward. The relationship between the nature of rewards and satisfactions and job level is also suggested by studies which have followed Robert Dubin's method of attempting to elicit whether the individual's *central life interest* lies inside or outside the work sphere. Dubin (1956) himself, in his original study based on a large sample of industrial workers, found that three out of four individuals in this manual work had central life interests *outside* their work. Yet Louis Orzack (1959) found that four out of five of the professional nurses whom he studied, using a procedure similar to Dubin's, indicated a central life interest *within* their work.

When we come to examine the material rewards of cash income and associated fringe benefits we find that these, like the actual working conditions which people experience, are distributed in an uneven way with the white-collar/blue-collar divide still apparent (Wedderburn and Craig 1974, Westergaard and Resler 1975 and Roberts *et al.* 1977). As was suggested earlier, work with higher potential intrinsic rewards is often that which also offers higher extrinsic rewards.

Apart from the type of evidence produced by the authors just cited, most of the data on which the generalisation which we have looked at is based is subjective material – it depends on accounts given to researchers. The evidence is such, however, that at the very least, we can take it that those in higher level work *expect* more by way of intrinsic satisfactions than do those in more routine manual work. Using Daniel's (1973) very helpful distinction we might say that routine manual workers both find and seek *satisfaction in* work less than do those in managerial, professional or highly skilled work. But this does not mean that they are not *satisfied with* their job. The 'affluent' car workers studied by Goldthorpe, Lockwood *et al.* appeared to be satisfied *with* jobs in which they achieved little or no intrinsic job satisfaction. They did not seek or expect such satis-factions. As Michael Mann (1973) points out in his study of workers moving with a relocated factory, the fact that the instrumentally-involved worker sets little store by intrinsic work activities is, paradoxically, all the more reason for his staying firmly attached to his job. One stays in a job in order to increase its stability and predictability, thereby lowering one's 'emotional investment' in work.

Lowering emotional involvement in work is not so easily done for the worker in the professional or managerial sphere. The prior orientation to work is likely to be quite different and the absence of intrinsic satisfactions may lead to a greater degree of dissatisfaction and felt deprivation than is likely among working-class employees operating in settings at first sight far more potentially depriving. Cyril Sofer (1970), in his study of managers in mid-career, reports how struck he was by the high expectations which these men had of their employing organisation and he expresses surprise that 'such a high proportion of the men we saw felt that they were under-utilised, more than this, that their personal resources were rejected'. Both Fletcher (1973) and Campanis (1970) indicate the degree of frustration which can be experienced in higher level posts within work organisations. The subjective experience of work, in practice, is very much influenced by the prior orientation which the individual brings to that work and the priorities, orientations and perceptions of the implicit contract vary considerably up and down the occupational hierarchy.

Turning now to the part which technology plays in the patterning of work experiences, we find that most of the existing discussions confine their attention to manual work. We may wonder why this should be, given that work of all types has its own technology in one way or another. The medical general practitioner has his medical bag, prescription pad and motor car for visiting patients and the concert pianist has his piano and his musical score. Why, then, has the relationship between working-class manual work experience and technology been the main centre of attention? The answer lies partly in the general point made earlier about the tendency to treat the working class as a 'problematic' group but it specifically relates to that major element of the input which the employee makes in his implicit contract with the employer: the surrender of autonomy and acceptance of control by the employer or his agents. Technology, for the majority of employees, is central to their work experience and is often something which, down to its finest detail, is chosen, is designed and its mode of use dictated by persons other than those applying it. In addition these persons are frequently ones with higher status, higher level of material rewards and, especially important, greater apparent autonomy in their own work experience than those directly applying the technology. Given cultural norms which encourage the valuing of personal autonomy, individuality and self-expression, we can see why technology is potentially such a source of resentment, conflict and opposition and hence concern among those studying manual work in industry. We are looking at a point where one of the major structural or cultural contradictions described in the previous chapter (where the culture values autonomy whilst the economy demands submission to control by many) comes to bear on the individual's work experience.

In stressing the importance of technology to work experience we do not need to revert to the 'technological implications' approach discussed earlier. If we follow Bechhofer's (1973) advice, we can retain our emphasis on individuals' motives and interests – their orientation to work – as a *source* of action which is to be socially located and recognise technology as a non-social *condition* of action (1973). The individual will tend to be aware of, and take into account, the general nature of the technology in his prior orientation to work but, once in work, his subsequent attitudes and behaviour may be conditioned by such factors as the extent to which the technology enables him to mix with others, the freedom it allows him to use discretion, etc. Wedderburn and Crompton (1972) in the study cited earlier found that, although they were studying 'a group of workers with primarily instrumental attitudes to work', there were nevertheless distinct differences of attitude and behaviour between different parts of the plants examined, and technology was taken to be the key variable in this. The degree of interest expressed in the job, the attitude to supervision and the level of grievance activity were all found to be more 'favourable', for instance, in the continuous flow plant than in the batch production plant (even though pay levels were higher in the latter area). These authors stress the importance of two factors which relate to technology: the structuring of the job itself and the way in which the relationship between the supervisors and the operators was shaped. It is thus not the technology itself which operates on the individual. It is the opportunity which the technology allows for personal discretion and the part it plays in the *power* relationships between the managers and the managed.

Robert Blauner in his influential study *Alienation and Freedom* (1964) attempted to bring together several of the major factors thought to influence work satisfactions and to relate those to work experience in different technological settings. He used the overall concept of alienation to bring together those factors influencing satisfaction. These four 'dimensions of alienation', as he termed them, were *powerlessness*, or lack of opportunity for control, *meaningless* or lack of opportunity to feel a sense of purpose by linking one's job with the overall production process, *isolation* or an inability to relate closely to others at work and *self-estrangement* or a lack of opportunity to achieve self-involvement or personal fulfilment at work. Blauner used a variety of research materials to measure alienation defined in this way in four types of industry: printing, textiles, car assembly and chemicals. There were four distinct types of technology here: craft, machine-tending, assembly line and process technology and Blauner found that alienation was relatively low in the craft printing industry and the process chemical industry, higher in the machine-tending textile setting and highest on the car assembly line. We thus get the famous 'inverted U-curve' shown in Fig. 4.5.

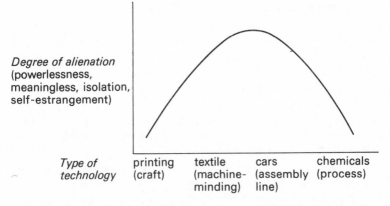

Degree of alienation (powerlessness, meaningless, isolation, self-estrangement)

| *Type of technology* | printing (craft) | textile (machine-minding) | cars (assembly line) | chemicals (process) |

Fig. 4.5 Blauner's 'inverted U curve' relating alienation and technology (based on Blauner 1964)

There are considerable problems with Blauner's thesis: he trivialises Marx's notion of alienation by conceptualising it in subjective terms; his inferences from attitude survey data can be questioned, and the representativeness of the areas surveyed can be doubted. Eldridge (1971) has provided a very full critique of the study but, whilst accepting that Blauner has important things to say about the relationship between certain technical settings and sources of work satisfaction, I would point to the greatest inadequacy of this study as its failure to locate technology within the essentially *political* context. Blauner suggests that as technology becomes more automated in the future so will the opportunity for people to experience control, purpose, meaning and self-realisation at work increase. What this does not recognise is that technology is a means to the ends of those who own and control capital and that, within any given industry, automation will only be introduced in those areas where its costs are less than employing human effort, and the replacement of human effort in such areas is likely to lead to the deskilling of various tasks within that industry and the tendency to require unskilled labour to serve the process as it is to lead to the evolution of a workforce of autonomous skilled, integrated and satisfied control room workers and maintenance engineers. Automation is merely one way of increasing control over work process on the part of the owner or manager and its combination with other methods of achieving control such as partial automation combined with deskilling is just as feasible, if not more so.

Justifications for the type of reservations expressed here can be found in a study done in the British chemical industry more than a decade after Blauner. Nichols and Beynon (1977) found that in six out of the seven plants of a major British chemical company which they visited, control room operatives – the archetypal non-alienated worker of automated industry – were a minority: 'for every man who watched dials another maintained the plants, another was a lorry driver and another two humped bags or shovelled muck'. As these authors point out, about 50 per cent of the work involved in chemical production in Britain is classified as demanding virtually no skill from the worker. Reading the authors' reports of the accounts given by the workers of their experience of what is recognised as 'donkey work' in one of these plants, one is very much reminded of studies of the car-assembly line.

What we have to be careful about, I suggest, is making broad generalisations about the effect of technological change on work experience on the basis of quite real differences of experience within specific and limited work settings and without recognising that any given technology is typically a mediating factor between those who control work and those whose efforts are controlled. Since the managers of work are typically under constant pressure to maintain and increase this control we can expect their efforts to introduce technical change to be a constant influence on the 'dynamic orientations' of the employee, that is, on their ongoing definition of their situation and their preparedness to act in certain ways. Huw Beynon's study of the car assembly plant in *Working for Ford* (1973) illustrates the major part which the technology plays in the battle between management and workers over a 'frontier of control'. Any management threat to what the worker regards as an acceptable balance in the implicit contract through technologically mediated interference with employee autonomy will lead to a shift in orientation and a preparedness to act.

Technology, then, is a major influence on people's orientations to work. But its influence has to be set alongside various characteristics of the workplace itself. The effect of socialisation within work has been stressed by writers in the interactionist tradition, for instance. Becker *et al.* (1961) in their study of medical students show how groups facing common problems and situational pressures tend to develop certain common perspectives or 'modes of thought and action' thus creating a peer group pressure on the individual's orientation to work. The individual's knowledge of a work setting is always likely to be relatively limited prior to his entry and a whole series of influences are brought to bear on him once he enters the new subculture whether it be that of industry generally (as described by Turner 1971) or that of the particular workplace. R. K. Brown (1974) attempted to measure the shifting orientations of apprentices over the period subsequent to their entry to work and it is instructive to note the ways in which the changes in their responses to the same questions asked at different times about intrinsic and extrinsic satisfactions, interests in promotion and the like can be interpreted as part of their adjustment to specific conditions as they experienced them. But factors inside the workplace are not the only ones affecting how the individual views work or acts within: non-work factors play their part too and it is to these which we now turn.

Work and non-work

The relationship between the work and non-work sphere is complex and two-way. At the highest level of generality the two spheres interrelate to form a particular type of society; the industrial capitalist type examined in chapter 3 being the one with which we are concerned. This society is ever-changing, with changes at work influencing those in society at large and vice versa. As was argued in the earlier chapter, much of the impetus to social change comes from structural contradictions, many of which derive from aspects of work organisation, control and experience. The structures of work and the technology used, we have suggested, are located in the power structure of the wider society and we have seen that the social class, family, education and various other social structural factors have a major influence on individuals' prior orientation to work: their socially conditioned predisposition to act and think in a certain way once in work.

Following entry to work, one's occupation, through the income earned and the other social class correlates of the position, is a major determinant of one's own life chances and those of one's dependents. The career structure of either the occupation or the employing organisation will offer or deny opportunity for social mobility and hence improvement in their life chances. Different approaches to mobility can be noted, however. For example, William Watson (1964) located a particular type of aspiring middle-class employee, the *spiralist*, who moves upwards in career by moving from organisation to organisation and locality to locality. This type of person, one who occupies what Alvin Gouldner (1957) has called a *cosmopolitan* latent role, can be contrasted with what he calls a *local*, someone more inclined to seek whatever advancement is desired within the local setting. These various categories of people, with their contrasting orientations to work and career, are recognisable in the recent study of what is seen as the fragmented British class structure by Roberts *et al.* (1977) who clearly distinguish the spiralist middle-class workers as a group with both distinct political, social and job attitudes within the middle class as a whole.

The above study supports what various studies have indicated over the years: that the social class images which people have are related to the work they do. The findings support what Goldthorpe, Lockwood *et al.* (1969) found in the mid-1960s; that achievement of relatively high levels of income by some manual workers does not lead to their assimilation into the middle class in either behaviour and attitude (thus invalidating the so-called 'embourgeoisement thesis'). Gavin Mackenzie (1975) has attempted to relate the specific factors in people's work situations which are likely to influence class imagery, arguing that this in turn influences such things as their child-rearing attitudes, political viewpoints and ways of using leisure time. The factors which he examines as conducive to either middle-class imagery or working-class imagery are those suggested by David Lockwood (1960):

the size of the factory, the organisation of the work group, its relation to supervisors and management, the degree to which the worker has control over his work process, the extent to which the job facilitates or prevents communication between workers, the rigidity of the distinction between staff and workers, security of tenure, the progressiveness of earnings, and job discipline.

The recognition that people's work situation influences their wider world view has led various authors to speculate that moves towards greater automation in the workplace would help create a 'new working class'. This view, a sort of 'technological implications' version of the embourgeoisement thesis mentioned above, has appeared in different versions. Blauner in *Alienation and Freedom* (1964) expected the typically non-alienated workers of the automated plant to become quite different in outlook and behaviour from the traditional working class, manifesting less loyalty to the trade union, more to the employer and generally a more characteristically middle-class orientation. In his version of the new working class ushered in with advanced technology, the French writer, Serge Mallet (1975), foresees an opposite tendency with workers making use of a new sense of power and a greater knowledge of the firm to act through their unions in efforts to challenge the employer and gain greater control. However, this type of argument, in both versions, tends to infer too much direct influence of work experience on outside orientations, underestimating that of structural and cultural factors in the wider society. This has been shown in Duncan Gallie's (1978) study of four oil refineries, two in France and two in Britain. His results question both the above theses, suggesting that advanced technology itself appears to have no significant effect on class attitudes and aspirations, or on attitudes to the employer and to trade unions. The study suggests that more significance has to be attached to the structure and culture of the society outside the plant, this being indicated by the distinctly more conflictful and class-conscious orientations of the French workers compared with the British.

In a way corresponding to that in which trends in the workplace have been taken to have major implications for working-class life outside of work, some writers have pointed to the ways in which various kinds of middle-class employment create a type of person whose first loyalty is to the corporation. These 'organisation men', graphically described by W. H. Whyte (1961), show a willingness to fit in and co-operate with others at work; they are unwilling to challenge or disturb the order of which they are a part and their superficial suburban home life reflects the lack of initiative and their docility at work. This thesis gained wide currency and is found in similar forms in various other American works such as Wright Mills's *White Collar* (1953). However, Kohn's (1971) investigation of the personality types associated with bureaucratic employment found little support for this popular stereotype, arguing that there was no evidence that bureaucracies produced placid conformists. It was argued in fact, that the reverse tended to apply, the secure base provided by the bureaucrat's employment enabling him to consolidate his own values and 'develop a life style reflecting his personal preferences' (1971). Nevertheless, it is clearly recognised that careers which involve long absences of the individual from the family setting and frequent geographical moves do create tensions in home life (Pahl and Pahl 1972, Tunstall 1962), this being exacerbated where both spouses work. But this is again an area where individual orientations to work are important. Rapoport and Rapoport (1976) in their study of *dual-career families* show that the stresses involved in this form of family life are reorganised and accepted as a 'cost' involved when such a way of life is chosen, and Sofer (1970) reports that where the managers in his sample were able to achieve a separation between their working and non-working lives, there was less mental conflict engendered by aspects of the husband's work career.

The family is the most significant setting for most people's life-cycle and here we would expect there to be a significant type of pressure on the individual's orientation to work. The arrival and different stages of children's growing up may, for instance, exert significant pressures on fathers' interests in such items in their implicit contract as income level and degree of security. But the part played by children in adults' life cycles is vastly more significant for women interested in or needing to find employment. As was suggested in the previous chapter, cultural pressures tend to lead to the defining of women's roles in such a way that married women and mothers working have an implicitly deviant status and this, together with their requirement to fulfil two roles at once, puts them at severe disadvantage in the work sphere (Myrdal and Klein 1968, Barker and Allen 1976).

Child-rearing practices themselves have been related by researchers to the employment of the parent. Kohn (1969), for instance, noted the commitment to different value-systems by manual workers and non-manual workers, these affecting the extent to which they stressed conformity or self-direction in the child socialisation patterns. He argued that the *restrictive* nature of working-class employment reinforced the relative lack of education of the parents in its influence on the higher level of conformity encouraged in their children. Similar findings have been reported by Miller and Swanson (1958) and Aberle and Naegele (1961) and, as Mackenzie (1975) points out, this indicates important influences on the class imagery of children. This, of course, has significant implications for the future work life of these children as well as for their non-work attitudes and behaviour.

The family is not only the unit for the raising of children and a contributor to the effective reproduction of class patterns. It is also the setting of a great deal of *leisure* activity, something which not only varies with individual taste but which can be seen to relate in different ways to various types of employment. The hours left free for leisure by different types of work and the money available to spend on leisure are factors which clearly relate work and leisure forms. However, other factors are also relevant and, to help indicate a pattern in these, Stanley Parker (1971) has suggested that we can see three types of relationship between work and leisure: extension, opposition and neutrality.

Where a relatively high degree of autonomy and intrinsic satisfaction is experienced in work there is a greater likelihood that leisure activity will be an *extension* of work, it is suggested. The academic's work and leisure reading may well shade one into the other and, as Gerstl and Hutton (1966) showed in their study, engineers may well apply their expertise to hobbies and read professional literature in their non-work time. Parker's (1971) research indicates that social workers tend not to see a sharp distinction between their working and non-working lives, and this may be the case with some businessmen. The extent to which businessmen are centrally involved in their work, eating business meals and playing golf with colleagues or clients in their leisure time may vary from country to country, and, as Child and Macmillan (1973) suggest, our impressions here are probably heavily based on American images, British managers being far less inclined to be so centrally involved in their careers.

In work where there is less autonomy and potential self-fulfilment the relationship between work and leisure may be one of *neutrality*, where those in jobs such as those involving routine clerical work reflect their lack of involvement and passivity at work in their leisure pastimes. Alternatively, the pattern may be that of *opposition*. Here the worker who is liable to be frustrated and unfulfilled at work may concentrate on the fulfilling and comfortable pastimes of home and family (this privatised life style fitting with the *instrumental* orientation to work considered earlier) or he may pursue the more gregarious and even riotous type of leisure associated with the coalminer or deep sea fishermen (Tunstall 1962); the sharing of social activities with workmates perhaps reflecting the love-hate attitude to work associated with the *traditional* orientation to work.

Some writers have pointed to the opportunities which some workers may find to compensate for work experience in the exercise of skill and the obtaining of social satisfaction in activities like pigeon-racing (Mott 1973). But the general likelihood of this type of compensatory effect has been strongly argued against by people such as Meissner (1971), who diagnoses what he calls the 'long arm of the job' and argues that the suppressing of the capacity for initiative in the work setting will tend to reduce the capacity for engaging in leisure activities which involve discretion, planning and co-ordination. As Parker and Smith (1976) say, following Argyris's (1973) objections to this compensation theory:

> If individuals tend to experience dependence, submission, frustration, conflict, and short time perspective at work, and if they adapt to these conditions by psychological withdrawal, apathy, indifference, and a decrease in the importance of their worth as human beings, these adaptive activities become more dominant in the person's life, and they will guide his leisure behaviour outside the workplace. Individuals will seek leisure activities that are consonant with the adaptive capacities.

What sociological research clearly indicates is that human beings' experience of work and their activity, experience and values outside of work are closely interrelated. The choices which face the members of industrial capitalist societies with regard to their futures are ones which must take into account this interrelationship. The nature of these choices to be made will inevitably be returned to later. For the present we will move our focus from the individual and his or her experience of work, to look more closely at the variety of structural contexts in which that experience occurs. Sight of the individual will not be lost during our examination of occupational and organisational structuring in the next two chapters but the way individuals react and adjust to their work situation will be a direct concern of the chapter which follows these two and which looks at the conflicts, challenges and defences which operate in these contexts.

Chapter 5

The structuring of work: occupations

Introduction

If we seek some pattern underlying the work which people do in modern societies we will find that there are two basic principles which contribute to the structuring which can be observed. These principles are partly complementary and partly in a relationship of conflict and rivalry. They are, first, the structuring of work on a bureaucratic, administrative or 'formal organisation' basis and, second, structuring on the occupational principle. In the first case, emphasis is on the ways in which work tasks are designed by certain people who then recruit, pay, co-ordinate and control the efforts of others to carry out these tasks. In the second case the emphasis is more on the patterns which emerge when we concentrate on the way specific work tasks are done. Here we take as our starting point the carrying out of a specific type of work operation, say driving a lorry, cleaning a house, catching fish or running a business. We then concentrate on the social implications of there existing within society groups of people regularly doing similar tasks. The implications of these occupational groupings arise at various levels, as we shall see in this chapter: they have implications for society as a whole and for social change; they have implications for the members of these groups in so far as the groups become collectivities, and they have implications for the individual engaged in a particular type of work.

It is important in defining an occupation to recognise that the concept is not simply a sociological tool of analysis but is also a notion used by the people whom the sociologist studies. A definition has therefore to take into account that whether or not any given work activity is to be regarded as an occupation depends in part on the decisions made by those doing the tasks and also by the wider public as to whether such an identity is to be bestowed. I therefore suggest that we conceptualise an occupation as *largely full-time engagement in a part or the whole of a range of work tasks which are identified under a particular heading or title by both those carrying out these tasks and by a wider public.* We should note that this conception is one which is wider than simply paid employment. Membership of an occupation may involve total independence of an employer, as in the case of a freelance writer, say, and it may mean that there is no direct financial reward from the work. In this latter case the individual will have to be supported by someone else. This will apply to the commercially unsuccessful poet and to the student, either of whom may receive a government grant. It also applies to housewives, who are typically supported by their marriage partner.

Occupational and administrative forms of work structuring

Practically every person who works can be assigned to an occupation. But for many individuals, their location in a work organisation may be more salient than this occupational membership. In trying to place a stranger we may ask either 'what do they do?' or 'who do they work for?' Traditionally, we locate people in society by their occupation – tinker, tailor, soldier, sailor – but with the growth of bureaucratised work organisations the specific tasks in which a person is engaged and the skills which go with it become less relevant for many people than the organisation in which they are employed. It is not uncommon for one person to say of another 'I don't know exactly what he does but it's something with the council' and the nearest to any occupational specification which is often achieved with regard to the work of friends, acquaintances or relatives may well be along the lines that 'she does something in the offices' or 'it's some kind of factory job'.

It is suggested that, for many people, the way they are seen by others and often the way they regard their own work is less in terms of the occupational principle than the organisational or administrative one. There are, however, two special cases where the *study* of people's work has tended to concentrate on the occupational principle. The first is where the tasks associated with a job are particularly distinctive. This may be through a certain public visibility (policeman, teacher, actor) or through their being somewhat peculiar or in some way deviant (prostitute, undertaker, dope peddler). The second case is where the tasks involved in a certain kind of work are such that control over the carrying out of those tasks can be sought by members of the occupation itself at the expense of control by an employer, government or clients. These will tend to be highly skilled 'trades' or, more especially, the 'professions'. The twentieth-century study of particular occupations by sociologists has tended to veer between a fascination with high-status professionals and various low-status figures like those of the Chicago *demi-monde*.

The history of western occupations has been very much one of the rise and fall of the degree of occupational self-control maintained by various groups. The occupational principle is seen very clearly in the occupational guilds which were at their height in the thirteenth century. The guilds developed as part of the urban world which was growing within the feudal structure. They originally served as protective societies for merchants trading in Europe but were then taken up by groups of artisans within the cities as an organisational form to provide them in a similar way with mutual aid and protection.

With the guilds we see an example of that common tendency in social life and social change for people to form coalitions of interest. The guilds, as such coalitions, helped mediate between the tradesmen and the city authorities, thus providing in part a defensive role for the group. But they also acted in a more assertively self-interested manner by maintaining a tightly controlled monopoly in their trade. They not only controlled raw materials, and restricted entry to trades, but laid down work procedures which, whilst maintaining quality of the product or service, ensured that any job took the longest possible course with the effect that technical change and any move toward an increased technical division of labour was ruled out. The guild gave the occupation a stratified structure of master craftsman, journeyman and apprentice, thus providing in theory a career structure for the individual. However, groups tend to exist within interest groups and those who find themselves with relative material advantages tend to operate so as to maintain that advantage. Thus the master craftsmen began to operate as an élite within the guilds, often preferring to pass on their advantaged positions to their own children rather than to aspiring journeymen. With the growth of the more competitive and market-orientated capitalism which was developing within and threatening the feudal order, master craftsmen were strongly tempted to break their guild monopolies and associate more with the growing class of merchant capitalists. These men helped break down the occupational principle of work organisation as they began to use former guild members as wage labour and as they made use of the former peasantry within the putting-out or domestic system of production. Later, of course, the development of factory production accelerated the dominance of the administrative principle, leaving the occupational form of organisation as a residual principle – a principle to be defended by groups whose trade skills were a resource sufficiently exclusive to allow them to maintain some autonomy.

The survival of the occupational principle among the growing working class was carried over into workshop and factory production in the first half of the nineteenth century in the form of a 'labour aristocracy' which retained an élite position 'through the force of custom, or combination and apprenticeship restriction, or because the craft remained highly skilled and specialised ' (Thompson 1968). The growth of the new skills accompanying the rise of engineering created a potentially new occupational élite or labour aristocracy but by the late nineteenth century the growing predominance of the administrative principle was such that the more important bodies formed by groups like the engineers were the more *defensively orientated* trade unions. Throughout the twentieth century the trade or occupational basis of unions has become undermined as occupational groups have amalgamated with each other to help in the primary union task of representing *employee* interests rather than occupational ones.

The occupational principle of work organisation did not only survive the growth of industrial capitalism in the vestigial form represented by skilled trade unions. It has survived and indeed flourished in parts of the middle-class sphere of work in the guise of professionalism. Those occupations, like law and medicine, widely recognised as professions can be seen as forms of work organisation which gave a place within industrial capitalism to those doing high status work whilst keeping them in part outside and above those processes which were bringing the work lives of so many people under the administrative control of employers.

The increasing influence of the work ethic in the developing industrial capitalist society meant that those upper-class practitioners in such areas as medicine, law and university teaching who had formerly seen their efforts as gentlemanly pursuits rather than as labour needed to redefine their position. We thus see the decline of what Philip Elliot (1972) calls *status professionalism* and the rise of *occupational professionalism.* Those who had previously been above having an occupation (the upper class being in many ways a leisure class in principle if not always in practice) now embraced the occupational principle as a way of engaging in work without becoming contaminated by industrialism and commercialism. The ideology developed by such high status groups existed beyond these specific occupations, however, being found among the military and senior civil servants and propagated in the universities and new public schools. This ideology of liberal education, public service and gentlemanly professionalism was elaborated, as Elliot (1972) stresses, in opposition to the growth of industrialism and commercialism:

> it incorporated such values as personal service, a dislike of competition, advertising and profit, a belief in the principle of payment in order to work rather than working for pay and in the superiority of the motive of service.

The essence of the idea of a profession is *autonomy* – the maintenance of the control over work tasks by those doing these tasks. It should not be surprising therefore to find groups of people who operate within formal organisations or within other restricted settings looking to the traditional high status 'free' professions to find ways of developing strategies to oppose control over them by others. This is something to which we will return later in this chapter. The concern of so many sociologists with the occupational strategy of profession-alisation is a justifiable one because it represents one of the major ways in which the prevailing mode of work organisation and control has been and will perhaps continue to be challenged. The possibilities of the occupational principle developing so as to reduce the conflicts and excesses of capitalism have been suggested by both classical and recent sociologists. The possibilities here will be raised again in our final chapter.

Occupational structure

In contrast to the term 'organisational structure', which refers to the internal patterning in work organisations, the concept of occupational structure is used by sociologists to refer to the wider pattern in society which is suggested by the distribution of the labour force across the range of existing types of work. Patterning may be sought, for example, by looking for *horizontal* differentiating factors. The dividing of the work-force into primary (agricultural and extractive industries), secondary (manufacturing) and tertiary (service) sectors is frequently used. As we shall see, this type of distribution, widely used by economists, has been used sociologically to study industrial-isation processes. However, various sociologists have looked for ways of grouping occupations on a basis other than a hierarchical one. The notion of occupational *situs* is the major contribution here and this refers to a grouping of occupations which is differentiated from other groupings according to various criteria other than or in addition to ones which imply status or reward-yielding capacity. Morris and Murphy (1959) took up this concept (which had first been applied to the occupational sphere by Hatt (1950)) using the criterion of 'societal function'. Hopper and Pearce (1973), who point out that the particular criterion used may vary with the purpose of the research being undertaken, classify occupations for their own purposes on the basis of economic function. They thus develop nine *situs* categories: distribution; manufacturing; finance and insurance; agriculture; building and transport; communications; civil service, church, military and government; education; and medicine and health.

Occupational *situs* as a tool of analysis is yet to be widely used. Up to now sociological researchers have been reluctant to divert attention from the all-permeating status-criteria which, many researchers point out, cannot be kept out of classifications. It is questionable whether we can say that the list of categories given above are unequivocally of equal prestige: does work in the manufacturing *situs* generally bestow prestige in the same way as work in the education, medicine and health *situs*, for example? It is therefore far more common for *hier-archical* structuring to be emphasised in studies of occupational structure. This is not surprising, given that an individual's occupation is the key indicator of his social class and social status – as those concepts are generally used, inside and outside of sociology. As well as the prestige which one derives from a job, one's market position and relationship to the means of production is generally dependent upon the job which is held. As we saw in the last chapter, the hierarchy of jobs based on material rewards tends to coincide with that based on intrinsic rewards which contribute to job satisfaction, and both of these factors influence the general life-chances not just of the workers themselves but also of their dependents.

Sociological researchers often develop their own set of socio-economic categories or classes to help in their particular investigations and a useful example is the scheme of class positions used in recent research on class mobility in Britain (Goldthorpe and Llewellyn 1977). The categories used here achieve differentiation in terms of *both* occupational function and employment status. Occupations are brought together in such a way that we can expect incumbents to share in 'broadly similar market and work situations' – these being taken to be the two major components of class position. The groupings, somewhat simplified for present purposes, are as follows:

Class I: higher-grade professionals, administrators, managers and businessmen;

Class II: low-grade professionals, administrators and managers; higher-grade technicians and supervisors of manual employees;

Class III: routine non-manual, largely clerical, workers; sales personnel and other rank and file service workers;

Class IV: small proprietors; self-employed artisans and other non-professional own-account workers;

Class V: lower grade technicians and supervisors over manual workers;

Class VI: skilled manual wage-workers;

Class VII: semi and unskilled workers.

Thus the study of occupational structure involves classifying occupations horizontally, vertically, or in a way which mixes both of these. The categories developed are used to do various things, including examining the numbers of people covered by certain sectors or socio-economic groups, the mobility of people between different categories, the characteristics of people in various positions in terms of such criteria of gender, race and age and, especially, the way these patterns change over time. All of these factors are central to understanding the social structure and processes of change occurring in society at large. We shall now look at some of the major changes which have been suggested.

At the basis of the study of changes in occupational structures is a concern with the *division of labour* in society. Durkheim saw this as central to the nature of a society's solidarity – the way in which a society achieves integration. In a simple society there would be little occupational differentiation with, say, most of the women carrying out one basic task, most of the young men occupied in another general task and so on. A similarity of outlook would develop between people, most of whom are engaged in more or less similar activities. Social order and stability would thus be maintained through *mechanical solidarity*. However, in the vastly more complex industrialising world where a large range of specialised occupations have developed, each with distinctive ideas, norms and values, a similarity of outlook cannot be depended upon to hold society together. The source for stability is to be found, instead, in the inevitable interdependence of members of occupations one with the other. The baker depends on the butcher for his meat, the butcher on the baker for his bread, and so on. We thus have integration through *organic solidarity*.

Where Durkheim's analysis is instructive, paradoxically, is not so much in its accuracy as in the way it brings to our attention factors which *weaken* rather than contribute to social solidarity. Durkheim himself observed that the increasing emphasis on material advancement and sectional interests of his own time tended to undermine social solidarity, leading, in particular, to the moral confusion and purposelessness which he conceptualised as *anomie*. But Durkheim treated such tendencies as pathological rather than as essential features of industrial capitalism. The more closely we look at Durkheim's assumed source of social order in modern societies – the organic solidarity achieved by interdependent occupation – the more we come to realise that the structure and dynamics of industrial capitalism can be better understood in terms of interests, power and control. The attachment of people to the prevailing social order is more realistically seen as deriving from their dependence on the material rewards to be gained from their relationship not to occupations but to bureaucratic work *organisations*; whether this relationship be more one of submitting to control within an organisation, exercising such control or servicing the organisation in some direct or indirect way.

Consideration of the division of labour in the Marxian tradition has seen the increasing specialisation of tasks which accompanies the capitalist labour process as essentially disintegrative. An important distinction is made between the general or *social* division of labour, which refers to the necessary allocation of general tasks to trades and occupations and the detailed or *technical* division of labour, that splitting down of tasks within a former craft at the initiative of the employer or his agents in order to increase the efficiency of the enterprise – efficiency as conceived by those extracting a surplus. As Harry Braverman (1974) puts it:

> the social division of labour divides society among occupations, each adequate to a branch of production; the detailed division of labor destroys occupations considered in this sense, and renders the worker inadequate to carry through any complete production process.

The dividing of tasks *within* occupations, with its alienating effects, is seen as fundamentally different from the dividing of tasks *between* occupations – the latter constituting a healthy and necessary part of any human society.

The Marxian view of the changing occupational structure, which in its basic form looks to the ultimate polarisation of all former occupational roles into those of capitalist and proletariat, can be contrasted with those analyses which have focused on the nature of industrialism rather than capitalism. Implicit in many of the discussions of the type of occupational structure which develops with industrialisation is some kind of attachment to the 'logic of industrialism' thesis discussed in chapter 3. It is suggested that the technological changes basic to industrialisation lead to the growth of occupational structures which are bound to be more or less similar in all industrial societies at the equivalent level of development. In the work of such writers as Aron (1967), Kerr *et al.* (1973) and Moore (1965), we see suggested a number of trends which accompany industrialisation: the fall in numbers occupied in the primary sector and the rise in numbers employed in the secondary, and later, tertiary sectors; the increasing differentiation of occupations and the appearance of new ones; the general upgrading of skill levels with an increasing proportion of skilled workers; an increasing proportion of professional, scientific and managerial jobs; an increase in the mobility of labour both within and between occupations as a result of the ongoing changes in the occupational structure and the need to appoint people on the basis of ability rather than status.

There is clearly a lot of truth in various of the above formulations and consideration of empirical evidence of changes occurring in distributions between occupational categories in the United Kingdom and USA suggests some continuing validity (see Brown (1978a) and

Montagna (1977), for example). Two types of reservation have to be raised, however. The first is with regard to the use of terms like 'skill' and 'professional' which are used in the statistical data drawn on by observers and which can potentially mislead us with regard to such things as the amount of professional autonomy or craft discretion experienced in practice by those whose work is labelled in this way in surveys. The second reservation is of a more fundamentally theoretical nature and arises out of the need to question the inevitability of a particular type of occupational structure arising with little variation in all 'industrial societies'. There is a strong implication of some kind of technological determinism behind this. Such analyses are misleading in that they tend to deny the part of human agency in the development of occupational structures and because they question the degree of human choice involved in the organising of social life.

Elizabeth Garnsey (1975) has shown the extent to which ideological factors and deliberate growth strategies can lead to significant variations in occupational structure between industrialised societies. She used Soviet evidence to make this point, showing for example the way in which the size of the lower white-collar category has been curtailed in the USSR by the holding back of administrative growth, this being the outcome 'not so much of the immaturity of the economy as of ideological objections to the employment of non-productive personnel'. Detailed comparison of the changing occupational structures of England and Scotland also suggests that economic and political decisions can cause significant differences in occupational structure, within the basic pattern associated with an industrial economy. As Geoff Payne (1977) suggests, with regard to this latter research, we must avoid using theoretical approaches which hide 'the agents of change from the people who are being changed' and instead of implying an impersonal inevitability about economic life should give full account of 'the dimension of capitalist decision-making (on investment, location, innovation, or closure and redundancies) and political policy (economic planning, "regional policies", infrastructure provision, etc)'.

In the same way in which sociologists generally have tended to observe a transformation occurring in occupational structures as societies industrialise, so have some writers recently suggested a further transformation in some industrial societies which is thought to be sufficiently significant to warrant recognition of the approach or arrival of the *post-industrial society*. Daniel Bell (1974) has made one of the most influential statements of this kind, suggesting that advanced industrial societies are entering a new phase in their development. This will make them as different from what we now know as 'industrial society' as such societies differed from 'pre-industrial' ones. The characteristic features of the post-industrial society are to be found in the spheres of technology, the economy and the social structure. The economy undergoes a shift from being a predominantly manufacturing one to a service one; in technology the new science-based industries become central, and in the social structure we see 'the rise of new technical élites and the advent of a new principle of stratification' (Bell 1974). The suggestion is that a new type of occupational structure develops in which white-collar workers outnumber blue-collar ones and in which the professional, scientific and technical occupations become predominant. This latter trend follows from the essential principle underlying the new type of society: the emergence of 'theoretical knowledge' as the basis for innovation and policy making. Post-industrial society is thus a 'knowledge society' and it is taken to follow that those occupations which possess theoretical knowledge will – on the principle that knowledge is power – come to exert a controlling influence on society. With the diminution of the manual working class a relatively stable order will follow as social and economic policy is rationally formulated and as individuals are tied into the social order through the operation of the meritocratic system of rewards which must accompany an occupational structure dependent on recruiting individuals with high ability. The potential for satisfaction at work is increased, it is claimed, by the increased opportunity created by the expanding service sector for people to relate to other people in their jobs rather than to machines.

Bell's assumptions about the changing nature of the work people *actually* do are ones which can be strongly questioned. Qualitative inferences about the nature of occupational life are made on the basis of statistical trends whereby tasks are allocated to official categories which tell us little about what people actually do in their work (Gershuny 1978). The greatest weakness in Bell's thesis lies in his assumption that there is anything novel about the centrality of knowledge to economic and working life. The growth of industrialism and the rise of capitalism were both dependent on the increasing application of rational-calculative thinking to social life – as was argued in chapter 3. Thus the growth of scientific and technical qualifications among the population is all part of the rationalisation process which Max Weber saw as characterising western history over several centuries. As Anthony Giddens (1973) suggests 'modern technology is not "post-industrial" at all, but is the fruition of the principle of accelerating technical growth built into industrialism as such'.

Advanced technology and the growth of educational institutions to train those who will apply and administer it can equally be taken to be a source of deep conflict in society as one of relative stability. This is the case in Alain Touraine's version of post-industrialism (1971) which, as with Bell, is a 'knowledge society'. In this French view of the new type of society and occupational structure the members of the predominating knowledge-based occupations (engineers, accountants, educators, skilled workers, etc.) form a new working class – one which is increasingly alienated, not by the way ruling groups economically exploit them, but by the way they involve them in *dependent participation*. The highly-skilled and the university-educated are seen as resenting the way in which they are required to apply their skills and knowledge in a system which does not give them the discretion and autonomy they increasingly expect. The new working class can thus be expected to mobilise itself against prevailing ruling interests, not to challenge this 'exclusion', as did the old working class, but rather to challenge the way they are 'integrated and used' (Touraine 1971).

Touraine's prognostications about an emerging new working class have not been borne out by empirical research (see above, p. 14) and the assumption which he shares with most other theorists of post-industrialism of the arrival of a post-scarcity society is wildly over-optimistic. However, the possibilities which he points to are ones which may yet become real. Touraine's analysis does at least have the value of recognising the centrality of a power dimension in the structure of societies. It recognises that the form which the occupational structure takes and the rewards which accrue to different levels (although qualitative rather than material rewards are stressed here) are to be understood as following from the interests and strategies of the most advantaged groups in society.

The relationship between the occupational structure and the stratification system of industrialised societies is not seen by all theorists as relating to the efforts of ruling groups to maintain their own advantage. A widely discussed theory which attempts to explain the difference in reward received by people in different occupational positions is the *functionalist theory of social stratification*. Although this theory has undergone a massive onslaught of academic criticism it must be considered here since I suspect that it is a theory widely held among non-sociologists as a kind of common-sense explanation of inequality. This theory, most associated in its academic form with Davis and Moore (1945), suggests that occupational roles vary in terms of their importance to the overall functioning of society (or to the 'common good', if you prefer) and those which require greater individual application, and motivation and willingness to undergo long training are more highly rewarded, materially and in terms of satisfactions, comforts, status or prestige. Many criticisms have been made of this type of analysis and these are usefully summarised by Hall (1975). However, we can point to the most fundamental weakness of such theories as their dependence on a notion of society as some independently existing thing to which human agency, choice, power and initiative are secondary. On one level we may question any suggestion that the work of, say, the highly paid and high-status surgeon is more important to 'society' than that of the lowly cleaner of public lavatories. On another level, it is very pertinent to ask whether it is at all possible to understand the extent of the differentials of reward accruing to these two occupations' members without taking into account the initiatives and efforts over the years of members of the medical profession and of fellow members of the social backgrounds from which they typically come.

To formulate an alternative account of the relationship between occupations and patterns of inequality we need not abandon all elements of the functionalist position. In so far as we can see the social world as having some kind of structure we may note the different degrees of contribution made by different groups to the continuation of that particular structure. If we see the structure of industrial capitalist societies not as a reified object but as a *pattern of advantage* in human relationships, as is suggested by the theoretical scheme outlined earlier (pp. 62) then we may note how those with relatively high stakes in that hierarchy act in such a way as to maintain the overall pattern of advantage and thereby continue to receive the relatively high rewards which are in part allocated or allowed by those further up the hierarchy in return for such a contribution. Aspiring groups may seek an opportunity to make such a contribution and thus gain access to higher rewards.

The level of rewards accruing to an occupational group generally depends on one or, more typically, a mixture of three factors. These are:

(1) The survival of some traditional criterion of superiority from the past – this in itself most likely giving superiority in prestige rather than material reward (the clergy might be an example in the British case).

(2) The possession of a skill or other attribute which is scarce and marketable. This may be a unique attribute (of an entertainer for example) or one controlled and restricted in supply by an occupational association (as in medicine, say).

(3) The contribution made by an occupation to carrying out tasks which, if neglected, would undermine the structure of advantage associated with the industrial capitalist order (as with accountancy, for instance).

The interplay of these factors which occurs with most occupations (and which will be theorised in a slightly different way in the following section) can be illustrated with the case of the legal profession. The traditional status criteria associated with the gentlemanly origins of the work are carried over (and are symbolised by the wearing of wigs in British courts for example); the restriction of entry by various means (including the restricted space in Inns of Court for barristers for example) helps maintain a scarcity of qualified practitioners; and a key role is played in servicing the economic order by dealing with property transactions, company taxation, employment legislation, commercial litigation, as well as by contributing to general 'law and order'. All these factors contribute to the material rewards, high status and other qualitative advantages associated with the occupation of law.

Class stratification follows from the hierarchical grouping of occupations which becomes apparent when we consider the work and market situations associated with these occupations. But this is not the whole story with regard to patterns of inequality existing in the occupational world. Given that access to scarce resources is gained by most people through their occupation we might expect there to be a constant look-out on the part of occupational (or organisational) members for means of reducing competition for entry to or advancement within occupations and employing organisations. One way of achieving this might be to exclude from a particular work milieu any group of people who possess an attribute enabling them to be labelled as *outsiders* in some way. Membership of certain of what Weber called status groups (*standen*) may be relevant here, where members of a particular race or religion are excluded. Otherwise attributes like age or sex may be used. For members of any occupation or area of an organisation to keep out, say, all blacks or all women or all Catholics is to serve the interests of these members, at least in so far as the potential numbers of people competing for scarce rewards or advancement can be reduced at a stroke. This is something to which we will return when we look at occupational recruitment and consider the possible existence of dual labour markets.

At this point we will begin to move our focus more towards particular occupations. Instead of simply describing a variety of particular occupations, I shall suggest a series of headings under which one can analyse any specific occupation. These headings are structural location; recruitment and socialisation; careers; autonomy, association and strategy; cultures and ideologies and occupational communities.

Structural location of the occupation

The starting point for analysing any particular occupation is to attempt to locate it in the wider occupational structure so far described in this chapter. By placing the occupation in the overall division of labour and noting how it is affected by changing patterns of work organisation and social stratification we will be made aware of the nature of some of the basic problems faced by members of that occupation – problems which affect the recruitment pattern, socialisation, ideology and strategy, associated with that occupation. For example, an occupation whose skills are being eroded by technical changes occurring within a society is likely to show a different pattern in many respects to one which is associated with some increasingly important and necessary skill.

A great deal of attention tends to be given to middle-class occupations since their location is often seen as ambiguous in industrial capitalist societies. The majority of members of such occupations cannot be seen as belonging to a capital-owning employing class yet neither can they be readily put into the same category as the manual working class, despite the fact that many of them share the same basic objective characteristic, that of selling their labour power on the market. Hence we see theorists attempting to cope with this ambiguity by either arguing that many middle-class occupations are undergoing a proletarianisation process (becoming increasingly identifiable objectively and subjectively with the working class) or, alternatively, that they are taking the place of the former property-owning ruling class and are forming a new ruling class or technocracy.

Managerial and administrative occupations have been seen by many commentators as forming part of a new technocracy and as playing an increasingly significant role in the control of enterprises as the separation of ownership and control has allegedly increased following the nineteenth-century appearance of the joint stock company. As business corporations and public bureaucracies have increased in scale and complexity, and as specialist knowledge and expertise has become crucial to running these organisations, fewer of which are under the clear control of private owners, what James Burnham (1945) called the 'managerial revolution' is said to have come about. A new class of professional salaried managers is said to be exercising significant *control*. This argument is highly questionable, however. Whereas there is much truth in the claim that the business functions once performed by owner-managers have increasingly been split down and allocated to holders of various administrative roles, it does not necessarily follow that the holders of these roles will necessarily perform their functions so as to achieve ends different from the ones which would be pursued by individual or family owner-managers.

The criteria of performance under which managers operate are, in practice, perhaps even more oriented to what have been traditionally seen as entrepreneurial goals than any new and less capitalistic ones. Pahl and Winkler (1974a), for instance, argue on the basis of their research on company directors that with regard to 'professional managers' as opposed to owner-managers 'the indicators of successful performance are profits, growth and return on investment. The essence of the professional manager is his rigorousness and exclusive dedication to financial values'. This research suggested that such managers were *more* oriented to profit, and were more capable of obtaining it, than the traditional owner-managers. Maurice Zeitlin (1974) has assembled a range of evidence which supports a view of this kind and he notes that 'growth, sales, technical efficiency, a strong competitive position are at once inseparable managerial goals and the determinants of high corporate profits'. As Zeitlin points out, these corporate profits are the prerequisites of high managerial income and status. Thus the high status and material rewards which can be achieved by membership of a managerial occupation are dependent on the contribution made to profit achievement, or at least to the continued survival of the corporation in a context where too great a deviation from profit-oriented performance would lead to collapse or takeover.

The managerial occupation is located in industrial capitalist society, then, on the basis of the contribution which its members make to the achievement of capitalistic criteria. It is thus in the interest of managers to aid in furthering the interests of whoever owns the enterprise (whether this ownership be concentrated or dispersed). Their position in the structure of advantage of society at large is not one of constituting a new ruling class but is one of servicing propertied interests and thereby gaining a share in the surpluses on capital produced. This analysis is helpful but it does not enable us to fully come to terms with the problem of the ambiguity of the managerial occupations' position. The ideas of G. Carchedi can be helpful here in indicating how we can locate any given occupation, or segment of an occupation, in the wider societal structure through identifying the part it plays in the *productive* relationships of industrial capitalism.

Carchedi (1975), working in the Marxian tradition, shows how the capitalist mode of production has a dual nature. It involves, on the one hand, the *labour process*, in which real use value is produced by people working within a social division of labour (this process not, of course, being specific to capitalism) and, on the other hand, a *surplus value producing process* which gives capitalism its defining features and which involves the conversion of use value into exchange value and the appropriation of surplus value. As capitalism has developed it has, first, formally subordinated the labour process to the surplus value process; second, increased the subjection of the labour process to the surplus value process by increasing the technical division of labour through the application of science and the development of technology; and, third, with the growth of advanced or monopoly capitalism, seen the role of the capitalist subdivided into specialist functions filled by non-capital-owning agents of capital. Under monopoly capitalism we therefore see the dual processes described above reflected in the existence of the *collective labourer*, on the one hand (which, to be effective, has to achieve unity and co-ordination) and, on the other hand, the *global functions of capital* (in which the various specialists engage in control and surveillance tasks to ensure that a surplus is realised, appropriated and the means of its production reproduced).

What is important in Carchedi's analysis, for our present purposes, is that members of managerial, administrative and supervisory occupations may contribute to either of these processes or to both. In so far as the occupation is engaged in co-ordination operations within the production process (bringing people and materials together at the right time, checking the quality of the product, for example) then it is part of the collective labourer and will find itself approaching an objective situation corresponding to that of the manual workers themselves, and as technical changes like computerisation and automation come about so the proletarianisation of so-called managerial roles which fall into the collective labourer category will increase. In contrast, the occupants of those managerial roles which are more closely associated with the global functions of capital will be correspondingly better rewarded and at the highest level will achieve closer identity with property-owning élites. However, for a large proportion of managerial occupations there are elements in the work which contribute to both the labour functions and those of capital. Hence the basis of their ambiguity. The value of Carchedi's analysis, which I have drastically simplified here (and do so even further in Fig. 5.1 to help with clarification) is that it helps us locate occupations in the overall societal structure of advantage not on the traditional (and 'vulgar Marxist') basis of ownership or non-ownership of property by their members but by the contribution made to the overall structural basis on which work is organised and wealth generated.

Still confining our application of Carchedi's scheme to the managerial sphere, for the moment, let us illustrate how it can assist in explaining changes occurring in two particular managerial occupations: that of foreman or supervisor and that of personnel manager. Foremen are frequently told by their employers that they are key men in the management structure and, indeed, there is a clear component in their work which is involved in the controlling of their charges, thus associating them with the functions of capital. Yet increasingly, it is their contribution to the labour process itself which predominates in their work. From a position in the early days of management when the foreman was indeed a key man (Child 1975) the foreman has increasingly been reduced to a role which has been described as that of 'the man in the middle' (Roethlisberger 1945) in which he owes

CAPITALIST MODE OF PRODUCTION'S
DUAL STRUCTURE

LABOUR PROCESS
(not specific to capitalism)

SURPLUS-VALUE PRODUCING
PROCESS
(a defining feature of capitalism)

Creation of real use value –
dependent on a social division
of labour and on specialised
occupational knowledge

Appropriation and realisation of
surplus value through control
over labour process

With growth of advanced or monopoly capitalism

Labour carried out by
COLLECTIVE LABOURER

Surplus-value producing
process carried out by GLOBAL
FUNCTIONS OF CAPITAL

Technical division of labour
associated with scientific and
technical development
requiring achievement of
UNITY AND CO-ORDINATION

Subdivided efforts of agents
of capital contributing to
CONTROL AND SURVEILLANCE

*LABOUR PROCESSES
developing here as a
consequence of
dispersal and
fragmentation of
these functions*

Primary function:
APPROPRIATION
Secondary functions:
REALISATION (accounting,
allocation, distribution
of capital)
REPRODUCTION (relations of
production reproduced in the
social formation)

*Fig. 5.1 Carchedi's approach to locating 'middle-class' occupations in the
class structure*

loyalty to both management and workers and yet is part of neither, or has been seen as that of the 'marginal man' of industry (Wray 1949) – the one who is held accountable for work carried out yet is excluded from managerial decision-making. The work done by supervisors varies from context to context but the four basic tasks which are covered, according to Thurley and Hamblin (1963) are planning the work, keeping a check on its progress, dealing with production difficulties and reporting back to higher management. These are not tasks which involve a great deal of initiative in deciding how the work is to be done. The initiative over systems and procedures lies more with specialist functions such as production control, work and method study, cost accountancy, quality control and personnel management. The declining status of the foreman, his poor relative income level and his willingness to unionise reflect his decreasing contribution to the 'functions of capital', and reorganisation of shopfloor activity may well remove the supervisory role altogether, as occurs with moves towards 'autonomous group' job design (clearly recognising the location of the supervisory task as it has developed in the 'labour process'). Alternatively, the supervisory role may be increasingly used as a *training ground* for qualified personnel who are expected to progress up through the management hierarchy. David Dunkerley (1975b) points to an increasing trend towards this use of what he calls 'middle-class foremen' (and Child (1975) calls 'cadets'), something which I have heard justified in the engineering industry as an excellent way of getting graduate management trainees to learn about the 'realities of the shop-floor situation' without having to make them manual workers proper.

The quality of the implicit contract which can be made by a member of the occupation of foreman with an employing organisation will depend on whether the tasks of that occupation are being defined as *more* crucial to the way in which efficiency a surplus or return on capital is achieved (through providing future managers with a first-hand knowledge of the production process) or *less* crucial (where the job is left as a low status 'marginal' one or is handed over to the work group itself). The occupation of personnel management is one of those whose status and reward level has increased in part at the expense of the traditional foreman. The increasing possibility for personnel managers to achieve levels of reward comparable to those of finance specialists (Watson 1977a) can be interpreted as reflecting the increasing centrality of their occupation in influencing the economic performance of their employing organisation. Handling problems which increasingly arise with the resource of labour and the contribution which it makes to achieving a surplus in a way which is dependent on occupationally-specific specialised knowledge and skills (especially with regard to employment legislation and collective bargaining strategies) associates them more closely with Carchedi's 'global functions of capital' and hence enables higher levels of reward to be received.

It is suggested by the above case of the personnel management occupation that the specificity of a given area of specialised knowledge and skill to an occupation is relevant to the social location of that occupation. Indeed a very common explanation of the relatively advantageous social and economic location of the various *professional* occupations is that they receive rewards which reflect the importance to society of the specialised knowledge which their members possess and control. This view suggests that because of the social importance and the sensitivity of the issues to which this knowledge is applied (people's souls, health, welfare, treatment under the law, etc.) the knowledge has to be carefully and ethically controlled to ensure benefit to the client and to the community and to prevent commercial exploitation or one-sided self-interest interfering with the functionally necessary occupational altruism. Although this account sounds very much like an ideological justification of the comfortable position of the established professions it has nevertheless been taken up by sociologists, many of whom have accordingly developed lists of attributes which any occupation would need to possess in order to be recognised as a 'profession'. George Millerson (1964), on reviewing such studies, found that the six most frequently mentioned elements of professionalism were: skill based on theoretical knowledge, the provision of education and training, the testing of member competence, the existence of a professional body, adherence to a code of conduct, and altruistic service (i.e. community orientation rather than self interest).

It is clear that few occupations in an industrial capitalist society can fully meet all these criteria – particularly since the possession of many of these attributes would conflict with employment in a setting based on the organisational or bureaucratic form of work structuring. Therefore sociologists have moved more towards looking at how the members of occupations frequently set out to organise themselves so as to 'professionalise' by conforming to as many of these criteria as possible, thus increasing their autonomy in the world of work. We will look at the strategy shortly but what we need to do at this stage is to identify the basis on which any occupation which is involved with specialist knowledge (and is thus 'professional' in the wider sense implied by this concept) achieves its particular position in the changing hierarchy of occupational advantage.

Earlier, we considered the view that advanced societies are increasingly becoming 'knowledge societies' and this has led various writers to see society as becoming increasingly professionalised as the locus of power moves from commercial organisations to those occupations upon whom society is increasingly dependent for specialised knowledge and its application. Eliot Freidson (1973), for example, sees post-industrial society as one in which the occupational principle of work control takes over from the administrative principle. On the other hand, M. Oppenheimer (1973) has pointed to an opposing trend: that by which professional work is increasingly devalued as increasing fragmentation of work associated with an extensive division of labour brings the 'expert' more under administrative control and hence subjects him more to treatment like a wage-worker. To help resolve these apparently contradictory views of how professional occupations fit into the changing occupational structure, Terry Johnson has taken up Carchedi's analysis to explain why some 'professional' occupations – or parts of them – should fare relatively well (hence partly justifying Freidson's optimism for the future of professions) whilst others fare less well (thus giving some validity to Oppenheimer's (1973) apparently contradictory thesis of a proletarianising trend). Basically it is a matter of whether the knowledge and skills associated with an occupation, or part of one, are such that they can be routinised, split down or taken over by machines (and thus are identified increasingly with the 'collective labourer') or, alternatively, are such that the degree of uncertainty of 'indetermination' in the knowledge and skills is of a kind which cannot be routinised and devalued without interfering with the contribution it makes to the 'global functions of capital'. If a specialist occupation contributes in such a way (requiring initiative and non-routine skills) to the global functions of capital through 'control', 'surveillance' and the 'reproduction of labour' it is thus 'protected from the processes of work devaluation which constantly affect the collective labourer' (Johnson 1977).

Johnson's application of the Carchedi scheme to professional occupations can be illustrated by pointing to the ways in which certain branches of the accountancy profession could be relegated to 'collective labourer' status through, say, computerisation of routine operations whilst other branches might retain or even increase status and associated rewards through their continued exercise of discretion and expert judgment at a strategic level in the management of capital. A more fictional illustration can be attempted if we imagine that some miraculous technological invention were made whereby all physical human diseases, disorders and injuries could be cured by instant treatment on a wonder-machine. This would lead to the rapid social and economic down-grading of medical practitioners whose expertise-dependent and critical role in the maintaining of a healthy labour force (Carchedi's 'reproduction of labour' component of the global functions of capital) had been severely curtailed. On the other hand it might be that the psychiatric branch of the medical profession, whose mystique and skills had not succumbed to technological change, continued to retain the prestige, income and occupational autonomy allowed to them through their role in the maintenance of a 'sane' population of producers and consumers of goods and services. The logic behind the *rationalisation* process to which occupations are here seen to be more or less vulnerable is one which we will look at more closely in the next chapter when we examine its involvement in the predominating *administrative* principle of work organisation and the connection between this and the management of capital. But what we can point to at this stage is that the place which knowledge plays in advanced societies is anything but one which is likely to push the locus of control away from formal organisations to knowledge-based occupations, as Bell's (1974) analysis discussed earlier, suggested. To make this type of inference on the basis of an increasing proportion of jobs which are labelled as 'professional', 'scientific' or 'technical' is to underestimate how much these labels can disguise the extent to which the principle of rationalisation and the increased technical division of labour (following from market pressures to maintain a certain efficiency in the use of capital resources) can lead to a deskilling of work which retains or even acquires such labels.

It might seem to be implied in what has been said so far about the structural location of occupations that the location of manual or 'blue-collar' work is unproblematic. This is not really the case, however. One of the major debates here has been over how far a new, more middle-class-like group has emerged among those manual workers who are either relatively well-paid ('affluent') or whose work involves a high level of skill. Such a thesis of *'embourgeoisement'* has not been supported by research, as was argued in chapter 4 on the basis of evidence presented by Goldthorpe and Lockwood (1968, 1969), Roberts *et al.* (1977) and Gallie (1978).

Our locating of the occupations which we have looked at so far in this section has concentrated on the part which they play, directly or indirectly, with regard to the management of capital and its associated factors of production. Other occupations may be less immediately analysable in such terms. The occupation of housewife, for example, has frequently been regarded more as a 'natural role' for women than as an occupation. Yet, as Anne Oakley (1975) has effectively demonstrated, a great deal of insight can be gained into the domestic labour performed by women if it is examined under the headings traditionally used in occupational sociology. In addition to this, various attempts have been made to locate the housewife in ways other than defining her by her husband's socio-economic position. Such discussions are inevitably complex, having to take into account that the occupation is an unpaid one, is based on a highly diffuse and theoretically long-term contract, and is peculiarly resistant to the rationalisation process (Davidoff 1976) whilst at the same time contributing significantly to the capitalist mode of production through the maintaining and 'reproducing' of labour power (Middleton 1974, Gardiner 1976).

Occupations such as shopkeeper are among those whose social location has been debated by sociologists and Bechhofer *et al.* (1974), in following the tradition of seeing small businessmen as *marginal* in industrial capitalist society, suggest that they are in a sense 'outside' the contemporary class structure. Their ownership of a certain amount of capital and their relative autonomy distinguish them from the manual worker whilst the lack of security, prescribed tasks and possible career ladder in the occupation similarly distinguish them from the mainstream lower-middle-class employees with whom they might at first be identified. This marginality presents interesting problems when it comes to the occupational strategies which members of this *petit bourgeoisie* may choose to adopt.

Marginality of another kind arises when we consider a final group of occupations: deviant, illegal and non-respectable ones. The problem which is presented for most people who gain their livelihoods in such work, whether it be as burglars, prostitutes or ticket touts, is one of integration into the wider community. One's occupation may be such that to admit to it outside a restricted community or network may be dangerous (leading to arrest) or may lead to disapproval and ostracisation. The latter may occur with various occupations which are anything but illegal but which because of their involvement in some taboo or morally doubtful area fall into the category of what E. C. Hughes (1958) calls 'dirty work'. We might include here the work of mortuary attendants, sewage workers or even prison guards. But these latter areas of work, despite the stigma which may be attached to them, clearly play an important part in servicing the social order generally approved of by the people who prefer to avert their eyes from such occupations – and their members. And the same could be said of various other pursuits of a more dubious or even illegal nature, with pornographers, prostitutes and 'exotic dancers' helping to cope with several dissatisfactions which might otherwise undermine marriages, for example.

The type of marginality which arises in the kinds of occupation considered above means that many of the problems which arise for most occupations arise in a particularly acute form in such cases. I will therefore follow the lead of the Chicago school of the sociology of work in the following sections by taking a number of illustrations from these occupations to illustrate principles about occupations in general, recognising that, as Hughes (1958) puts it: 'processes which are hidden in other occupations come more readily to view in these lowly ones'.

Occupational recruitment and socialisation

A large proportion of people are recruited into work by an employing organisation which may not necessarily view its recruits so much in terms of the occupation in which they will engage as in terms of the specific organisational tasks which have to be carried out. However, for many jobs, including those where an employer rather than an occupational representative performs the selection, there is sufficient coherence in the tasks which are to be formed and sufficient social organisation of people engaged in those tasks for an occupational identity to be seen to exist. What we are concerned with here is not the extent to which entrants to these occupations *choose* their occupation – this was a major concern in chapter 4 – but the pattern of recruitment which can be seen to exist with regard to any given occupation.

Certain occupations will restrict their entry in terms of the recruit's age. This may be a trade stipulation relating to the requirement of a long apprenticeship – something which serves as a protection for members of that occupation by presenting a barrier to sudden or uncontrolled recruitment into the occupation. The stipulation of youth may also help with the problem of socialising new members of the occupation, not only in terms of learning skills but in order to aid the acquisition of appropriate attitudes and values. This is as likely to apply to a professionally oriented occupation as much as to a trade-based one. In some cases the age requirement may relate to the physical attributes necessary in the occupation as would be the case with professional sportsmen, dancers and models.

Associated with age requirements may be certain educational or qualification barriers to occupational entry. This may be specific to the skills to be developed in the occupation – the requirement of some certification of mathematical ability in the case of engineering apprentices for example – or it may have far less specific functions. Melville Dalton (1959), in his study of industrial managers for example, pointed out that the 'total experience of going to college' may be more relevant to occupational success than the technical content of what is learned. The future executive learns, as a student, how to analyse his teacher's expectations and manoeuvres, how to utilise social contacts, how to cope with competition, meet deadlines, co-operate with others, cope with intangibles and ambiguities and make rapid adjustments to frequently encountered new personalities and situations. The type of education which one receives is also relevant to social background and the educational requirements of occupations may involve the use of *ascriptive* criteria of eligibility alongside the more obvious *achievement* criteria suggested by the demand for a certain kind of schooling or higher education background. The relevance of educational background for entry to élite occupations and the social class and family implications of attendance at prestigious schools and universities has been widely demonstrated (see Boyd 1973, for example). Salaman and Thompson (1978) have closely examined the behaviour of officers engaging in recruitment for commissions in the British Army and note the 'inevitable residue of flexible *ad hoc* practices' which takes place within what is claimed to be an objective and scientific selection procedure. These practices ensure that class and cultural factors intrude into the apparently 'neutral' procedure so helping the 'legitimised perpetuation of a social élite' in this occupational élite.

Family background is not only relevant to the way individuals are recruited into high status occupations. Stephen Hill (1976), in his study of dockers, has shown how the kinship system of labour recruitment has survived intact in the London docks. Hill shows how, at least in the past, the family networks in this occupation were encouraged by employers who were able to look to the family connections between dockers to cope with problems of training and the maintenance of discipline. Bennie Graves (1970) has shown how in the American situation holders of pipe-line laying contracts find it particularly convenient to depend on the kinship networks which exist within gangs to mobilise a gang which includes all the requisite skills to meet a specific contract.

It is clear that a variety of patterns of occupational recruitment exist but we should not forget just how casual such entry may be for many people. A study which stresses this in the case of striptease dancers is that of Skipper and McCaghy (1970) who show the extent to which entry is 'spontaneous, nonrational, fortuitous, and based on situational pressure and contingencies'. The appeal of monetary reward urged upon them by agents, friends and others encourages them to move on from work as singers, dancers, models and the like to strip.

Despite the fact that individuals may frequently appear to drift casually into a particular occupation, the social scientist may nevertheless observe patterns at the wider level of occupational structure when it comes to the various characteristics of people who enter certain types of occupation. In recent years, for example, economists have begun to observe how labour markets tend to become stratified. Occupations may take their recruits from the *primary sector* of what is seen as a dual labour market, where the work is characterised by good working conditions and pay levels, opportunities for advancement and fair treatment at work, and especially stability of employment. Occupations which draw on the *secondary sector*, however, are worse off in each of these respects and are particularly characterised by considerable instability and a high turnover rate (Piore 1972). Members of this secondary workforce will tend to be people who are dispensable, possess clearly visible social differences, are little interested in training or gaining high economic reward and are ones who tend not to act together collectively (Barron and Norris 1976). Given these features and the social and cultural features of the wider society we tend to find recruitment to this secondary labour force drawing to a disproportionate extent on women, blacks, immigrants, unqualified teenagers, students seeking part-time work, disabled and handicapped persons (Doeringer and Piore 1971).

The dual labour market model is particularly useful for analysing the way women and certain racial groups are the predominant recruits in certain occupations, especially if, developing the arguments of Barron and Norris (1976) that dualism can cut through firms, industries and industrial sectors, we note that a particular occupation can draw on its own dual labour markets. Thus the occupation of teaching, for example, will draw more on men and on whites for higher status or 'advanced' work than it will on women and blacks, who will tend to be employed more predominantly in the nursery or other lower-status areas of teaching. It is interesting to note that many service occupations tend to draw to a large extent on the secondary labour market, most notoriously the catering industries. This suggests major qualifications to the optimism seen earlier to prevail among theorists of the post-industrial or 'service' society. As Montagna (1977) points out: 'according to dual labor market analysis, if we are to be a service-producing society, we are also to be a society of mostly secondary jobs'.

Once the typical pattern of recruitment to a given occupation has been noted attention can be turned towards the way in which the individual 'learns the ropes' (Geer *et al.* 1968) of the particular milieu which has been entered. The more coherent and socially self-conscious is the occupation the more likely is there to be a ceremonial initiation ceremony at some turning point in this socialisation process and the more pressing will be the need to learning the special language (Meissner 1976), formal and informal rules, and attitudes of the group as well as the technical skills involved in the work.

The informal rules, values and attitudes associated with an occupation are of great importance in helping the newcomer to adjust to the exigencies of the occupation which has been entered. Becker and Geer (1958), for example, observed the way in which the low status of the medical student within the hospital setting was adjusted to by the students through their suspension of the idealism with which they entered their training and its replacement by a relative cynicism which pervaded the student culture. The idealism which re-asserted itself later as the students moved closer to graduation and professional practice is consequently a more realistic one than had previously existed – an idealism which would not have helped the practitioner cope with difficulties to be confronted in the real world of medical practice.

A significant element of cynicism developed by the socialisation process is also suggested by Bryan's (1965) study of the 'apprenticeship' of call girls – an apprenticeship which has little to do with skills and is aimed at developing appropriate values and rules. Central to these values are those which stress the maximisation of gain for a minimum of effort and which evaluate people in general and men in particular as corrupt (the prostitute thus becoming defined as no more reprehensible than the public at large). Rules which follow from this include the regarding of each customer as a 'mark' and avoiding emotional involvement or pleasure with the client. As Roberta Victor, the 'hooker', says in Studs Terkel's collection of interviews *Working* (1977): 'You always fake it. You're putting something over on him and he's paying for something he didn't really get. That's the only way you can keep any sense of self-respect.'

The socialisation process which the occupational entrant both undergoes and participates in will contribute to the extent to which the individual identifies with and becomes committed to the occupation. Howard Becker (1960) uses the term *investment* to conceptualise the processes by which commitment can come about. This can refer to the investment in time, effort and self-esteem which the individual makes in his job and in acquiring the relevant skills but it also covers a series of 'side bets' which are external to the occupation itself but which discourage movement out of the job which might break up friendship networks, disturb children's schooling, etc. A factor which may either encourage or discourage individuals' commitment to an occupation is the career structure which they find associated with it.

Occupational careers

As was suggested in the previous chapter, where the emphasis was on the individual's experience of work, we can understand the way in which people achieve a sense of coherence in their working lives through the use of the idea of the subjective career. It was pointed out that the structural context which influences that processual self-view may be the objective career pattern provided by either an occupation or an organisation. These two are frequently related but, here, we are concerned with the sequence of positions through which individuals will typically pass within a given *occupation* in the course of their involvement in it.

Different positions within an occupation generally involve different levels of prestige and give varying levels of reward of various other material and psychological kinds. We therefore tend to see careers in terms of the upward, downward or horizontal movement which they imply for the individual. It is commonplace to observe that many professional and administrative occupations provide career structures of a 'ladder' type: a series of positions of improving status and reward through which the successful individual can expect to move, but other occupations involve quite different career patterns. For many manual workers there may be little change in the work done over the whole of a working career and, although a certain status may accrue from 'seniority' in later years, it is just as likely that rewards may decrease as physical strength falls off (see Beynon's (1973) account of assembly-line work, for example). In other occupations the only changes which can be made are horizontal ones of the kind observed in Becker's (1952) study of Chicago teachers in public schools.

It is an important part of the analysis of any given occupation to note just what shape the typical career, or variety of careers, may take. The shortness of the typical career of the sportsman, soldier, or policeman, the insecurity of the typical career of the actor, and the risk involved in certain business careers are all factors which must seriously influence the orientation to work of the occupational member. Involvement in the occupation of lorry driver, as Peter Hollowell (1968) shows, holds promise of advancement from initial shunting work to tramping and then to trunking but is later likely to return to the earlier lower-status shunting work. Of course, any one occupation can offer more than one typical career pattern, depending on certain characteristics of the individual and various other career contingencies (what Ritzer (1972) defines as 'chance events which occur at critical points in a career'). The high-class call-girl, for instance may progress to work as a madam, given the appropriate abilities and opportunities, or she may be reduced to the status of a street-walker – the difference between these two 'career grades' of prostitution being graphically illustrated by Roberta Victor in Terkel (1977) as equivalent to the distinction between an executive secretary and somebody in the typing pool. In the former role 'you really identify with your boss' whereas in the latter 'you're a body, you're hired labour, a set of hands on the typewriter. You have nothing to do with whoever is passing the work down to you. You do it as quickly as you can.'

Autonomy, association and strategy

The work which people do is, we have seen, bound up with the distribution of power and resources of society at large. Most individuals are not in a position to defend or improve their location in the wider structure of advantage on their own. Some form of collective action to defend or further individuals' interests is inevitable. A variety of ways in which people attempt to control the extent of their autonomy in work will be looked at in chapter 7 but our present concern is with the way the members of any identifiable occupation form an association for such purposes *by virtue of their membership of that occupation* rather than on the basis of commonly experienced problems arising from their position as employees.

As was suggested earlier, the trade union as an occupational association is of decreasing significance as amalgamation between former trade groups increasingly occurs to deal with the more crucial problems experienced by people as employees or organisational members rather than as holders of specific skills and knowledge. The trade union strategy, traditionally associated with working-class values and interests, is essentially defensive. It is a coalition of interest arising from the recognition of a common problem of defending individuals' implicit contracts in a situation where the other party to that contract, the employer, is bound to treat the rewards allowed to employees as a cost to be minimised. But where the members of an occupation recognise in their skills, expertise or knowledge a potential basis for their own monopolistic control over their work they may look towards an alternative strategy: one which draws their eyes towards the traditionally middle-class symbol of professionalism. This, in contrast to the current trade union trend towards seeking power through amalgamation of occupational groups (following what Parkin (1974) has called a *solidaristic* attempt at *social closure*), is a move towards *exclusivity*, involving, in Weber's (1968) terms 'the closure of social and economic opportunities to outsiders'. It is the members of the *occupational* group, not a group of employees, who define who is an outsider.

It is clear that in a society where the great majority of people work as employees rather than as independent fee-paid practitioners, any given group strategy is likely to involve some mixture of elements from both the trade union and the professional ideal types of strategy. Hence we see the high-status medical profession using, from time to time, trade union tactics in its relations with the government which, in Britain, mediates between the professional and the client. Similarly, we can occasionally see a group of manual workers acting on an occupationally-exclusive basis as Hill (1976) shows has occurred in the London docks. What we need to do when engaged in the sociological analysis of occupations is to identify the extent to which any given occupational group is able to act as an occupational collectivity, that is on the professionalisation model. To help us here we need to identify the conditions which influence the capacity of any group to act in this way. Before we do this, however, we must clarify what we mean by the process of professionalisation.

The position taken here is that there is no clearly definable category of occupations which can be recognised by their possession of a series of traits or elements of professionalism (see above, p. 165). There is, however, what Howard Becker (1971) has called a *symbol* of professionalism. This is a 'folk concept' or image based on traditionally independent occupations like law and medicine and, as Becker puts it, the 'professions' are 'simply those occupations which have been fortunate enough in the politics of today's work world to gain and maintain possession of that honorific title'. To acquire the professional label and the prestige and economic benefits associated with it, any given occupation will, *to the degree to which its material situation allows it*, organise itself on a basis resembling the traditional élite occupations. An occupation following the professionalisation strategy will therefore tend to stress a claim to esoteric competence, the quality of which it will argue must be maintained for the sake of client and society, and will accordingly seek for its licensed members the exclusive right to do work in its sphere of competence whilst controlling who enters the work, how they are trained, how they perform their work tasks and how this performance is checked and evaluated. The fact that many occupations by their very nature can never approach the level of autonomy traditionally associated with lawyers and physicians does not prevent occupations as varied as industrial managers, estate agents and embalmers getting together and pursuing some elements of the professionalisation strategy (cf. Larson, 1977).

There are a range of factors determining the capacity of any occupational group to achieve the benefits associated with professionalisation strategies. Parry and Parry (1977) in their historical analysis of the fortunes of the occupations of medicine and teaching note the importance of the relatively lower involvement of the state in the regulation of medicine in the nineteenth century than in the control of education. The relative success of the occupation of medicine in the professionalisation strategy (a success which, of course, has been influential in defining the very symbol of professionalism) is reflected in their relatively successful resistance to the acquiring of employee status. Within groups whose status is that of employee, such as scientists and engineers, the looking towards professionalism as opposed to trade unionism by specific groups will be influenced, as Kenneth Prandy's (1965) study shows, by the extent to which their situation is perceived as different from that of manual employees. Particularly salient here is the presence or otherwise of opportunities for individual career advancement, something which helps foster the traditionally middle-class *status* view of work rather than the more proletarian *class* view of work which reflects the experience of subordination and tends to attract the individual more to a union-like body. As Rosemary Crompton (1976) has argued, using an analysis very similar to those of Carchedi and Johnson considered earlier, the more the contribution to the *capitalist function* of the work of white-collar groups is itself routinised and rationalised and the more its conditions coincide with those of the *labour function*, so will such groups look more to trade union oriented strategies.

Occupational culture and ideology

The forming of occupational associations as part of the strategy followed by members of an occupational group is an example of the process taken to occur throughout social life by the theoretical scheme developed in chapter 2 whereby coalitions of interest are formed between people. These coalitions, which are formed around *objectively* existing common interests, are dependent on the recognition and articulation of such interests by leaders or 'spokesmen'. The spokesman's role is to ensure that the underlying objective (or 'potential') interests are converted into *subjective* ones thereby encouraging mobilisation and the consequent defence or advancement of group interests. To justify or legitimate this group activity to both members and relevant outsiders a set of ideas will be developed and propagated, thus creating a *group ideology*. An *occupational* ideology, then, is a set of ideas developed by an occupational group, and especially by its spokesmen to help legitimate the pursuit of the group members' common and occupationally-related interests. The ideology associated with an occupation is a component of the wider *occupational culture*: the set of ideas, values, attitudes, norms, procedures and artifacts characteristically associated with that occupation.

The tasks in which an occupation is involved, the occupational culture and the ideological component of that culture are all closely interconnected. Bensman and Lilienfeld (1973) argue, for example, that the specialisation of occupational members in handling certain materials creates 'habits of mind, attitudes and loyalties' and that these craft attitudes interlock with interests and attitudes which are based on the historical success of the occupation in developing its professional acceptance and claims in the society at large'.

Occupational cultures and ideologies are to be found in occupations of varying status levels. Among the higher status occupations (and many other less prestigious but aspiring ones) the symbol of professionalism is frequently drawn on. It is an invaluable ideological resource which typically assists occupational members and spokesmen in seeking legitimacy for their claim to exclusive involvement in certain tasks and in justifying the high rewards which are felt to be appropriate. This is done by pointing out how it is in the interest of clients and, especially, of *society at large* for the tasks to be carried out on the occupation's terms. An occupational claim is 'ideological' regardless of the truth of the claim. Doctors may or may not be right in arguing on the grounds of patients' interests against the licensing of rival osteopaths to carry out treatments and solicitors may or may not be justified on similar grounds in their insistence on an exclusive right to do conveyancing work. Either way, the claim made is an illustration of professional ideology in action. Self-interest and altruism may often clash in the politics of work but this is by no means necessarily the case. The best way for a group to serve its self-interests may well be to do the best for others.

At the lower status levels the occupational culture is less likely to be expressed in ideological form by any official group spokesman as is frequently the case with professionally-organised types of occupation. Any occupational member (as in all groups) is likely to articulate the culture when talking about his or her work in a way which will vary with the audience (again, as with all groups). With the more lowly type of occupation, however, the content is more likely to function in a defensive way – helping occupational members cope with problems created for them by the hostile environment in which they operate. To illustrate the varieties of function and emphasis found in different occupational cultures we can look at examples found in studies of both 'professional' and deviant occupations.

Philip Elliot (1973), in a study of two occupational groups involved with the treatment of cancer, observes how different positions are taken up by doctors on the one hand and scientific researchers on the other with regard to how the disease is to be approached. The two major positions are related to and bound up with the occupational situation of each group. The occupational and organisational positions and problems of the doctors are reflected in their adherence to a 'therapy ideology' whilst the different situation and career interests of the scientists influence their adherence to a 'basic science' ideology. Elliot's important article illustrates the need for the public, as consumers of occupationally created goods and services, to be sensitive to the ideological accounts given by occupational members. It is an important question of public policy as to how resources should be allocated to dealing with diseases like cancer. In relying on the experts to whom laymen must turn for advice it may be vital to take note of the occupational interests behind the advice which is given as to how resources should best be allocated. However sincere occupationally related advice or actions may be they are unlikely to take a form which undermines the major career investments which practitioners have made in their occupation.

Certain features of the occupational culture of prostitutes were discussed earlier when we considered some of the values and associated rules which are met in the process of occupational socialisation. The defensive function of aiding the occupational members' retention of self-respect was important here. The legitimatory function of certain ideas upon which prostitutes typically draw is also illustrated in the accounts given to Lionel James (1973) in interviews with ten Soho prostitutes, all of whom 'felt they were helping people in some way by providing a service'. This might involve giving 'paid consultations', acting as a kind of 'psychological doctor', 'helping society' by providing an alternative to rape and generally keeping down the number of 'sex crimes'. The echoes of professionalism here in the 'oldest profession' are quite apparent and similar attempts at rationalisation and enhancement of the occupational image are reported in studies of strippers who may alternatively stress the quality of their work as entertainment, sex education or therapy for men who would otherwise be lonely and sexually frustrated (see Salutin 1971 for example).

Occupational communities

We can expect an occupational culture to be especially strong and to spill over into areas of members' lives outside the work sphere itself in occupations where the work and non-work lives of its members are closely related. This tends to be particularly the case with what some sociologists have described as occupational communities.

The notion of the occupational community is implicit in the analysis of Kerr and Siegal (1954) who suggested that the high propensity to strike of such groups as miners, longshoremen, sailors and loggers could be related to their living in an 'isolated mass': the communities found in the 'coal patch, the ship, the waterfront district, the logging camp, the textile town' are all seen to have 'their own codes, myths, heroes and social standards'. The notion was further developed by Lipset, Trow and Coleman (1956) to characterise the interlinked work and non-work life of printers and Blauner (1960) followed up their arguments in his discussion of factors which can contribute to job satisfaction. Blauner suggests that the essential feature of the occupational community is that workers socialise more with persons of their own occupation in non-work hours than they do with members of other occupations. To this he adds that participants tend to 'talk shop' in their off-hours and that the occupational community constitutes a 'little world' in itself. It follows from this that its members regard it as their key reference group in such a way that 'its standards of behaviour, its system of status and rank, guide conduct'. Blauner suggests that occupational communities arise either where there is spatial isolation or where communal identity is encouraged by the kind of shifts worked by some printers, by steel workers, firemen and railway workers.

It is clear from the above discussion that the concept of occupational community implies more than the geographical proximity of members' homes. The concept of community in sociology implies a type of relationship between people which need not, in a society with relatively developed means of communication, necessarily involve geographical identity. The essence of *community* is an integrated set of social relationships, a system which provides its members with a sense of common identity and a shared values system. William Goode (1957) suggested that professions constitute communities in this sense, an argument which encourages Graham Salaman (1974) to propose that we can usefully talk of two types of occupational community. One of these is that which is based on the occupation as a whole and the other on a common geographical location. Salaman suggests that both the architects and the railwaymen whom he studied can be seen as members of occupational communities and he notes that both were strongly and positively involved in the work they did, gaining satisfaction from carrying out their work tasks, using their valued skills or from such things as the responsibility or autonomy intrinsic to the work they do.

The suggestion that occupational communities may be important sources of job satisfaction, as Blauner and Salaman suggest, is one important reason why occupations should be examined in such terms. The presence or otherwise of a sense of occupational community is also relevant to understanding certain dynamics of political and industrial conflict behaviour as well as occupational and professionalisation strategies. I. C. Cannon's (1967) study of compositors, for instance, suggests a connection between these printing workers' occupational community and ideology and their relatively radical class and political affiliations. However, membership of an occupational community need not, in the case of manual workers, necessarily lead to an oppositional 'them and us' class conflict view. As Robert Moore (1975) has pointed out, coalminers may well note a common market situation *shared* with supervisors and employers, i.e. their particular industry, and Trevor Lummis (1977) has observed that the work milieu of the East Anglian driftermen discourages an oppositional class view since it makes them independent of the on-shore small-town social hierarchy 'without placing them into conflict with their employer' – people with whom they are involved as co-venturers.

In examining the way in which certain occupations involve their members in a particularly significant way in occupational communities, we are brought back to fundamental sociological issues such as the meaning which work can potentially provide for people and to the relevance of such matters for the wider social and political structures and processes which they inform and by which they are influenced. Interestingly, it was to some kind of restored occupational communities that Durkheim looked for a source of integration in what he felt to be an increasingly normless industrial capitalist society. This is a consideration to which we will return in the final chapter.

Chapter 6

The structuring of work: organisations

Introduction

In the previous chapter the occupational aspect of the way in which
work is patterned was examined. Implicit in that analysis was a
suggestion that, although the occupational principle partly com-
plements the structuring of work on the basis of the administrative or
formal organisation principle, it is also in a relationship of tension or
conflict with it in the contemporary industrial capitalist society. The
growth of industrial capitalism necessarily involved a considerable
erosion of the type of occupational self-control represented by the
medieval guilds. Yet vestiges of the occupational pattern of
organisation survive in some of the more trade-based trade unions and
are found in certain manual worker 'occupational communities'. A
much stronger bid for occupational independence (and thus for our
recognising the salience of the occupational principle in work
patterning) was seen, however, in those areas where groups are seen as
coveting the symbols and pursuing the strategy of professionalisation.

All the above tendencies towards occupational strategy or initiative
must be seen in the light of what is to be regarded as the dominant and
currently prevailing aspect of work patterning in industrial capitalist
societies: structuring in the form of administrative institutions or
'formal organisations'. Here the emphasis is not on the way in which
people with similar skills, traditions and values co-operatively
conceive, execute and regulate work tasks, as would occur in an
ideal-typical occupation-based situation, but on the ways in which
some people conceive of and design work tasks in the light of certain
ends and then recruit, pay, co-ordinate and control the efforts of other
people, who do not necessarily share those ends, to achieve the
fulfilment of these tasks.

The concept of 'organisation', used in a general sense, is fundamental to sociological analysis. A basic insight of the discipline is that life is socially organised in various ways – that it displays certain patterning and exhibits regularities. Indeed the occupational aspect of working life is as much a part of this overall *social organisation* as is the administrative component which we are examining in the present chapter and which is often referred to as *formal organisation*. It therefore needs to be made clear that in the ensuing discussion the terms *the organisation* and *organisations* are being used to refer to just one aspect of the wider social organisation of society. Reference is to institutions which have been deliberately set up at some historically distinguishable point in time to achieve certain tasks and which, to meet these ends, make use of various administrative or bureaucratic techniques. Organisations thus include such things as banks, firms, hospitals, prisons, but exclude families, tribes, social classes, spontaneous friendship groups and the like.

What ultimately distinguishes organisations, however ramshackle they may become and however diverse and confused may be the interests and concerns of their members, is some initially inspiring purposiveness. The differentiating feature of the business, the educational institution or the charity organisation is, at least in its early period of existence, some kind of relatively explicit charter or programme of action. The increasing pervasiveness of organisations is to be understood as part of the wider trend of increasing rationalisation which underlies the development of industrial capitalism: the process identified by Max Weber whereby deliberately calculated means are adopted in the pursuit of consciously selected ends.

Organisations are being portrayed, then, as specifically purposive and characteristically rational constructs. Whilst this characterisation is to be retained this will only be in the light of certain massive qualifications. These qualifications derive from two centrally important elements of social life which are identified in the theoretical scheme outlined in chapter 2. These are the tendencies within societies towards social conflict and, related to this, towards structural contradictions. Basic to our theoretical scheme is a conception of social structure as dependent on the institutionalising by dominant groups of the advantages which they have with regard to scarce and valued resources. The stability of social structure – seen as a 'pattern of advantage' – is constantly threatened by social conflict, where less advantaged groups challenge the current order, and by closely related structural contradictions, whereby the institutionalised means chosen by advantaged groups (contemporary work organisations being especially important here) tend to develop unintended consequences which may undermine the achievement of the ends for which they were designed.

In accord with the frankly power-conscious and conflict-oriented model of social life which is being used in this book, work organisations are indeed to be seen as purposive human constructs but nevertheless as ones whose great complexity derives not only from their complicated technology and large size but also from the conflicts and contradictions with which they are riddled.

The general perspective on social life being applied here to organisations has not been adopted as a simple result of a personal fascination with the Machiavellian aspects of social life and far less out of any individual taste for social conflict. The sociological perspective being utilised is the one felt to have the greatest utility in interpreting the problems which real human beings experience, as managers, workers and consumers of organisational outputs. It is felt that the great bulk of material written about work organisations is analytically inadequate and is biased in favour of certain social interests. Analysis and ideology is frequently confused, largely as a result of a deliberate or accidental unwillingness to pay full attention to the essentially political nature of all work organisations. Since the present chapter, like every other in this book, is intended to report on existing literature as well as to advance on existing analyses, we must, before proceeding with our substantive considerations, examine those tendencies in the current literature which leave much of it open to accusations of partiality.

Organisation theory and its ideological implications

By far the largest part of what has been written about organisations has been less part of a relatively disinterested sociological enterprise than a contribution to furthering the interests of those involved in running organisations. The general body of writing and teaching which can be termed 'organisation theory' involves attempts to generalise about organisations with a view to aiding the development of better *techniques* for achieving organisational efficiency. It is only recently that sociologists have begun to distinguish their efforts from this body of work. The emerging orthodoxy among organisation theorists has become one of conceptualising the organisation as a system of interdependent parts whose structure is rationally devised by its management to meet certain 'organisational goals' in as efficient a way as possible within prevailing circumstances. We cannot say that this approach is in any simple way 'wrong'. At first sight, in fact, it looks eminently sensible. But what we can say is that it is highly *partial*.

By saying that the bulk of modern organisation theory is partial, two things are being claimed. First, the conception of the organisation sketched above is partial in the sense that it is *inadequate*. The organisation tends not to be set in the wider power structure of society of which, seen sociologically, it is a part. As a result of the common emphasis which is placed on the co-operative aspects of organisational functioning, inadequate attention is given to the extent to which conflicting interests exist among members of the organisation and the degree to which the structure and behavioural pattern of the organisation is as much an outcome of the initiatives and attempts at resistance on the parts of those not nominally in control of the organisation as a result of official corporate policies. Second, the orthodox conception of the organisation is partial in another sense of that word: it is *biased*.

The image of the organisation which is commonly fostered is one which is consonant with the interests of those who run organisations. Through the use of neutral and technical-sounding terms like 'efficiency' and 'the pursuit of organisational goals', the self-interested actions of those who own and control organisations are obscured. Power is mystified and the dominance of some human beings within organisations over others, and the exploitation of certain people by others, is as good as denied by the absence of a vocabulary with which to refer to it.

Efficiency, we must remember, is only efficiency from a certain point of view. Yet the organisational literature frequently ignores this. An organisation may be efficient from its owner's point of view, for example, but might not be efficient from an employee's point of view. This would be most clearly the case in the not untypical event where an employee (either a manager or a manual worker) is sacked as part of an attempt to 'increase efficiency'. Correspondingly, we need to recognise that talk of 'organisational goals' frequently obscures the existence of sectional interests. The goals of managers may sometimes be met only at the expense of workers' goals and the converse may also apply. Logically, the organisation cannot have a goal. Only its members can have goals and these will only coincide within certain and strict limitations. To pretend otherwise is to underestimate the extent of conflict existing between organisational members and subgroups. But whereas, as sociological observers, we may bemoan this analytical inadequacy, we must also recognise that such a bias may well suit dominant interests. A pretence of consensus is often believed to encourage consensus. This is where the concept of ideology is important. We need to be sensitive to the ideological purposes which may be served by the partiality of much existing organisation theory.

It was argued in chapter 2 (pp. 61) that the fabric of social life is woven out of the interplay between *interests* and *ideas*. In the process whereby realities are created interests are articulated and legitimated (and vice versa). Social science thinking is part of our socially constructed reality and, given that the application of this type of thinking to organisations has largely occurred in contexts where the main markets for ideas have been managerial ones, it is not surprising that much of the resulting analyses are congruent with managerial interests.

Ideas act *ideologically* in so far as they support particular material interests and where certain ideas perform this kind of legitimatory function for a particular social group we can say that these ideas contribute to a *group ideology*. The managers of organisations, although not necessarily acting as an organised group in society at large, do have certain objective interests in common by virtue, as Reinhard Bendix (1963) puts it, of 'the common problems and experiences' to which they are exposed. As Bendix points out, 'whenever enterprises are set up, a few command and many obey. The few, however, have seldom been satisfied to command without a higher justification even where they abjured all interest in ideas.' Even where knowledge is developed with an ostensibly purely technical purpose, as with much writing on organisations, it may nevertheless be framed in a way which meets this kind of group need and is thus 'partial' through its striving to be consistent with the way managers may prefer to see, and prefer others to see, the enterprise. Much organisational theory thus parallels the bulk of published managerial thinking to which it is closely related in having, as John Child (1969a) points out with regard to 'management thought', both a *legitimatory* and a *technical* function, with the former 'primarily linked to the securing of social recognition and approval for managerial authority and the way in which it was used' while the latter is 'primarily linked to the search for practical means of rendering that authority maximally effective'.

The problem with this kind of partiality and bias in organisation theory is not just one of a failure to provide concepts of value to those wishing to look at organisations from an objective, external or critical viewpoint. It may also do a disservice to those involved in managing organisations themselves. As was suggested in the earlier discussion of the general value problem in the sociology of work (p. 29), to tell people what they want to hear or to ensure that their preferred image of the world is left intact is hardly the best way to improve their understanding of their analytical ability. To put it another way, the danger to managers of managerially-biased organisation theory is that they may be encouraged to believe and act on the basis of what is, in effect, their own propaganda rather than on the basis of analyses grounded in something closer to the 'realities' of the situation.

The highly prevalent tendency to view organisational structure and performance in terms of 'organisational goals' has already been referred to. Not only does this approach mystify the power relations inherent in organisations by turning political issues into technical ones (through the translation of the problems of organisational controllers' achievement of their particular goals into neutral-sounding problems of 'efficiency') but it also encourages us to see the organisation merely in terms of that *part* of the organisation which officially serves those *sectional* purposes which are mystified as 'organisational goals'. Goals, purposes and activities of organisational actors which do not service official goals in this way are thus seen as residual, peripheral or incidental to the basic structure or the organisation. In the Human Relations tradition (see p. 42) these are relegated to a twilight zone of *informal organisation*. They are elements of organisational life which do not possess the rationality displayed by managerial activity and they must, it is argued, be dealt with by management to avoid their becoming more than minor irritants to the organisation as a smoothly functioning and healthily organic *system*.

The 'systems strand' of the sociology of work and industry introduced in chapter 2 is most strikingly manifested in the analysis of organisations. It was suggested in the earlier discussion that the systems model ultimately relates back to that classic metaphor of traditional social thought, the organic analogy. In the same way that an image of society as some kind of integrated organic whole was said to have potential as a political legitimating force in implying that the *status quo* is the only natural, and therefore inevitable, way for society to be, so the organisation theorists' penchant for viewing organisations as systems may function to support managerial efforts to justify their way of organising the efforts of others.

The basic insight of the systems perspective on organisations is a simple and a necessary one: that the various components of the organisation are closely interrelated and that what occurs in one part of the 'system' will have ramifications for other parts. The organisation must be seen as a whole, it is suggested. The major difficulty with this systems perspective, in practice, is that the notion of 'the whole' tends to be given primacy over the parts which make it up and, very easily, an image of the organisation as a unitary and consensus-based entity forms in the eyes of the observer. This tendency is reinforced by the efficacy of such an image as a component of managerial ideology. Theo Nichols (1969) noted the importance of the organic analogy in the ideologies of the northern city managers whom he studied, and Alan Fox has pointed out the popularity within managerial ideologies of seeing organisations as *unitary* 'families' or 'teams', with the consequent tendency to play down the plurality of interests existing within the organisation (1966) and ignore the involvement of the enterprise in the wider conflicts and inequalities of society as a whole (1973). The tendency present within the systems perspective on organisations, pointed to in particular by David Silverman (1970), of implying that organisations as systems have 'needs' for survival and 'behave' to ensure this survival, both commits a logic fallacy (which leads to major methodological problems) and also reinforces these tendencies towards organic and unitary thinking. From this follows an underplaying of the importance of power, conflict and multiple interests in organisations. This may help managers as *ideologists* (which at times they must be) but it hinders the managers, sociologists and critics alike, as *analysts*.

What I have noted as a double partiality in much organisation theory has been increasingly recognised by writers concerned to develop a better *sociological* understanding of organisational life. Their efforts have involved looking more towards ideas which were introduced in chapter 2 as part of the third, fourth and fifth strands of industrial sociology. Silverman (1970), Anthony Elger (1975) and Angela Bowey (1976) draw on the Weberian and the symbolic interactionist strands to develop a 'social action' or 'processual' approaches to organisations whilst the value of ideas in the Marxian tradition have been shown as needing to be put alongside Weberian ones to help develop a 'critical' study of organisations (Clegg and Dunkerley 1977) or to achieve a more fully 'sociological' understanding of organisational structures (Salaman 1978).

Our concern here is to join these writers and to develop a *sociological* account of how organisations contribute to the ways in which work is structured in industrial capitalist society. In what follows an attempt is made to counter the partiality of much of what exists. However, in attempting to move beyond the goal-based and systems-oriented orthodoxies, we must recognise that there are important insights in these perspectives. The 'rational' organisational-goal notion cannot be totally abandoned whilst we still recognise some overall relatively purposive aspect of organisational processes, for example. Also, by avoiding the systems trap we must not abandon all the insights provided by the systems tradition by, as Bowey (1976) puts it, 'throwing out the baby with the bath water'.

A sociological conception of organisations

To analyse *sociologically* any given area of life we have to meet the very basic requirement indicated in chapter 1 (p. 11) to do full justice to the *interplay* which occurs between the patterns, regularities or structuring of social life (the detection of which provides the basic rationale of sociology) and the varied interests, initiatives and values of the individuals which create this structuring. By giving primacy to only one aspect of this dialectical process, organisation theory has left us with a highly partial literature.

To achieve a more fully sociological account of organisations we need to do three things: first find a way of recognising the importance of much of what is discussed in the existing but 'partial' literature on organisational structure; second, develop a wider conception of organisational structure than those which have largely prevailed and into which the above ideas can be incorporated, and third, set the organisation in the wider structure and processes of industrial capitalist society. These three issues relate to the three circles which make up Fig. 6.1.

First, we need to reconceptualise what is often regarded as the total structure of the organisation as merely one part of it. John Child (1972), one of the most sociologically-sensitive writers on organisations, has chosen to define organisational structure in a way which typifies the prevailing 'restricted' approach: it is conceptualised as 'the formal allocation of work roles and the administrative

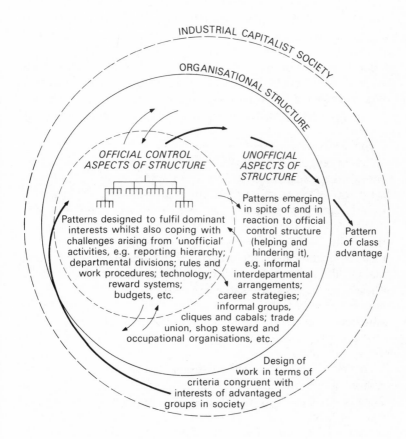

Fig. 6.1 Aspects of organisational structure

mechanisms to control and integrate work activities including those which cross formal organisational boundaries'. This I shall relabel the *official control aspects of structure*. It includes all the official arrangements made by those who control the organisation – and by their agents – to achieve the goals of those in control whilst at the same time coping with challenges and contradictions which may arise and threaten to undermine this goal achievement. In this is included the hierarchy typically represented by the official 'organisation chart', the contents of the organisation's rule book, the range of prescribed work procedures and techniques, the budgeting and reward systems, etc. None of these things, analysed in isolation as they tend to be to various degrees by many writers, contains the key to understanding actual behaviour in the organisation. Even the identity of those who, in the end, are in control of the organisation in the sense of making strategic decisions may not be officially identifiable. To understand the official aspects of structure we have to set them within a wider conception of structure.

To meet the second requirement established above, that of using a wider conception of organisation structure than has been prevalent among organisation theorists, we turn towards a more social-action based way of conceiving of 'structure' in social life. This leads us towards seeing the organisation's structure not in terms of the pregiven official arrangements into which individual actors are slotted but as the *emergent* pattern of the relationships and behaviour of organisational actors. All aspects of this behaviour and these relationships are to be understood as influenced to some degree by the official control structure of the organisation: had not some official structure been set up in the first place there would clearly be no subsequent members of the organisation. Nevertheless, a great deal of what actually goes on cannot be accounted for solely in terms of the official apparatus.

To understand organisational life we cannot depend on a conception of the organisation based on a notion of one integrating 'organisational goal', with structure seen as the means of meeting this goal. We have, rather, to recognise that the organisation contains members with a vast range of different, cross-cutting and often mutually exclusive goals. As a result of this we find a multitude of activities going on which are oriented to goals quite separate from anything conceivably definable as organisational goals. We find workgroups setting up output norms in opposition to managerial efforts to increase outputs; we find individuals and trade union groups acting in pursuit of increases in reward, which puts up the organisation's costs; and we find supervisors holding back information from subordinates or administrators to safeguard their jobs, even at the expense of their department's 'efficiency'. All this is part of organisational structure – in the sociological sense of that term – despite its negative implication for official performance goals.

Alongside these 'negative' unofficial activities we may equally well find unofficial relationships existing between departmental heads which, in effect, speed up performance by by-passing 'correct' procedures; we may find trade union intervention resulting in simpler management through the establishment of formal bargaining procedures and we will almost inevitably see example after example of rule-breaking and circumvention of rules helping to keep the job running (witness the paradoxical destructiveness of 'working to rule' as an oppositional strategy). By the same token, we may find off-the-record arrangements and payments of 'backhanders' vitally necessary to the success of organisational policies whose initiators and beneficiaries have made such activities officially 'illegal'. Since, as we shall stress later, the hierarchical control structure of the organisation constitutes, in addition to its control functions, a career ladder for many of those who are part of it, we are likely to see the unofficial and essentially self-interested actions of individual careerists both contributing to official aims as well as undermining them.

These two aspects of organisational structure, the official and the unofficial, we must stress, are not two separate structures on the lines of the traditional Human Relations school's formal/informal dichotomy. They are merely conceptually or analytically distinct aspects of one overall structure. They are dialectically related: each one is influenced by and contributes to the other. A payment system devised by officials to increase output may invite unofficial strategies among work-groups who choose to resist pressure to speed up their work, for example. But this, at the same time, may lead to some redesign of the official structure in the form of changes in the supervisory arrangements, modifications to the work study department or even the introduction of a plant industrial relations or personnel officer.

Organisational structure, then, is the *outcome* of the activities of a range of people with a multiplicity of goals and purposes. Official structures and procedures are constantly being changed to cope with structural contradictions which they develop and are modified in reaction to the ways their performance is challenged by unofficial activities. However, further unofficial activities consequently develop which, again, may either help or hinder the achievement of official success goals.

However, what is implied in all the above discussion is that although there is clearly no ultimate 'organisational goal' behind these processes there are nevertheless certain overall tasks or purposes to be achieved without which the organisation is unlikely to continue to exist. If we are not to conceptualise these in terms of 'systems needs' with a consequent reification and mystification we have to identify these higher level goals or purposes with particular actors' or group interests. This means seeing every work organisation as a power structure with its essential dynamic lying in the exercise of and the resistance to power. To appreciate the basis on which this dynamic operates we must now set the organisation in its societal context.

The third requirement for an understanding of organisations which is *sociological* in the terms which have been established here is that organisations are not isolated from the societal form of which they are a major and essential part. In the following two sections of this chapter I shall attempt to show that what occurs within organisations (the two inner circles of Fig. 6.1) can only be understood in the light of the structure and processes of industrial capitalist society (the outer circle). The basic argument is that organisations are designed to meet performance criteria which are congruent with the interests of those who are most advantaged in society (to a large extent, but not exclusively, through the making of profits). In this way the organisation is an *outcome* of the class structure. At the same time, it is also a *contributor* to this aspect of social structure in that it rewards those who are recruited to carry out its various work tasks on a differential basis, so allocating organisational members to different positions in the class structure (the societal pattern of advantage with regard to the range of things which are scarce and valued in society – these varying from the material rewards of work to the quality of experience at work itself).

In every organisation there will be an individual or a group seen as 'in control' in that they make certain strategic decisions and are likely to achieve a level of rewards from the organisation which is greater than their subordinates. Their goals come nearest in our present conception of the organisation to the idea of 'organisational goals'.

However, it must be stressed, these goals are strongly bounded by what is achievable in terms of the organisation's own resources and by the constraints existing in the social, political and economic institutions of industrial capitalist society.

To meet all the requirements set out above, and especially that of recognising the purposive or task-based nature of organisations whilst at the same time noting the multiplicity of interest existing with whatever is nevertheless an 'unequal' power structure, the following conceptualisation is offered. Formal organisations are *social and technical arrangements in which a number of people come or are brought together in a relationship where the actions of some are directed by others towards the achievement of certain tasks.*

Power, conflict and contradictions

Work organisations have grown as central institutions of industrial capitalism and display both the rational calculative features of the general rationalisation process associated with the rise of this type of society as well as the specific characteristic of making use of human labour-power, this being purchased as a means towards ends which are not necessarily those of the people needing to take employment. To recognise the implications of this we must now refer back to the account of the rise of industrial capitalism provided in chapter 3. Two elements of that account are important. First is the recognition that particular social groups and often historically identifiable individuals took the initiatives which established early work organisations. This was done in the furtherance of *material interests* within society and not as a consequence of some mystical historical force such as 'inevitable technical progress'. The second argument which we need to bring forward from chapter 3 is the exceedingly important one that points to the various ways in which industrial capitalist society suffers from a 'paradox of consequences' and hence contains various structural contradictions: a range of tendencies within the overall social and economic organisation which would lead to its collapse were initiatives not taken to accommodate to them. The process of adaptation by those in power, occurring in the face of resistance and challenges from the less powerful, has been the motor of social change within industrial capitalist society and accounts for a large proportion of organisational dynamics.

We must now observe that many of these structural problems manifest themselves within the formal organisations which constitute basic institutions in this type of society. Organisations use rational calculative techniques as means towards the ends pursued by their controllers and they use human beings as resources – as *means* in a similar way. But human beings as assertive, creative, and initiating animals – characterised earlier on as different from other animals in their capacity to develop *conceptions of alternatives* about how they live – are always problematic when used as instruments, as they must ultimately be in an organisational society with an asymmetrical distribution of power. Every organisation is thus confronted by a basic paradox: the means used by the controlling management of the organisation to achieve whatever goals they choose or are required to pursue in an efficient way (i.e. at the lowest feasible cost – short and long term) do not necessarily faciliate that efficient achievement of goals since these 'means' involve human beings who have goals of their own, which may not be congruent with those of the people managing them. Not only does this paradox account for many of the problems which organisational managements continually experience in their work but it also provides the starting point for explaining many structural features of organisations themselves. It provides the key to explaining the growth of inspection and auditing functions within organisations, work study and management services departments, personnel and industrial relations departments as well as the very existence of organisations such as those government and quasi-government agencies involved in regulating the activities of other organisations. These are all involved in coping with potentially destructive contradictions.

This view of organisations caught up in a paradox is very much in the spirit of Max Weber's view of modern society and is developed from his key distinction between formal and material rationality, explained in chapter 3 (p. 89). Yet, ironically, many sociologists and organisation theorists – who frequently look back to Weber as some kind of father of organisation theory – completely miss the point of Weber's view of bureaucracy through their assumption that when he wrote of the high degree of formal rationality achievable by bureaucratic organisation he was claiming that it is necessarily 'efficient' in its meeting of goals. As Martin Albrow's (1970) important reappraisal of Weber's position shows, Weber did indeed recognise, in pointing to the high formal rationality of bureaucracies, their 'technical superiority' and their virtues of calculability, predictability and stability but he was nevertheless well aware that although these were necessary conditions for 'efficient' achievement of goals they in no way constituted a sufficient guarantee of such success. Formal rationality (choice of technically appropriate means) as was argued earlier (p. 90) does not guarantee material rationality (achievement of the original value-based goal). In the light of this argument it is indeed ironic that attempts to refute Weber's imputed belief in the efficiency of bureaucratic organisations have provided a key motivation behind much organisational sociology. At this point we can introduce some of the key studies which have been done in this tradition, noting that their mistaken intention of 'correcting Weber' does not in itself invalidate their findings. In a sense they are extensions of the Weberian view rather than refutations.

The basic mistake made by many writers on organisations is to take Weber's ideal type of bureaucracy (a construct of what a bureaucracy would look like if it existed in a pure form) as if it were some kind of prescription of what an efficient organisation should be. Ideal-typically, a bureaucracy has, according to Weber, the following features (bureaucracy being the administrative form characteristic of modern legal-rational types of political system or type of 'domination' and being increasingly found in every sphere from government, to industry, to church and army): it composes a clear *hierarchy* of offices whose functions are clearly specified; officials who are subject to a *unified control* and disciplinary system are appointed on a *contractual* basis having been selected because of their specific *expertise*; the officials' posts, which they may not appropriate for their own ends, are their sole occupations. They are rewarded by a *money* salary (graded according to their position in the hierarchy) and they may be promoted up the hierarchy at the discretion of their superiors.

One of the first sociologists to point to negative aspects of the above approach to administration was Robert Merton, who concentrated on certain of what he termed *dysfunctions of bureaucracy* – a dysfunctional aspect of any system being some aspect of it which undermines the overall functioning of that system. Merton (1957) argued that the pressure put upon the individual official by the above type of arrangement, which encourages accountability and predictability through the use of rules, could encourage a counter-productive inflexibility on the part of the officials themselves. Rules and operating procedures thus become ends in themselves rather than means towards organisational goal achievement. Here may develop the 'bureaucratic personality' whose existence as such was questioned earlier (p. 141) but who inhabits contemporary folk-lore as the 'jobsworth' – the petty official who if asked to interpret any rule flexibility (such as unlocking a door half a minute before the appointed opening time of a building) characteristically responds with the words 'it's more than my job's worth'.

Philip Selznick (1966) observed an equivalent form of goal-displacement arising from a different source. The sub-units or departments resulting from delegation of authority within organisations may set up goals of their own which may come to conflict with those organisational purposes behind the setting up of that sub-unit. Responses to such problems involving the setting up of further departments to cope with these difficulties only exacerbate the situation as further sectional interests or goals are created.

Alvin Gouldner's classic factory study *Patterns of Industrial Bureaucracy* (1964) illustrates in a corresponding way how attempts to cope with contradictory tendencies within the organisation may merely set up a kind of vicious circle of increasing organisational dysfunctions. Impersonal rules in the workplace contribute to control and predictability in task-performance and they also function to reduce the visibility of the power relations between supervisors and workers. But the tendency of rules to be interpreted as minimum standards of performance may in certain circumstances reduce all activity to an apathetic conformity to this 'official' minimum. Should this happen there is likely to be a managerial response whereby rules are tightened or direct supervision increased – with the effect that power relations become more visible and overt conflict between managers and managed is increased. Through this the achievement of management's overall goals is increasingly threatened as their control is challenged.

The rules, procedures and administrative devices shown in these studies by organisational sociologists to create problems for those in charge of organisations are all means by which power is exercised. The so-called 'dysfunctions' arising within organisations are, in effect, limitations on the successful exercise of power within the organisation. What we must note is that these contradictions relate in large part to structural problems in the society and economy outside the organisation. As the whole thrust of chapter 3 indicated, there are contradictions inherent in the context in which organisations operate.

The challenge by administrative and manual worker alike to the power of those running the organisation come about in large part as a result of expectations for personal satisfaction, individual freedom and autonomy, desire for material gain, etc. engendered in employees by the culture of industrial capitalism itself.

In the same way that the bulk of the employees of organisations are, in a sense, creatures not just of the organisation but of the wider society, so are those exercising so-called 'power' in the organisation similarly bounded. The dominant coalitions within managements who make the strategic operating decisions for the organisations are, correspondingly, not fully autonomous beings but are people operating within tightly bounded constraints set by external financial, economic, social and governmental forces. As Stewart Clegg (1975) has suggested, it is illegitimate to see power ultimately residing in individuals or groups *within* organisations: the greater freedom to act of some rather than other organisational members is dependent on their relationship to the power located in the 'deeper structure' of the society in which the organisation is located. In the final analysis the continued appointment of the top executives of any organisation, be they paid officials or owner-managers, will be dependent on their running the organisation in a way which contributes to the continuation of the basic industrial capitalist pattern of social organisation with its characteristic structure of advantage. Government reorganisation, private or public takeover, legal dissolution or financial bankruptcy all present close constraints on the executive body and in fact help *define* what are tradition-ally and naïvely frequently conceived of as *organisational* goals.

The above argument helps account for the range of adjustments made externally to organisations to cope with the contradictions affecting them – especially those legislative and economic measures taken by governments to cope with problems arising from the industrial capitalist mode of employment. In noting all this we must not lose sight of the fact that those in élite positions in large organisations tend, as we shall see in the next section, to be closely tied in to what is in effect the most advantaged and powerful class within the social structure. In many respects these people create the contexts of each other's organisations. Thus the environment in which organisations operate is not a totally hostile one. As we shall now see, to a large extent the environments of organisations can be 'managed', this being the first of three basic ways in which organisations cope with the ambiguities and contradictions in which they are involved.

This first way in which adjustments are made to cope with contradictions involves not so much adaptations made *within* the organisation as attempts made by influential organisational interests to bring about adjustments in their *external* environment. Kenneth McNeil (1978) points out that organisational sociologists have concentrated on the internal adaptive strategies of organisations at the expense of what, in following up certain concerns of Max Weber, he calls *external domination strategies*. The need for organisations to pursue this type of strategy arises from a particular fundamental contradiction or paradox of industrial capitalism: that which McNeil calls the tension between market and administrative logic: 'the market logic of supply and demand for labor, commodities, and capital is inherently unpredictable, yet the administrative logic of economic organisations demands a high degree of calculability'. Managements of organisations tend to act to reduce the type of uncertainty implicit in a free market. This would cover those strategies associated by economists in the Marxian tradition with the rise of *monopoly* capitalism. We must note the ways in which the heads of large organisations seek to influence governments, legislatures and local authorities, can manipulate the affairs of smaller or weaker organisations and attempt to manipulate their clients and consumers in ways ranging from advertising to bribery. The activities of ITT in Chile, the relationship between large drug companies and the British National Health Service, the foreign investment programmes of the Ford Motor Company, and the activities of Lockheed across the globe, are among the more spectacular illustrations of the importance of organisational power strategies which can be related to fundamental structural contradictions.

The second aspect of organisational reaction to ambiguity and contradictions is the internal tendency of organisations to be continually modifying and redesigning both administrative structures and specific work tasks. These are adaptations in the official control aspects of organisational structure – the inner circle of Fig. 6.1. Organisation and job design has been a major concern of organisational sociologists and will be looked at here shortly.

The third aspect of structural adaptation is also internal but occurs within what I have represented as the unofficial aspects of organisational structure. Here I refer to the unofficial activities of managements which despite their not being part of formal procedures nevertheless help fulfil the overall goals of the interest dominant in the organisation. To illustrate this we can again refer to Gouldner's study (1964) which we used earlier to illustrate the dysfunctional aspects of rule-conformity. The same study illustrates how, conversely, unofficial rule-*breaking* may in fact help meet the ends which those rules were originally intended to serve. Gouldner noted the existence of an *indulgency pattern* whereby supervisors avoided the potentially negative effects of workers taking certain rules as minimal performance standards through their own demonstrating of flexibility by conniving at the breaking of certain other rules by subordinates. Such a pattern is very common and industrial foremen frequently find that one of the few devices left to them to obtain flexible and more than grudging co-operation from those they supervise is to be willing to turn a blind eye to illegally extended tea-breaks, late arrivals at work and various other minor rule infringements.

Peter Blau (1963) in an important study of two government agencies reveals what he calls the *dynamics of bureaucracy* through observing the various ways in which employees avoid what could become 'dysfunctional' aspects of official procedures. 'Procedural adjustments' constitute one form of adaptation in which the officials, when faced with alternative courses of action choose the one more congenial to themselves, typically justifying this choice as the one more in the interests of successful organisational performance. Law enforcement agents, for instance, justified their preference not to obey the rule of officially reporting bribes which were offered to them on the grounds that keeping the offer to themselves gave them a psychological advantage over the offender which would help them complete their investigations. Another tactic is to redefine a rule or procedure in a way which 'deliberately sacrifices the original objective of a procedure in order to achieve another organisational objective more effectively' as in the case of the employment agents who more or less abandoned counselling clients in order to concentrate on getting them speedily placed in jobs. In reaction to this type of unofficial activity, Blau observes, managerial attempts are made to elaborate or 'amplify' procedures. These, in turn, lead to further unofficial adjustments. Here we see an ongoing dialectical relationship between what I have called the official and the unofficial aspects of the organisation. In the end all this helps the functioning of the organisation through accommodating the interests and preferences of employees to the wider purposes of those running the organisation. In these ways, and in others to be seen in the next chapter, individuals adjust to their being used as instruments within organisations and structural contradictions are thus coped with.

Organisational control, social class and organisational structure

Work organisations in industrial capitalist societies are typically hierarchical in their official structure. They make use of human beings at all levels but the ways of using people's efforts and the ways they are rewarded vary with their level in the hierarchy. To continue linking work organisations with the wider social structure of which they are a part I shall now examine how the class pattern of society is both reflected in and reproduced by the way organisations are structured.

For both the unequal distribution of valued resources in society at large and the hierarchical distribution of rewards within organisations to continue in the face of potential opposition some source of legitimacy is necessary. An ideology appropriate to this task of justifying the contemporary pattern of stratification has been found, according to Claus Offe (1976), in the form of a widely accepted *achievement principle*. This refers to the general feeling which people are said to have that the distribution of rewards in society is 'fair'. It is felt to be fair because the rewards which people get from their work are believed to be related to what they actually achieve within work organisations or are related to what they had to achieve in order to be able to do that work (gain qualifications, etc.).

Despite the *ideological* efficacy of a general belief in the achievement principle, Offe argues not only that the principle does not apply in practice but that it *cannot* apply given the nature of modern work organisations. The achievement principle would apply in what is called a 'task-continuous status organisation' – one like a medieval guild where those further up the status ladder have more of the *same* skills as those on the lower rungs. But modern organisations are increasingly 'task-discontinuous status organisations', where those in lower positions have *different* skills from those further up. Technical change makes this increasingly the case. There cannot, therefore, be a general scale of rewards based on a unilinear measure of technically equivalent performance. To cope with this problem, symbolic substitutes for performance are found by organisations and are used as criteria for recruitment and promotion. These criteria tend to be normative and ideological ones relating to the individual's displayed conformity with and willingness to accept the organisation's power structure. To interpret Offe's subtle arguments at the risk of oversimplification: he is suggesting that people get higher rewards and promotions in organisations not so much because they are 'good at the job' (since, technically, there can be no clear and general criteria of what 'good performance' is) but because they show a willingness to fit into the organisational power structure and exhibit features such as an appropriate racial, cultural, educational and social status background. Such features indicate the likelihood of the individual's 'fitting in'. Since these features are generally class-related, we find organisations thus helping to reproduce social class and status patterns which are, at the same time, legitimated by a spurious claim to their being performance or achievement-related.

To claim that senior appointments in organisations are made to a large degree on the basis of class-related rather than task-relevant criteria is not necessarily to question the ability of those appointees to achieve the tasks for which they are recruited. In fact, their possession of what Bourdieu and Passeron (1977) call *cultural capital* – the various linguistic and social competences derived from and certificated by the educational system and manifested in a certain manner, ethos, style, know-how and aspirations – can help them to gain compliance from both subordinates and peers who are likely to respect such attributes as appropriate to executives. The education system, through the 'correspondence principle' described earlier (p. 104) inculcates at each level among those it prepares for work appropriate attitudes and expectations with regard to unequal rewards and associated work experiences and, very importantly, towards authority.

The élite jobs in organisations in Europe and America are increasingly being filled by individuals with graduate-level qualifications. This does not necessarily mean a move to more meritocratic modes of recruitment, as might be inferred. The new pattern is interpreted by Bourdieu and Boltanski (1978) as involving a method of class reproduction no less effective than the older mechanism of direct inheritance of wealth. This, they attempt to demonstrate, is because the upper classes are making increasing use of educational institutions in recognition of the increasing trends for business profits to be realised in the form of salaries rather than dividends. In these countries the qualifications gained may well have some generally task-relevant or technical element. In Britain, however, it would appear that, even in the business sphere, a non-technical but high social status and associated educational background is most important in gaining access to the very top jobs. Research indicates that public school and Oxford or Cambridge university backgrounds (these institutions recruiting largely from upper social strata) are more helpful in obtaining the top posts than possession of a postgraduate business qualification (Marceau, Thomas and Whitley 1977). Public school background may be more important than university attendance. Alumni of the prestigious business schools nevertheless gain privileged posts, if not membership of the business élite itself, with the level they achieve tending to reflect the occupational status of their own fathers (*ibid.*).

Again on the basis of research, Giddens and Stanworth (1978) show a trend among the British business élite for there to be an *increasing* significance of public school and Oxbridge education among both industrial and financial directors. These authors review evidence of the ties which exist between members of the business élite themselves and between the business and other organisational élites (legal, educational, political, etc.). When this pattern is related to the evidence of a heavy and unequal concentration of private wealth in Britain a conclusion is drawn that the various organisational élites (those occupying 'high positions of authority' within organisations) 'still compose a unitary dominant social class' (*ibid.*).

When all the evidence on the concentration of wealth and the social connections between owners of wealth and those involved in managing the organisations which create wealth is taken into account and this is put alongside the fact that the rewards accruing to senior managers (in the form of salaries, bonuses, fringe benefits, dividends on their own shares and personal prestige) relate to their performance with regard to wealth creation, we can see any claim that organisations are run in the interests of a dominant social class is well founded. An assumption of a managerial revolution separating managerial and ownership interests is, as was argued earlier (p. 160), not tenable.

We can see the hierarchical control structure of the organisation, then, as a device for ensuring that these dominant interests are met, the compliance of those filling the posts in this hierarchy being gained through their being rewarded by being allowed varying degrees of participation in the benefits of successful organisational performance.

Contribution to the fulfilment of the goals of dominant interests by those lower down the ladder is encouraged by the promise of increased rewards which may be gained through career promotion. But this mechanism for gaining compliance is only one of two which are used in organisations, as I shall explain shortly. First, however, we have to note a second function fulfilled by the hierarchical distribution of rewards in work organisations.

One of the most significant contradictions underlying the organisational aspect of work structure, and industrial capitalism as a whole, is that deriving from the fact that individuals are brought together to enable their work efforts to be better controlled whilst, at the same time, their being brought together creates the conditions in which potential collective opposition to that control may develop. If, however, groups within the great majority of the population who sell their labour power can be differentiated in terms of status and material rewards and persuaded that their respective interests differ, then the degree of potential unity and solidarity among employees as a whole is reduced. In this way Marx and Engels' predicted growth of a class-conscious and unified proletariat is avoided. Something like the 'fragmentary class structure' identified by Roberts *et al.* (1977) can thus be seen, in part, as an outcome of the way formal organisations are structured.

Whilst the Marxian two-class model, based on ownership and non-ownership of property is still useful analytically (given the importance of the ownership of wealth argued above) we nevertheless need to recognise that the ways in which work is organised and rewarded provides us with two other possible ways of viewing the class structure: in terms of a three-class and a five-class model. The three models are shown in Fig. 6.2. The models each have some value and, I would argue, they are not necessarily incompatible since their differences are based on which of the *divides* (the four horizontal lines in the diagram) we choose to emphasise. The divides stressed by each model – and the relevance of each of them is empirically demonstrable – do not necessarily exclude the relevance of those stressed in the other models.

In most of the discussion so far the emphasis has been largely on the divide stressed in the two-class model, this being applied to organisations to bring out the relationship between a dominant class which largely benefits from the work done by a subordinate class which sells its labour-power to organisational employers (with there being an important overlap at the point of this divide). But at this point I wish to turn to the three-class model in order to take up the point made earlier: that there are two basic types of control or compliance-gaining mechanisms used within work organisations. These mechanisms are related to two kinds of employment relationship.

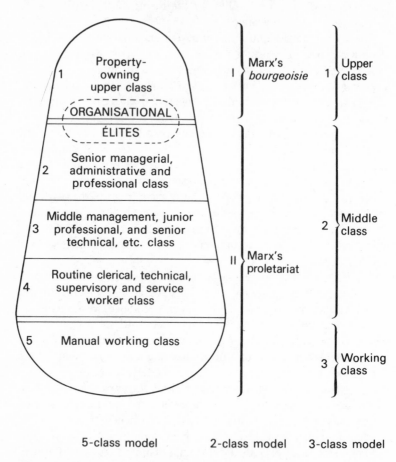

5-class model   2-class model   3-class model

Fig. 6.2 Three ways of looking at class structure

People employed in jobs which locate them in the middle-class and working-class strata of the three-class model, respectively, are typically employed in the organisation on the basis of two different types of implicit contract. Those above the manual/non-manual divide tend to have a relatively *diffuse implicit contract*. Alan Fox (1974) notes that those employed on the basis of a diffuse contractual commitment are required to use *discretion* in their work and are involved in a *high trust* relationship with their superiors. The high trust which is put in this type of staff and the relatively high level of rewards (in the form of cash, status, opportunity for intrinsic satisfaction and career advancement offered) are reciprocated on the part of the employees with a willingness to comply with organisational requirements on their own initiative. The type of control to which they are submitted is characterised by Andrew Friedman (1977) as *responsible autonomy*. It relates to what Blau and Schoenherr (1971) call 'insidious control' and is the type of control viewed so pessimistically in its potential for eroding real individual autonomy in William Whyte's *The Organisation Man* (1961). Organisational norms are, in the psychologist's terms, 'internalised' and individuals, in other words, control themselves (as well as their subordinates) on behalf of their superordinates.

This type of employment relationship and its associated method of control can perhaps best be regarded as ideal-typical and as forming one end of a continuum in the way represented in Fig. 6.3. Despite the fact that, as we shall see shortly, there are both trends for the responsible autonomy control mechanism to be applied below the manual/non-manual line and, conversely, for direct control approaches to be applied to those above it, this divide is nevertheless a significant one in forming a break in the continuum.

Manual work and, increasingly, routine clerical and service work is typically characterised by a *restricted type of implicit contract*. The generally lower level of rewards is associated with what Fox (1974) describes as institutionalised *low-trust* relationships with superiors. Work tasks are much more closely *prescribed* and these are *executed* (their *conception* occurring elsewhere, as Braverman (1974) emphasises) on the basis of a contractual commitment which is specific rather than diffuse. This specificity is represented by there typically being an hourly or weekly wage as opposed to an annual salary, by the much tighter specification of what is required of them and, especially, by the lack of an inducement in the form of potential career promotion. The control mechanism is traditionally that referred to by Friedman (1977) as *direct control* which in effect 'treats workers as though they

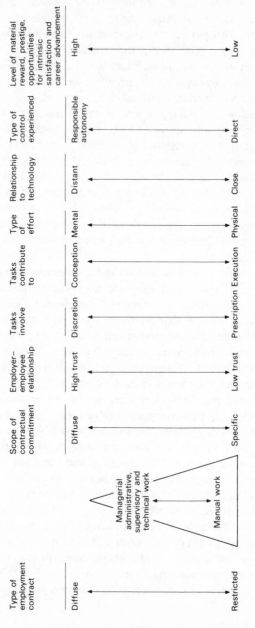

Fig. 6.3 Two ideal types of relationship between individual and employing organisation (seen as two ends of various continua related to hierarchical structure of organisation)

were machines', removing responsibility and submitting them to close supervision.

Associated with these two methods of organisational control and the two types of employment relationship (these being closely related to a significant divide in the wider social structure) are two approaches to organisational design. These are represented in Fig. 6.4. The approach to organisational design typical of the top part of the hierarchy drawn in the diagram is a bureaucratic one which provides a generalised expectation of potential career advancement for the individual. We shall look at this in the next section. Following this we shall turn our attention to the lower part, noting the only partially bureaucratised nature of the structure here – a facet which replaces the career type inducement to compliance of individuals with far more direct and typically 'Taylorian' ones.

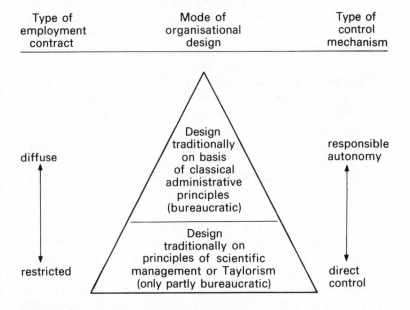

Fig. 6.4   Two modes of organisational design

Organisational control and organisational careers

Although work organisations are basically bureaucratic bodies it is increasingly the case that the full set of bureaucratic features which make up the Weberian ideal type described on p. 197 only apply to the top half of the hierarchy – the half which relates to the middle-class stratum of society. Where the principles of scientific management have typically applied at the lower levels we find a set of administrative principles being advocated for the control part of the structure by a series of writers who have followed the classic work of Henri Fayol (1949). This classical school of management writers, whose efforts and interests were quite distinct from those of Weber, converted into practical managerial precepts the approach to organisation identified sociologically by Weber as of growing importance in western societies. Writers in this tradition have strongly influenced the design of administrative structures across the range of modern organisations through the following of various structural prescriptions which are taken to be universally applicable. Writings of people like Fayol, Urwick, Mooney and Reiley tend to specify an ideal 'span of control', assert the necessity for a formal specification of functions and call for a clear chain of command with direct or 'line' managers differentiated from functional or 'staff' specialists.

The essentially hierarchical basis of the widely applied principles of this classical administrative school not only provides a control mechanism but provides a potential career ladder and thus a reward mechanism for individuals. This point is of fundamental importance and is central to the organisational sociology of Tom Burns who points out that organisational members are 'at one and the same time co-operators in a common enterprise and rivals for the material and intangible rewards of successful competition with each other' (1961). The bureaucratic structure thus has both an integrative and a disintegrative aspect. The fact that the career rewards available to individuals are necessarily scarce ones means that those who are officially intended to work co-operatively are likely to find themselves in conflict with each other. Although a certain amount of competition between individuals may be 'functional' for the organisation, as Harold Landsberger (1961) points out, it equally may create organisational problems. Following the common tendency in social life for people with common interests to form coalitions or groups we are likely to see the kind of cliques forming which Melville Dalton (1959) observed in his classic study of managerial behaviour. Sectional interests may be served at the expense of those of senior management. Burns (1955) has shown how cliques which develop norms and values contrary to the dominant organisational ones may develop among older managers who lack promotion prospects and feel a need to act defensively. However, Burns contrasts these coalitions with the 'cabals' which develop among younger men whose individual interests may be served by compliance with dominant norms and values. Conflicts between these cliques and cabals are inevitable.

The provision by organisations of career advancement as a motivational inducement is frequently systematised in administrative procedures in the form of 'career development' programmes, annual assessments, promotion boards and the like. Yet again the paradox of consequences manifests itself since such systems may well create unrealistic expectations of advancement with consequential demotivating results when these expectations are not met (Watson 1977a). The potentially disruptive effects of internal promotion procedures are well illustrated in Burns's (1977) study of the BBC where promotion procedures are so highly stressed that the corporation appears to put a 'positive value on careerism, on the energetic pursuit of promotion' with the effect that, as one interviewee said to the author, 'I get the feeling that people tend to adapt themselves to being acceptable to Appointments Boards, rather than to being successful in their jobs.'

Officially, the criteria for career advancement are meritocratic ones but since, as we saw from Offe's analysis considered above, there are no clear technical criteria to make unambiguously achievement-based appointments possible, unofficial factors inevitably come into play. Advancement is likely to be based in part on the basis of what Offe called 'peripheral' characteristics. Melville Dalton (1951) showed the importance of extrafunctional promotion criteria in the organisations which he studied where particular importance was attached to membership of the Masonic Order, not being a Roman Catholic, being Anglo-Saxon or Germanic in ethnic origin, belonging to the local yacht club and affiliated to the Republican Party – in this order of importance. Coates and Pellegrin's (1962) investigation of factors relating to the promotion of managers and supervisors indicates the importance not of 'native ability', hard work or the 'demonstration of ability' in the explanations given by interviewed individuals of their career success or failure but of what the authors recognise as varying normative orientations. Such things as cultural and educational background together with early career experiences lead individuals to 'adopt attitudes, values and behavior patterns which function as important positive or negative influences in subsequent career progress and occupational mobility'. Burns' (1977) study of the BBC provides an outstanding empirical illustration of the type of process being considered here. He shows how individuals attempt to appear as 'BBC types' through carefully managed impressions of self, thus contributing to 'a latent system of approved conduct and demeanour'. Although this was by no means uniform, it was nevertheless 'always consonant with the prevailing code by which individuals . . . were selected and gained approval and promotion'.

We have to take care here not to stress the interpersonal career competitions and the striving for individual power outside the context of the departmental structures in which people are located. Power, I suggested earlier, can be seen as the capacity of any group or individual to affect the outcome of any situation so as to achieve or maintain access to scarce and valued resources (p. 60). To understand the basis of any individual's power we have to locate them in their particular organisational sub-unit noting that, as Charles Perrow (1970a) puts it, not all sub-units are equally powerful. In eleven of the twelve industrial firms studied by Perrow, managers felt the sales department to be the most powerful. Perrow explains this in terms of the 'strategic position with respect to the environment' of these sales departments. In line with this argument we find various authors arguing that coping with organisational uncertainties may be the key to power within organisations. This is stressed by J. D. Thompson (1967) who sees leadership within organisations going to those who deal with the sources of greatest uncertainty for the organisation and by Michel Crozier (1964) who identifies power with the ability to resist the removal by others of uncertainty in one's sphere of activities. Thus, in this sense, maintenance workers in a factory will have more power than those who operate the machines which they maintain. Similarly the personnel manager in an organisation where labour is in short supply or where trade unions are well organised will be more powerful than the personnel specialist in an organisation where the resource of labour is less problematic.

The above type of insight is developed by Hickson *et al.* (1971) in their *strategic contingency* theory of power. This theory suggests that the power of a department depends on three things: first, on the extent to which it is not *contingent* or dependent on other sub-units; second, on its not being *substitutable* by any other sub-unit and, third, on its *centrality* to the organisational system. This centrality derives from the part played in coping with strategically important uncertainties. There is a lot of value in this analysis although, as Clegg (1975) suggests, we need to avoid confusing 'power' with what is, in effect, 'less dependency' on the part of some sub-units compared to others. This analysis suggests that if any individual or departmental grouping within an organisation wishes to increase its access to the material and qualitative rewards available within the organisation, a successful claim must be made to being independent of other parties, irreplaceable by other parties, and capable of dealing with whatever uncertainties face the dominant interests within the organisation in the pursuit of its goals. In the end, however, it is very important to emphasise that this 'power' of the individual or group is dependent on the contributions made to the maintenance or reinforcement of an overall structure of advantage. This needs to be recognised to avoid attempting to explain organisational dynamics in terms of fictional 'system needs'.

The location of individuals within the administrative structure clearly influences their relative autonomy and their access to rewards but it is important to note that these structures are not pregiven patterns into which people are simply slotted. Organisational structures, it was argued earlier, are the outcomes of an interplay between official and unofficial influences. The organisational structures within which individuals both contribute to organisational performance and pursue sectional interests are in part the outcome of their own initiatives. As Andrew Pettigrew (1973) shows in his study of organisational decision-making, 'by their ability to exert power over others, individuals can change or maintain structures as well as the norms and expectations upon which these structures rest'. Pettigrew's study shows how the head of a management services department is particularly able to influence key organisational decisions on computerisation through being in a 'gatekeeper' role – one which enabled him to bias the information which reached the formal decision-makers. Fred Goldner (1970) in his study of industrial relations specialists points out that organisational departments may develop to cope with uncertainties, as does the labour relations function. This is not an automatic process: individuals may seek out uncertainties and thus create a role for themselves: 'In fact, it is advantageous to an individual's career to find such activities if they are not already apparent.' In the personnel management field one may indeed watch personnel departments 'expand ("empire build") as career advantages and structural "uncertainties" are brought together by individual personnel specialists who see the need for a "job evaluation manager" today and a "remunerations manager" the next' (Watson 1977a).

Organisational control and organisational jobs

In the previous section we have looked at the upper half of the hierarchy of work organisations where individuals are controlled on a basis of *responsible autonomy* and are motivated by a *diffuse* kind of employment contract in which potential career reward is an important factor. Turning now to the lower half of the hierarchy we find people in jobs rather than careers (to use everyday rather than sociological terms). The organisational design principles are those of scientific management, which attempts to prescribe as closely as possible how tasks are to be done. Individuals are *directly controlled* and their employment contract is relatively *restricted*, it being unlikely to promise potential promotion as a reward.

Following the basic assumptions of scientific management or Taylorism (see pp. 36–7 above) jobs are designed to achieve the maximum technical division of labour through advanced task fragmentation; the planning of conception of work is divorced from its execution; skill requirements and job-learning times are minimised and material handling is reduced as far as possible, with indirect or preparatory tasks being separated from direct or productive ones. Various techniques and administrative devices are then devised to co-ordinate otherwise fragmented efforts. Included here are managerial attempts to 'scientifically' standardise procedures, the setting up of time study and monitoring systems and the use of incentive payment systems to both stabilise and intensify worker effort.

L. E. Davis (1972) has characterised the employment relationship implied in Taylorism as following a 'minimum interaction model' which allows the organisation to 'strive for maximum interchange-ability of personnel (with minimum training) to reduce its dependence on the availability, ability, or motivation of individuals'. Craig Littler (1978) takes up this point to argue that it is with this non-career-oriented element in the employment relationship that Taylorian principles diverge from general characteristics of bureaucratic organisation (as in Weber's ideal type) which fully apply to the upper parts of the hierarchy and which prevailed throughout in other organisational models which were available at the turn of the century and which were applied in public service bodies like the police, the railways and the post office. A diffuse, rather than a restricted, kind of commitment was encouraged at all levels in these organisations.

The *deskilling* logic behind scientific management is emphasised by Harry Braverman (1974). The splitting down of work tasks and the assignment of these minimal operations to different workers on the basis proposed by Adam Smith in *The Wealth of Nations* is seen as giving a double advantage to the employer: he gains through increasing both productivity and management control. According to Braverman, the most compelling reason for the spread of this advanced technical division of labour (an approach accelerated and codified rather than devised by Taylor and his disciples we should stress) is that emphasised in 1832 by Charles Babbage: the dividing of a craft 'cheapens its individual parts'. This follows from the fact that detail workers can command lower rewards in the market than craftsmen. Labour power as a commodity is thus cheapened by its being broken into its simplest elements.

The limits of scientific management

Taylorism is part of a wider process whereby work is subjected to a process of rationalisation. As both Braverman and Davis, Canter and Hoffman (1972) argue, its principles are still fundamental in work design. Scientific management not only contributes to productivity and cheapens labour resources but helps reduce the uncertainties which face managements when their labour force has the greater bargaining power (as individuals and groups) of the skilled worker. As with all attempts to apply formally rational techniques, there is the tendency for opposition to develop and for other counter-productive tendencies to manifest themselves. At the same time as the increasing application of Taylorian techniques is made possible by the introduction of electronic and other technical devices to more and more spheres of working (ranging, as Braverman shows, from printing to retailing and engineering to clerical work) so we also find employer interests undermined or challenged either by lack of motivation or interest on the part of individual employees or by organised opposition.

Andrew Friedman (1977) suggests that Braverman's analysis of an increasing trend towards scientific management is too simple in its inadequate treatment of organised worker resistance. Given the capacity of working people to oppose managements in many circumstances, managements often simply cannot afford to introduce techniques which reduce worker goodwill. Where the *direct control* strategy of scientific management tends to prove counterproductive, Friedman suggests that the alternative strategy of encouraging *responsible autonomy* may be followed. In this strategy employees are given status, autonomy and responsibility. An element of diffuse commitment is introduced into the employment relationship whereby employees are themselves expected to 'adapt to changing situations in a manner beneficial to the firm'. We will shortly review several manifestations of this willingness to implement responsible autonomy or 'participative management' strategies but, first, we have to note the nature of the circumstances which make more likely adoption of Friedman's direct control or his responsible autonomy approach.

Friedman suggests that the chosen control strategy is dependent on whether top managers perceive individual employees or groups of workers as *central* or *peripheral*. In the business world, employees are central when they are considered to be essential to the securing of high long-run profits, especially when business conditions are depressed. This centrality may derive from the possession of certain skills, knowledge, contributions made to managerial authority or, alternatively, to the strength of their collective resistance. Responsible autonomy strategies are more appropriate here, whereas direct control strategies remain viable with those peripheral employees whose weaker employment situation is also reflected in their lower wages, greater vulnerability to lay-off and their 'suffering the greater oppression engendered by direct control managerial strategies'. This centre-periphery pattern which Friedman observes as existing between firms as well as within them is very important for understanding the dual-labour market pattern discussed in the previous chapter (p. 171). Individuals with the various disadvantages attached to certain racial, gender, life-cycle or health characteristics are pushed towards the peripheral types of employment where their disadvantaged position outside work is reinforced by the greater vulnerability to exploitation within work.

Angelo Pichierri (1978), in discussing the different approaches followed in Europe and America in coping with what he calls the crisis in scientific management, suggests that moves towards what Friedman calls responsible autonomy are, in America, more the result of managements having to react to turbulent environments (market and product life-cycle problems, governmental regulations and changing cultural expectations among employees) whereas, in Europe, the explicit demands of organised workers are added to these factors as a spur to 'enlightened' managerial practice.

Scientific management or direct control strategies, then, are widely used, and are being increasingly applied, especially in areas where technical change facilitates deskilling. Whereas in certain circumstances dominant organisational interests are well served by these techniques through better productivity, cheaper labour costs and reduction of uncertainty facilitated by closer control and prescription, there are other circumstances where significant *costs* build up to undermine such advantages. This may be manifested in the stultification of the employee (a danger noted by Adam Smith), on their demotivation and consequent unwillingness to be adaptable in changing environmental conditions or, yet again, by organised employee opposition. Managements then turn to a variety of responsible autonomy techniques to temper still popular direct control ones. The various techniques used often relate to various theoretical approaches to understanding work behaviour and we will now examine some of these approaches.

The Human Relations movement represented an important questioning of many of the assumptions of scientific management as the account given earlier (pp. 37, 42) indicates. This movement not only produced a theoretical approach to understanding work behaviour but provided a managerial ideology more fitted to the American inter-war period when trade union representation of employees was increasing (Bendix 1963). The common tendency to describe the Human Relations approach as rediscovering the social aspects of work which scientific management is said to ignore is quite mistaken. As Littler (1978) points out, Taylor knew all about work-groups and in place of his attempts to destroy work-group solidarity, the Human Relations approach prescribes an alternative tactic: that of integrating the work-group so as to control it better. As Friedman (1977) puts it, 'the variable aspect of labour power is harnessed for managerial ends rather than subdued.' Charles Madge, in his account of the Hawthorne studies and their influence, notes the use of human relations ideas in countering trade unionism in America and suggests that the adoption of personnel counselling was a particularly significant effect. Despite the systems element of the Human Relations stance the prescriptions provided by it tend not to involve *structural* redesign within organisations. The most important manifestation of Human Relations thinking within organisations has perhaps been in the form of supervisory and junior management training schemes. These schemes, which are very popular across a range of contemporary organisations, tend to emphasise the importance of 'communications' and the careful 'handling of people'. Instead of altering work organisation, existing structures are marginally humanised through more sensitive 'man management'.

The writings of the more directly social-psychological neo-Human Relations theorists discussed earlier (p. 38) are also very popular in contemporary management training. This approach, however, in its concern to create conditions in which employees can achieve *self-actualisation*, does suggest a need for structural modification. Hence, for example, we find advocacy of *job enrichment* following from the 'motivation-hygiene' theory of Fred Herzberg (1966) where, typically, jobs are expanded either by reintegration of maintenance or inspection tasks, an extension of the work cycle or by an increased degree of delegation of decision-making opportunities for employees. Structural implications are also found in the work of Rensis Likert, another proponent of so-called participative styles of management. Likert (1967) advocates integration of individuals into the organis-ation through *groups* which are, in turn, integrated into the organisation's official structure of decision-making by their being made to overlap by means of their continuing 'linking pin' members who belong to more than one group.

Among the variety of approaches to job redesign one of the more theoretically sophisticated is that developed by the Tavistock Institute of Human Relations in London. This approach encourages a view of the organisation as a *socio-technical system*. The essence of this approach is the recognition that, to achieve its 'primary task', the technical and the social components of the overall system must be designed to take each other into account. One does not design a technology and then fit a social organisation to it but devises one alongside the other in order to jointly optimise the two. It is assumed that the precise technical form required to achieve tasks is variable, as is the social structure to accompany it. Both can therefore be *chosen* to get the best *fit*, one with the other. Trist *et al.*, in their influential study *Organisational Choice* (1963), showed how technical innovations introduced in post-war British coal mines failed to give either the social and psychological satisfactions traditionally expected by miners or the levels of productivity and on interrupted working sought by management. This was because the technical pattern of such things as new occupational roles and the shift arrangements associated with new machinery took away the relative autonomy of work groups and removed the opportunity for the coal miner to use a variety of skills. The researchers devised a different approach to the use of new machinery which allowed retention of some of the traditional features of the social and cultural arrangements preferred by miners. A better *fit* having been obtained between the social and technical arrangements, there was said to be a marked improvement in productivity, worker-management co-operation and absenteeism levels.

Probably the most important single innovation of the Tavistock researchers is that of the 'autonomous workgroup'. Work tasks are grouped together to form a logical 'whole task' which can be performed with minimal interference. The work designer attempts to devise 'a group consisting of the smallest number that can perform a whole task and can satisfy the social and psychological needs of its members' this being 'alike from the point of view of task performance and of those performing it, the most satisfactory and efficient group' (Rice 1958). A parallel movement towards devising work groups organised around 'whole tasks' which can be carried out relatively autonomously is the 'group technology' approach increasingly initiated by work engineers. Typically, shopfloors (or offices) are rearranged so that machines (or desks) are grouped together not on the basis of their doing similar work (drilling, grinding, invoicing or whatever) but on the basis of a contribution to a certain product or service. Thus a group of people all involved in making, say, small turbine blades or dealing with house insurance are brought together in such a way that greater integration is obtained and a greater degree of job satisfaction is facilitated by members' greater relative autonomy and through their productive co-operation with colleagues.

The types of organisational innovation outlined here will be returned to in our final chapter when we examine the scope for choice in future work organisation. What can be said at present, however, is that all these innovations are fairly peripheral to the way work is generally organised in industrial capitalist societies. They represent relatively isolated or marginal modifications introduced in situations where the limits of scientific management techniques are perceived by managements to significantly undermine the level of efficiency sought.

The limits of classical administrative prescriptions

Most of the innovations in both practice and theory considered above relate to the lower levels within work organisations. It is the one-best-way of scientific management thinking which has been questioned. Alongside these changing ideas has developed a tendency to suggest that the official structures of the wider or the whole organisation may similarly be capable of variation according to circumstance. In place of the tendency of classical administrative theorists to seek and then advocate universally applicable guiding principles on the *best* vertical and horizontal span of hierarchies, the *best* degree of specialisation, formalisation, centralisation, delegation and the like, it is increasingly suggested that managements should seek the most *appropriate* shape of organisation to achieve their purposes given prevailing situational *contingencies*.

The so-called *contingency approach* to the design of the official aspects of organisational structures has grown in popularity in organisation theory since the late 1950s. Two studies were particularly important in establishing this new flexibility in thinking: those of Joan Woodward (1958, 1965) and Burns and Stalker (1961).

Woodward's study of a hundred manufacturing firms in Essex started with an interest in seeking relationships between successful business performance and organisational structure. However, it was only when the variable of technology was introduced into the researchers' thinking that sense could be made of the variations which were found in such features as the spans of control within firms, the number of levels in the hierarchy, and the extent to which communications were verbal or written. When firms were examined in terms of their place on a scale of complexity of production technology (a scale ranging from unit and small batch production, through large batch and mass production to process production) it became clear that different structural configurations were appropriate to different technologies. Thus it would be appropriate for, say, a petro-chemical company to have a relatively tall and narrow hierarchical shape whilst a firm turning out custom-built perambulators might be better suited to a short and wide configuration.

Burns and Stalker's study can also be taken to show the importance of technology as a contingent factor, although technology itself is emphasised here less than is the environment to which the technology relates. The authors observed that a different organisational pattern is likely to be appropriate in an industry like textiles where the environment is relatively stable compared to the pattern appropriate to an industry like electronics where the environment produces a constant pressure for innovation. To cope with pressures for innovation an *organic* type of structure will be appropriate. The structure here will be loose and flexible with a relatively low degree of formalisation and task prescription. Where conditions are more stable, however, *mechanistic* structures may be more appropriate, these approximating far more to the ideal type of bureaucracy and the prescriptions of the classical administrative writers.

Contingent factors of *technology* and *environment* are stressed in these now classic studies but other contingencies are emphasised by later contributors. Researchers at Aston University, for instance, argue that Woodward's analysis does not sufficiently take into account the *size* of the organisation (Hickson *et al.* 1969). The Aston studies are interpreted by their authors as indicating that Woodward's generalisations about organisational shape and technological complexity may only apply in smaller organisations and in those areas of larger organisations close to the production process itself. Generally valid organisational principles may well be applicable, it was argued, at the higher levels of management. Thus, once you move away from the 'shopfloor' or operating level of any organisation the structural pattern will be more influenced by the organisation's size and its degree of *independence* from other organisations (within and without a parent group).

Lawrence and Lorsch's (1967) work has concentrated on environmental contingencies, stressing the influence of the degree of certainty and diversity in the environment on ways in which organisations are structured in terms of *differentiation* and the *integrating* mechanisms used to cope with problems arising from the operation of differentiated units. Charles Perrow (1970b), on the other hand, has argued for the centrality of technology, something which he conceptualises in a much wider way than have other writers.

Perrow concentrates on the nature of the 'raw material' processed by the organisation, whether this be a living material as in an educational organisation, a symbolic material as in a financial institution or an inanimate material as in manufacturing. These raw materials clearly differ in their variability and hence their processing will create different problems to be faced by the organisational structure. The more routine such materials processing is the more a formal centralised structure is appropriate – and vice versa.

There are many valuable insights to be derived from the studies briefly examined above. There are a number of difficulties which arise, however, not the least of which is the tendency for the various studies to rival each other in the particular contingency which they emphasise. An overview of the contingency literature does suggest that a variety of contingencies are likely to be relevant to any given organisation. Even if we accept this we are still left with the problem of incorporating the insights of this literature into a general *sociological* theory of organisations which sees organisational structure as arising out of the interplay between official and unofficial activities within what is an essentially humanly initiated and political competitive process. To help us here we can turn to John Child's invaluable discussions of the contingency approach.

Child (1972) stresses the dangers of seeing organisational structures as automatically reacting to or being determined by contingent factors like environment, size or technology. He points out that those effectively managing the organisation, whom (following Cyert and March 1963) he calls the *dominant coalition*, do have a certain leeway in the structures which they *choose* to adopt in their strategic directing of the organisation. In pointing to the *strategic choices* made by a concrete group of motivated actors as part of an essentially political process, Child is indeed providing a 'useful antidote to the sociologically unsatisfactory notion that a given organisational structure can be understood in relation to the functional imperative of "system needs" which somehow transcend the objectives of any group of organisational members'. There are clearly always going to be a range of contingent factors limiting the decision-making of senior managements but, as Child argues, their strategic choices are not limited to establishing structural forms. They also include the *manipulation* of environmental features (as stressed earlier p. 200) and the choice of relevant performance standards.

In a review of the factors which lead to different levels of organisational performance, Child (1977) suggests that there are a range of relevant contingencies which bear on the structural patterns adopted. These fall under the headings of environment, diversity (e.g. product diversification), size, technology and the type of personnel employed. This latter factor is an important one, which takes into account the fact that managements, in the structural arrangements made, need to take into account the expectations and perceived needs of their employees if they are to achieve their purposes. To qualify the importance of all these contingencies, Child cites research which suggests the importance of two factors which may be relevant over and above the various contingent factors. These are, first, the degree of consistency between elements of the organisational structure, both in themselves and with the overall philosophy of management and, second, the attributes of the managers themselves. Child's investigations suggest that an organisation's management is more likely to be successful in achieving its purposes if its members are relatively young, appropriately trained and qualified, have a personal stake in the ownership or success of an undertaking and, finally, if it tends to concentrate on a range of key objectives in such a way that efforts are not dissipated and conflicts generated through attempts being made to achieve too many different aims at once.

Overall, then, organisational performance is to be understood as deriving from a combination of contingent and generally applicable factors, and these generally applicable features, it is important to note, relate to matters which are ultimately social and political. Organisations are devised by advantaged groups in society (and by their agents) to fulfil tasks which contribute to or at least do not undermine the prevailing societal pattern of advantage. The official aspects of organisational structures, the technology utilised and the people employed are all *means* chosen to fulfil these tasks. Despite the variety of structural forms chosen in the light of particular external contingencies and societal contradictions, and in the light of particular internal contingencies and unofficial interests and aspirations, the ultimate constraint upon the way work organisations are structured in industrial capitalist societies is one which requires them to be involved in the maintaining and the reproducing of a particular social structure.

Chapter 7

Conflict, challenge and defence in work

Introduction

To do justice to the subtlety and the complexities of the phenomena which it studies, sociology has to take account of the interplay which occurs in social life between initiative and constraint, involving recognition of the importance of both structural factors and the experiences and intentions of individuals. The emphasis in the preceding two chapters has been on tendencies towards structure, in the form of occupations and organisations. The accounts given of these tendencies towards a patterning in work life were not, however, ones which reified these structures, giving them a concrete existence over and above the human efforts which create them. These structural tendencies were, rather, seen as the outcomes of various human processes of initiative, power-seeking and negotiation. The occupational and, especially, the organisational structures have been shown as reflecting to a large degree the greater success of some social groups compared to others in the securing of control over their own lives and over parts of the lives of others and hence in their gaining of access to scarce and generally desirable rewards. Our emphasis here will be on various reactions to these efforts to control and, inevitably – given the continuous dialectic which occurs between initiative and structuring – on the resulting institutionalisation of these reactions, giving us once again patterns or structures. We will not be so much looking at something different from the earlier concerns with occupations and organisations as looking at a different aspect of the same things. Whereas, for example, the emphasis in our discussion of work organisations was on attempts of dominant interests to exert control over work and its products, we shall now give greater emphasis to the efforts and accommodations of the subordinate, the disadvantaged and the aspiring. The view from above, so to speak, will be complemented by the view from below.

Much of the present chapter will be concerned with the area of academic study which takes the title 'industrial relations'. This existing academic specialism is one which is recognised, in part, by our dealing with much of its subject matter in one particular chapter. Yet it is a specialism which is ultimately to be rejected. It is rejected on the grounds that only a limited understanding of the conflicts which occur within work, about work and over the rewards of work is possible whilst we concentrate attention too closely on the relationships between managements and trade unions and on the institutions of collective bargaining. Our sociological interest in conflict at work goes beyond the territory of the typical industrial relations specialist in two respects. First, it sets specific conflicts and activities in the wider context of the structure and dynamics of the type of society in which they occur and, second, it looks to the opposite end of the spectrum to consider the unofficial, the informal and the relatively spontaneous activities of conflict, challenge and defence in work.

Since the experience of work for the majority of people in industrial capitalist societies occurs in an employment relationship, employer-employee conflicts will be central to our concerns. These conflicts are indeed the most crucial ones and they provide the context in which many other work conflicts occur. However, employer-employee conflicts are by no means the only ones which occur. It is most important to remember – as we will throughout this chapter – that people at work not only come into conflict with their bosses and their subordinates but with their peers, their customers and their clients. Divergence of interest and orientation between individuals and groups in the course of their work experience is our concern here and justice must be done to the range of these divergences and to the variety of ways in which they are manifested in the different contexts and at the different levels at which people work.

Understanding conflict at work

For social life to proceed at work as in any other sphere, be it leisure activity or political life, there must be co-operation between people. Co-operation is not only vital for necessary tasks to be achieved, it also gives stability to daily life. The minimising or controlling of differences of interest between people required by it suggests some positive psychological significance for co-operative activity. Co-operation is comfortable, we might say. From this it is not difficult to make the leap to the suggestion that co-operation is 'good' and conflict 'bad'. But co-operation and conflict cannot really be opposed in this way, either ethically or theoretically. As the theoretical scheme underlying this study suggests (p. 60), conflict and co-operation are omnipresent and inevitably co-existent in social life. Given the scarcity of humanly valued goods in the world and the competition which tends to follow in order to obtain access to these, we find that co-operation with one interest group may automatically imply conflict with another. Conflictful activities are as much part of life therefore as 'co-operative' ones.

Conflict and co-operation are two sides of the same coin. Yet there is a common tendency in everyday thinking about social life to see examples of co-operation as healthy and conflicts as pathological. This no doubt relates back to the psychologically comforting overtones of the notion of co-operation. But it is none the less a nonsense: co-operation cannot *of itself* be evaluated as good or healthy any more than can conflict *per se* be seen as bad or unhealthy. We can only judge it by the ends to which it is related. Co-operation with a murderer would be as widely deprecated, for example, as conflict with a rapist would be applauded. By the same token, to enter into conflict with one's employer (or one's employee) cannot of itself – without reference to the point at issue – be judged right or wrong, desirable or undesirable, healthy or unhealthy. Yet in our contemporary society such judgments do tend to be made. This probably results from the effects of various ideologies combined with the negative psychological overtones of the idea of 'conflict'. This tendency, it is argued here, presents a major barrier to the understanding among academics and laymen alike of work conflicts and 'industrial relations' activity. For sociological analysis of these spheres to proceed, issue has to be taken with a formidable array of conventional wisdoms and everyday evaluative tendencies.

To come to terms with some of the difficulties of analysing issues of work conflict and to deal with the frequent confusions of description and prescription which characterise this field, it is helpful to look at the various *frames of reference* which are typically used in discussions of industrial relations issues. Following the approach of Alan Fox (1973, 1974) we can note the existence of three analytical frameworks which are available to us: the unitary, the pluralist and the radical. Each of these stresses particular aspects of work relations. The unitary framework assumes a fundamentally common interest between all of those operating in the workplace or in society at large. The pluralistic view recognises a variety of interests but sees these as more or less balancing each other out in practice. The radical perspective, however, concentrates on the basic inequalities and power differentials characterising industrial capitalist society and relates work conflicts back to these structural patterns.

These three frames of reference are clearly rivals as tools for analysis. But our problem in evaluating them is made particularly complex by the fact that these three perspectives not only tend to describe the world differently but are frequently used to support arguments for how the world should or should not be. In other words, these analytical models also function as ideologies. Our consideration of these three approaches will primarily be concerned to judge their relative *analytical* utility. To do this we will need to take note of the ambiguities which often occur in their use whereby their descriptive and prescriptive elements are confused. Fig. 7.1 outlines the three perspectives to be discussed.

Frame of reference	Level at which applied	Basic assumptions	Typical ambiguity in use
Unitary	At either organisational or societal level	Harmony of interests – conflict activity aberrant or pathological	Between what is the case and what ought to be the case
Pluralist		Variety of interests – these more or less balanced – conflicts can be managed	
Radical	The continuity between organisational and societal factors stressed	Major inequalities and imbalances of power – conflict endemic and fundamentally challenging to *status quo*	Between what is the case and what ought not to be the case

Fig. 7.1 Three ways of looking at industrial conflict

In what Fox characterises as the unitary frame of reference (1966, 1973) the employing organisation is seen as being based on a community of interest. The management are the best qualified to decide how these common interests are to be pursued. Hence

employee opposition is irrational and 'industrial action' on the part of
the employee is generally misguided and frequently the outcome of
the successful agitation of troublemakers or 'politically motivated'
individuals. The ideological value of such a perspective to the owner
or manager of the work organisation is clear to see: the employee who
questions the authority of the manager can readily be compared to a
disloyal family member or to a footballer who challenges the captain of
his own team. In this way the employee challenge is rendered
dishonourable or misguided.

At the national level the unitary frame of reference makes much use
of the concept of 'national interest', a notion which is popular with
government spokesmen – whose task is not dissimilar at times to that
of the manager in the work enterprise – in a way directly analogous to
the industrial manager's talk of football teams, families and the like.
The effectiveness of such appeals is questionable in practical terms.
Nevertheless some general legitimacy given to them in the culture at
large is suggested by the popularity in everyday talk of references to
trade unions or groups of workers 'holding the country to ransom'. As
Fox (1973) points out, the unitary framework offers a variety of ways
of questioning the legitimacy of trade union activities suggesting,
alternatively, that unions are historical carry-overs, no longer needed
in an age of enlightened management; that they are outcomes of
sectional greed; or that they are vehicles for subversive political
interests.

There is no denying the sense behind leaders of enterprises' or
governments' advocacy of 'team spirit' or community of interest. All
leadership requires legitimacy and this involves ideological utterances. Where such utterances become a threat to the understanding of
what *is* the case is where prescription and description become
confused. Managers or politicians are as likely to be misled as are the
rest of us if they come to believe their own propaganda. To attempt to
run an organisation or a government on the assumption that there are
in fact no fundamental conflicts of interest between employers and
employees, producers and consumers and so on would be folly
indeed. Hence the increasing popularity, at least among academics,
of viewing both industrial and political issues through a pluralistic
frame of reference.

Pluralism as both an ideology and an analytical perspective has been
the subject of extensive debate among both political scientists and
industrial relations analysts. The use of the pluralist model at the

societal level was discussed earlier (p. 95). At the level of the work organisation this perspective recognises the existence within the enterprise of various different and indeed conflicting interests. However, these differences are not such that they cannot be accommodated. The benefits of collaboration between these fairly evenly balanced interests are such that compromises can be achieved to enable collaborative activity to proceed – to the benefit of all parties. Employees do have to surrender autonomy at work and recognise certain managerial prerogatives. This should not be seen as unreasonable or as reflecting any basic inequality, since management has to accept corresponding constraints. These involve recognition of a right on the part of employees to organise themselves to 'loyally oppose' and bargain over rewards and procedures. In this view, trade unions and the mechanisms of collective bargaining are necessary for the 'managing' of the conflicts of interest which exist between employers and employed and whose existence it is naïve and foolish to deny. At the national level the state tends to be seen becoming involved as only one among the range of different stakeholders or as the protector of the public interest where that may be threatened by any one interest group becoming too powerful. This pluralist doctrine was supported by the Donovan commission on industrial relations in Britain, which reported in 1968. It argued for the continuation of the British voluntaristic tradition whereby managements and unions are left to settle their differences, as far as this is possible, on their own terms.

The pluralist frame of reference became almost an orthodoxy among British industrial relations experts in the 1960s, but for a variety of reasons it became increasingly subject to critical scrutiny in the 1970s. This was largely as a result of its being found to be inadequate *sociologically*. As has been pointed out by one of those who became a leading critic of the pluralist perspective, which he had once advocated, the pluralist framework offers a fairly appropriate set of *working assumptions* for those involved in the practical world of industry and politics, given that 'irrespective of personal philosophy, a working acceptance of the basic structure, objectives, and principles which characterise industry is usually a condition of being able to exert influence towards reform' (Fox 1973). Nevertheless, it is felt that the radical alternative, as well as offering what Fox sees as a 'necessary stimulus and guide to the pursuit of more fundamental change', also has 'greater intellectual validity'. Before we consider this radical frame of reference, however, we need to establish the nature of the inadequacies which have been shown to undermine the analytical validity of the pluralist perspective.

Some of the 'crucial limitations' to the pluralist framework have been summarised by Richard Brown (1978a). First, he notes the failure of analyses offered within this framework to recognise the extent and persistence of 'marked inequalities of condition and opportunity'. He follows John Goldthorpe (1974) here in noting the absence of any 'principled basis for the distribution of income and wealth in British society'. As a result of this, industrial relations settlements rest ultimately on the power of certain groups to impose settlements on others. There is thus an inherent instability rather than a steady balancing of plural interests. This instability became more visible in the 1970s as British economic performance was seen to compare badly with that of other countries and thus offer less than might be expected by way of full employment and rising living standards; as increasing inflation disturbed previously unquestioned differentials; as governmental incomes policies encouraged public debate about the criteria on which relative incomes should be based, and as industrial reorganisation increased the size of bargaining units and hence both prompted the questioning of relativities and encouraged more ambitious pay comparisons. Brown's example in this latter case of the shipbuilding industry can be multiplied across a range of other industries.

The second inadequacy of the pluralist framework noted by Brown is its emphasis on procedural matters at the expense of the necessary recognition of substantive and material conflicts of interest. What to the pluralist is seen as achieving 'order' in the workplace may, in practice, involve shifts in power which are to the advantage of managements. The third weakness of the pluralist picture lies, according to Brown, in its underestimation of the degree to which the state has been forced to become directly involved in industrial relations. The example is given of the use of wage restraint by both Conservative and Labour governments as measures to help check inflation – something made necessary by wider economic policies. Fourth, Brown argues that the pluralist perspective, with its emphasis on institutionalising conflict, underestimates the importance of various characteristics of the British industrial infrastructure which may militate against stable regulation of conflicts. Such is the diversity and differentiation of the infrastructure that there is no basis for the growth of a formalised and centralised set of institutions for the regulation of industrial conflict.

To question further the validity of a pluralist framework – one which sees the trade union movement as a 'countervailing' force balancing the power of employers – we can look at the ability of trade unions in practice to defend their memberships against threats to their livelihoods which are presented by large industrial conglomerates and multinational companies. We need only to look at the number of large companies which closed factories in Merseyside in the late 1970s to make our point. According to a report of the protest which took place in Liverpool in March 1979 against the intended closure of the Speke Dunlop tyre factory, where two thousand people were under notice of redundancy, there was a clear recognition among the protestors of their near powerlessness in the face of the policies of a multi-national company able to gain a better return on capital in other countries (Reynolds 1979). We may also note that a year previous to this event, three thousand jobs were lost in Speke when the nationalised Standard Triumph factory was closed. This was the result of a decision made not, as in the Dunlop–Pirelli case, by a multi-national company, but by a company taken into public ownership by a Labour government (see Beynon 1978). Worker opposition to this closure, as with many others in this reputedly militant region, proved ineffective.

In putting forward this evidence about redundancies occurring in an area of Britain with an unemployment rate of over 30 per cent (at the time of writing), no judgment about the rights or wrongs of such actions is being offered. The point, rather, is to question the validity of any analytical framework which assumes a stable balance of power between employers and employed labour. Such balances may indeed exist in certain cases and over specific issues but, nevertheless, we need to recognise that ultimately there are particular interests which predominate in industrial capitalist societies, and an analytical framework is required to help us understand the implications of such power imbalances. In saying that a pluralist framework is analytically inadequate I am not saying that a pluralistic society would not be desirable, were it possible, any more than by finding the radical *frame of reference* more 'realistic' in current circumstances am I necessarily advocating any kind of radical *politics*. The popularity of the unitary framework among the politically conservative and the preference for the pluralist perspective on the part of liberals do not in themselves constitute grounds for questioning these two ways of looking at industrial conflict. In the same way, the validity of the radical perspective is to be judged on the basis of its analytical power rather than on the grounds of its attractiveness to those who seek radical change in society, or the discomfort which it may engender in the minds of those who would prefer to avert their eyes from the conflicts and inequalities which sociological analysis tends to reveal.

Despite the popularity of the pluralist framework among 'enlightened' practitioners and analysts, it has been questioned by a number of sociological writers, as has been suggested. This perhaps reflects the tendency of contemporary sociologists to look back to the classical sociological tradition. This is the tradition of Durkheim, Weber and Marx, thinkers who, in their different ways, examined the underlying structures and assumptions of industrial capitalist society. In this their analyses can be said to be *radical*: going below the surface phenomena to the *roots* of issues. Contemporary sociologists who have attempted analyses of industrial conflict in terms of what Fox calls a radical frame of reference have, in a number of ways, shown that the various manifestations of conflict which arise can only be understood if they are related back to basic characteristics of the overall societal structure and, particularly, to some of its inherent inconsistencies or contradictions.

To talk of contradictions in social, economic and political structures is to discuss the ways in which the various principles which underlie social organisation are inconsistent or clash with each other. To analyse contradictions is to locate internal tensions or strains which exist within 'systems' and which may lead to either collapse of that system or some kind of adaptation of it by those wishing to retain the basic features of the system.

The concept of contradiction is traditionally associated with the Marxian perspective but we can argue that the same notion exists in various forms throughout sociology. The very wide way in which the concept can be utilised is indicated by our central use of it in chapter 3, where a range of contradictions within industrial capitalism were discussed (see especially pp. 90–1). S. M. Lipset (1976) has noted the close correspondence between the Marxian notion of contradiction and structural-functionalist ideas of 'strain' (structural-functionalism having been seen by many as the most conservative brand of sociological theory) and he cites Eisenstadt's (1973) observation that 'both Durkheim and Weber saw many contradictions inherent in the very nature of the human condition in society in general, and saw them articulated with increasing sharpness in the developments of the modern order in particular'. As Eisenstadt points out, these sociologists were far less optimistic than Marx about overcoming the ubiquitous and continuous 'tensions between the creative and restrictive aspects of modern life, of potential contradictions between liberty and rationality, between these on the one hand and justice and solidarity on the other'.

In stressing the idea of structural contradiction we are drawing attention away from the *specific* conflicts which may arise between different actors or groups in social life to the *general* problems which give rise to these. For example, within the Marxian perspective it is not the particular conflicts which happen to take place between capitalists and workers that are crucial but the more basic contradiction between the collective production of wealth and its private appropriation. A basic sociological issue is thus raised: are the organisational principles of collective production and private consumption compatible in the long run? Such questions correspond to ones raised by Max Weber's notion of a 'paradox of consequences' in social life. In the long run can the formally rational *means* of wage-labour, advanced technical division of labour, instrumental motivation, etc. serve the materially rational *ends* of those who devised them? The answer may well be no because of the constant tension between formal and material rationality in social life (see pp. 89–90).

The particular strain or contradiction with which Emile Durkheim has commonly been associated is that whereby social inequalities lead to a situation in which certain goals are stressed by the culture but to which access for many is systematically denied (see Merton 1957). Durkheim's observation of industrial capitalism in action led him to an increasing awareness that persisting inequalities threatened the kind of social solidarity which he thought to be possible within the 'organic division of labour' which characterises modern economic life. For economic life to be regulated there needed to be some kind of moral basis underlying it, otherwise *anomie* would prevail, but he could not see how such a 'normative order' could be achieved whilst inherited inequalities of opportunity and condition existed. As Goldthorpe points out, industrial capitalist society, with its basic class inequalities, has to *impose* order, and, to the extent that this is so, 'fundamental discontent and unrest persist if only in latent form' (1974). From his reading of Durkheim, Goldthorpe infers the futility of trying to bring lasting 'order' to industrial relations activity, on the lines advocated by pluralist thinkers, whilst major inequalities of wealth and opportunity persist in society at large.

On the basis of the various discussions of structural contradictions, and the centrality to them of a concern with the implications of structured inequalities, we can draw together certain basic factors in the structure of industrial capitalist society which give rise to conflicts in work. Industrial capitalist society involves the buying and selling of labour power. These transactions are not made on a basis of equality between the parties. Inequality itself does not create a problem: the threat to the stability of industrial capitalism arises from it in two indirect ways. First, instability arises from the fact that industrial capitalism has been historically dependent on a rhetoric of social equality and of rewards based on achievement, a rhetoric which conflicts with the actual or effective distribution of rewards and opportunities for advancement in society. This gap between rhetoric and 'reality' is less likely to be visible during periods of economic growth and changing occupational structures than when growth slows down or stops. Inequalities of distribution, for example, are more likely to become contentious when there is a 'cake' of fixed size to share out, than when this cake is growing. The second source of instability arises from the fact that in a culture where individual freedom, choice, independence and autonomy are central values, the great majority of people in their work experience find themselves coming under the control and instruction of others to a degree which potentially clashes with cultural expectations.

Many of the conflicts which arise between employers and employees can be seen as paradoxical outcomes or unintended consequences of the actions and means which have been chosen by employing interests themselves in the course of the history of industrial capitalism. Collective resistance to employers could not have arisen had not employers brought together employees in single workplaces, for example. Further, the instrumental and calculative approach to work of many employees which employers frequently bemoan reflects the logic of employers' own policies as much as anything else. As E. P. Thompson (1967) points out, 'the first generation of factory workers were taught by their masters the importance of time: the second generation formed their short-time committees in the ten-hour movement; the third generation struck for overtime or time-and-a-half'. The low level of moral involvement of junior employees can also be seen as reflecting the very way their work is designed. Whilst employees are given narrowly restricted tasks to do, are closely and often coercively supervised by 'superiors' and are treated as dehumanised factors of production, managements can expect little more than grudging compliance. As Alan Fox (1974) argues, such untrusting management policies and control techniques are likely to be reciprocated with low trust employee attitudes and behaviour. What results from this is what Fox characterises as 'low trust industrial relations' in which we see the very familiar features of bargaining on a win-lose basis, attempts to bring the other side under closer prescription and control, and a screening and distortion of communication between bargaining parties.

The logic of the above type of analysis, with its radical concern to 'go to the roots', is fundamentally sociological. It not only questions the validity of many of the assumptions upon which the pluralist frame of reference is based, it also inevitably takes issue with many of the simplistic and psychologistic common-sense beliefs which are held about industrial conflict by numerous men and women in the street and by many politicians and contributors to the communication media. Industrial strikes, go-slows, restrictions of output, large pay-demands, etc. are now seen not so much as the outcome of greed, bloody-mindedness or envy but as natural and rational reactions of people living in a certain type of society.

Having striven to establish a distinctively sociological perspective for the study of work conflicts, we are in danger of losing sight of the individual working man and woman. This is always the danger when we concentrate on patterns of social organisation and find ourselves talking almost exclusively of systems, structures, cultures and the like. What we now need is something to link the situation of the working individual to his or her structural context. To help us here we can look to the work of W. Baldamus.

Baldamus (1961) focuses upon the relationship between the employee and the employer and the fundamental conflict which exists between them: 'As wages are costs to the firm, and the deprivations inherent in effort mean "costs" to the employee, the interests of management and wage earner are diametrically opposed.' This conflict of interests is manifested in the struggle which takes place to achieve 'wage disparity' in the favour of either the employer or the employee. In certain circumstances the employee may achieve an improvement in the amount of reward which he gains for a certain effort but, more typically in a capitalist economy, the tendency is towards disparity in the favour of the employer. This is partly because employees have been socialised into accepting a certain level of work obligation 'as a duty', thus conceding some effort to the employer 'free of compensation'. The second reason is probably more crucial: the employer, in the context of a capitalist market economy, simply cannot afford – in the long run – to concede wage disparity in the favour of employees. The capitalist context obliges the employer to intensify the work effort derived from the employee at a given cost.

Baldamus' concern with the ongoing conflict over what Hilde Behrend (1957) called the *effort bargain* tends to emphasise the material rewards available from work and concentrates on the factory shopfloor situation. The concept of the *implicit contract* seen to exist between employers and employees at all levels and playing a central part in the basic theoretical apparatus of the present work was developed to make more widely relevant some of the insights offered by Behrend and Baldamus. Something similar to shopfloor wage and effort bargaining goes on in all types of employment and over a wide range of issues, it is suggested. At this point we need to look back to the theoretical scheme set out on pp. 58–68. Within this scheme there is a general theory of industrial conflict which incorporates many of the points discussed above. It is important to look at the detail of the scheme to appreciate it fully but we can pick out a number of key points from it to enable our current analysis to proceed.

1 In a world where valued resources are scarce, people form coalitions of interest to help in the pursuit or defence of interests with regard to these resources.
2 Over time, some groups win out over others in the competition for scarce resources and attempt to consolidate their advantage through their control of institutions and through the propagation of ideologies.
3 Industrial capitalism emerged as 'bourgeois' groups became successful in pursuing their interests in certain societies, but the advantages which accrue from their use of such formally rational means as bureaucracy, technical division of labour, wage-labour, advanced technology and the rest are constantly threatened. The threat comes not only from challenges on the part of less privileged groups but also as a result of various contradictory tendencies in the industrial capitalist system itself (discussed above, pp. 90–1).

4 The relationship between the employer and the employee
centres on an *implicit contract* (discussed in detail on pp. 130–1.
See especially Fig. 4.4). This is an agreement between unequal
parties in which the employee, in the light of his or her particular
motives, expectations and interests, attempts to make the best
deal possible, given his or her personal resources (skill,
knowledge, physique, wealth, etc). The bargain which is struck
involves a certain relationship (in part explicit but largely, owing
to its indeterminacy, implicit) between the employee *inputs* of
effort, impairment and surrender of autonomy and employee
rewards of cash payment and fringe benefits, job satisfactions,
social rewards, security, power status, career potential, etc.

5 The bargain is essentially unstable, especially as a result of the
market context in which it is made. Market 'viability' on the part
of the employer creates a constant pressure to minimise costs –
this in turn leading to a pressure to either cut the rewards or
increase the efforts of the employee – either way to the
employees' disadvantage. However, employees are bound to
defend themselves, especially since they buy goods and services
on the same market. Paradoxically, the advertising and
marketing ef orts of employing organisations create a pressure
on their employees to increase, or at least hold stable, their
rewards (employees and customers being ultimately the same
people). The contradictory pressures operating on the
employment relationship here are illustrated in Fig. 2.4 on p. 67.

6 To increase efficiency or market viability, employers introduce
various organisational and technological changes, but any such
change, however minor it may seem, potentially invites
opposition from employees whose implicit contracts may be seen
to be threatened. This may be because of a tendency to reduce
'rewards' like job satisfaction or the opportunity to use craft
skills or because of a tendency to call for increased employee
'inputs' in the form of increased effort or a further reduction in
the amount of autonomy which the employee has at work.
Potential conflict, we can see, arises with practically any kind of
managerial initiative in employment situations.

7 Both to improve their market position and to defend themselves,
employees tend to form various coalitions of interest to present
the kind of group challenge which is necessary to have any effect
in the face of the greater power of the employer (the exception

here being where the individual employee has unique skills or knowledge on which the employer is dependent). Thus we get, within employing organisations, trade union organisation, 'professional' group mobilisation and 'informal' office and shopfloor groupings. All of these present challenges to the managerial prerogative.

8 In every workplace there is a constantly negotiated and renegotiated agreement about what goes on and what rewards accrue. Only a fraction of this negotiating process is formal and much of the agreement is tacit. External conditions are never constant and therefore there are always threats to the stability of arrangements. The underlying conflicts of interest between employer and employee may become overt and apparent at any time and will tend to centre on two main issues: the amount of material rewards available to the employee and the extent of control over employees conceded to the employer.

9 We can say that a grievance situation arises whenever a particular implicit contract is perceived to go out of balance. The grievance may lead to any of a range of employee reactions, from striking to absenteeism and from obstructive behaviour to resigning. A grievance can be settled or accommodated not only by a return to the prior *status quo* but by a rebalancing of the implicit contract in a new form; an increase in cash being agreed to compensate for a loss in autonomy resulting from a technical change, for example.

Here we have a frame of reference which can be used to analyse conflict in the widest possible range of employment situations. Having established this framework we can now turn to the variety of ways in which people adjust and defend their interests and their very selves in their work situation.

Adjustment and defence

When an individual takes up employment, he or she inevitably surrenders a certain amount of autonomy. In effect, all employees are *made use of* in some sense when they submit to the control of others in the work setting. We now turn our attention to the ways in which people adjust to the variety of ways in which they are made use of in the employment situation. We will also see that individuals adjust to being made use of in different but corresponding ways in service occupations where adjustment has to be made to being made use of by customers or clients as well as or instead of by employers.

One of the most direct ways of reacting to the deprivations of a given work situation is to leave the job. Indeed, levels of 'labour turnover' in employing organisations are often taken to be useful indicators of the level of conflict within that organisation. A. J. M. Sykes (1969), in his discussion of navvies, points out that 'jacking suddenly and for little or no reason was regarded as a demonstration of freedom and independence of the employer'. The importance of the idea of 'jacking' in the navvies' occupational ideology reflects the men's strong desire to feel and be seen as being independent of any particular employer and as indicating a basic hostility to employers in general.

The same grievances or dissatisfactions which are reacted to by people leaving their job may equally take the form of absence from work or the collective application of formal sanctions. Even accidents may reflect industrial discontent, and L. J. Handy (1968) has argued, for instance, that in the British coal-mining industry these various expressions of conflict have been utilised as *alternatives* by miners in the post-war period. Our major concern here, however, is with the adjustments which take place when the individual stays at work.

One very significant way in which the employee may come to terms with work deprivations is by taking his or her identity not so much from the occupation but from their home life. Thus, for what Goldthorpe, Lockwood *et al.* (1968) call the instrumental privatised worker, it is the non-work life which forms the central life interest. Work deprivations are coped with by their being rationalised as necessary means to other ends. Here, for instance, we find manual workers accounting for their acceptance of the negative aspects of work by pointing to the way that their income is enabling them to give their children a better 'start in life'. In addition to or as alternatives to deriving vicarious satisfactions from children's advancement people may daydream at work about the material goods or the holidays which their work enables them to buy and this may be extending into fantasising about the delights of, say, winning the pools (Ditton 1972). Elinor Langer (1970), in her study of a large office of telephone company customer service representatives, interprets the strong consumer orientation of these women as a compensation for work alienation: they express their individuality through the products which they purchase and continually discuss with their colleagues.

Sennett and Cobb (1977) in their discussion of what they call the 'hidden injuries of class' argue that for people to accept a circumstance whereby they are constantly given orders by others they may have to adjust by viewing themselves in a self-disparaging way and even by feeling secretly ashamed of what they are. The problem of establishing freedom and dignity in low status work is a considerable one and the ways of meeting it may be seen in the measures which such employees use to get through a working day.

Perhaps the simplest expedient for getting through an unfulfilling day's work is for the individual to allow himself to be 'drawn along' by the technology which he is operating – what Baldamus (1961) calls 'traction'. Nevertheless the typical seven- or eight-hour shift represents a long period of time for the manual worker to pass in this way. For long periods of unchallenging work to be psychologically manageable, the experience has to be structured and broken down into manageable components. Donald Roy (1952) illustrates this type of structuring in his participant observation study of a group of machine operators who alleviated the monotony of their daily routine by creating games and rituals within the workgroup and by devising a series of work-breaks: coffee time, peach time, banana time, window time, and so on. An alternative strategy is for workers to devise ways of imposing their own pacing on even the most mechanically paced of jobs. On the car assembly line, for example, the individuals may work 'back up the line' to 'build a bank' (by completing operations before the car reaches their station on the line) and hence buy time for themselves (Walker and Guest 1952).

Joking and horseplay can play a major role in people's adjustment to work deprivation. Such activities may be seen as a way of simply taking 'leisure in work' (Brown *et al.* 1973) or as a way in which people attempt to 'cling to the remnants of joy in work' (Henri de Man, quoted by Roy 1952). However, joking behaviour can be seen as having functions in addition to these, as is suggested by the parallel which can be drawn between joking at work and certain behaviour patterns noted by anthropologists in other settings. The classic discussion of the so-called joking relationship in social life is that of Radcliffe-Brown (1965). He points out how playful antagonism and teasing may help individuals in a potentially conflictful situation to accommodate to each other thus enabling them to co-operate and interact successfully. Such relationships are typically seen to develop in families between new spouses and their various 'in-laws'. P. Bradney (1973) has shown how such relationships and associated humorous behaviour developed between sales assistants in a London department store. It was in the interest of each assistant to increase her own sales, something which put her in conflict with colleagues. To avoid hostility and strain, joking was regularly resorted to. For example, a new assistant seen to be working too hard and seriously was told by an old hand 'You want to sell up the shop today, don't you?' Bradney notes that this was said 'in a friendly joking manner even though it did conceal a reprimand'.

The type of joke described here can hardly be seen as riotously funny, and the humour indulged in by Roy's subjects (1952) in his 'banana time' article is funny only in its pathos, as we see in the case of one of their standard themes where one might be asked, 'how many times did you go poom-poom last night?' The perfunctory nature of much workplace communication is something that has been pointed out by Martin Meissner (1976), who draws a parallel between the hidden injuries endured by the worker and those experienced by many wives – both of whom are 'used as a resource', despite the fact that in each case the entry to the situation was formally a voluntary one. The fact that economic dependence makes it impossible to leave the relationship (even when partners are changed) at work or at home results in a form of communication which *depersonalises* the dilemma. In this way the 'obscene joking, ritual and desultory relationships at the workplace' function in the same way as does the 'perfunctory code' of marital conversation or nagging. In the same way that spouses tend to bicker with each other as a mere routine so people joke and indulge in horseplay at work – without a great deal of zeal or interest. Meissner sees workplace humour, it would seem, as very much an alienated form of activity in itself. Such a suggestion is clearly made when he claims that the kind of obscene joking frequently observed among female manual workers is participated in more 'as a matter of defence against male presumption and dominance than for fun'. If it is at all funny, it is only in a 'self-destructive sense'.

Whereas Meissner stresses the alienation in workplace informal activity, Paul Willis (1977) emphasises the ways in which manual workers 'thread through the dead experience of work a living culture which is far from a simple reflex of defeat'. He notes how in the shopfloor situation and in the classroom situation of boys destined for the shopfloor there is the same kind of informal groupings with the same counter-cultural 'complex of chauvinism, toughness and machismo'. He argues that 'the lads'' attempts to control their own routines and life spaces at school parallel their fathers' informal work control strategies. He also notes continuities between the attitudes to conformists and informers ('earoles' and 'grassers') in both situations as well as their common 'distinctive form of language and highly intimidating humour', where many of the verbal exchanges which occur are 'pisstakes', 'kiddings' or 'windups'. The way in which the working-class counter culture can be seen as a reaction to middle-class culture is illustrated by the fact that the shopfloor 'abounds with apocryphal stories about the idiocy of purely theoretical knowledge', an example being the story of the book enthusiast who sent away for a book which he has yet to read – it having arrived in a wooden box which he is unable to open!

Whether one chooses to see shopfloor humour and practical joking (which, as Willis notes, is, indeed often 'vigorous, sharp [and] sometimes cruel') as a manifestation of work alienation or as a creative reaction to it, it clearly contributes to group solidarity in various ways. In our earlier discussion of occupational socialisation and occupational cultures (p. 177) we noted how norms are developed which help protect the autonomy and self-respect of lower status workers. The strong emphasis on masculinity in many workgroup sub-cultures may help provide male employees with the kind of 'counter culture of dignity' (to borrow a phrase from Sennett and Cobb *op. cit.*) needed by males whose potency is symbolically threatened by their being 'under the thumb', so to speak, of employer and supervisor. Here, we may have a clue to the association which we noted earlier between industrial conflict and the rate of accidents. Although many accidents occur, as Nichols (1975) suggests, in the context of pressures from managements and workmates to keep production going, they may also result from the not unrelated willingness to disregard safety rules and to refuse to wear safety clothing on the part of employees who feel the need to appear 'tough' to compensate for the loss of dignity in their being employed and managed. Hanna Meara (1974), for instance, observed how the butchers whom she studied regarded as 'weak' those who insisted on wearing heavy clothing when working in the walk-in refrigerator.

The cursing and obscene language which typify many workplace subcultures are usefully seen in the context of the connection which exists between sexuality, potency and autonomy in contemporary western culture, but such language does not always exist in isolation from the technical component of work group life. Meissner (*op. cit.*) notes the double meanings of many words which are used in the workplace. His own research on the sign language used by workers in the very noisy setting of a sawmill illustrates this well. Meissner notes that the same sign is used for 'pin' as is used for 'fuck' whilst the rubbing together of index finger and thumb may alternatively signify a requirement to advance a log *a little bit* or stand as a reference to sexual intercourse (as in 'going home to get a little bit'). In this way the language and subcultural practices provide both a technically necessary form of communication and a way of breaking the routine of repetitive and demanding work. A great deal of work jargon fulfils this dual social and technical role. As Ned Polsky (1971) puts it in his discussion of poolroom hustlers, 'argots develop partly to provide a short-hand way of referring to technical processes but partly also as an elaboratively inventive, ritualistic, often rather playful way of reinforcing group identity or "we-feeling"'. Polsky also claims that nicknames or 'monickers' serve a primarily social function, adding 'colour' to the work. This is probably correct but the frequency with which, at least in English factories, people are given the most obvious nicknames (John Macpherson becoming Jock, Thomas Jenkins becoming Taffy and William Clarke becoming Nobby) reminds us again of Meissner's point about the routine or perfunctory nature of much workplace communication and suggests, once again, the pathos of much shopfloor humour.

The counter cultures which grow up in work settings do in part represent a challenge and an opposition to dominant interests and values, but in the end these cultures often enable the less privileged to adjust to their lack of freedom and privilege at work. To this extent they provide an integrative mechanism within work organisations. As was argued in the previous chapter, organisations are constituted by the interplay between official and unofficial practices of participants. Even those activities which are 'against the rules' or are illegal in the narrowest sense can often be seen as integral to the way work is organised rather than as aberrant and constituting an unambiguous threat to dominant interests.

If we look at the type of pilfering and fiddling which Gerald Mars (1973) observed among hotel waiters, it is clear that the money made – which is seen, as one waiter put it, as 'a part of wages' – is a form of theft from the employer. Yet we need to bear in mind that these losses by theft may constitute very reasonable 'costs' from the employers' point of view. This is not only because they enable wage rates to be kept low but also because they constitute a form of reward which is not conducive to official negotiation. Because of this, unionisation is unlikely. By maintaining what Mars argues is a particularly individualistic form of activity, the potential for collective organisation and opposition to managerial control is effectively reduced. Jason Ditton's (1977) participant study of bread salesmen also shows how illegal gains can become part of the implicit contract of the employee. Here it is the money 'fiddled' from customers which makes up the wage and Ditton (1974) interprets the way 'the firm's entry and training procedures are explicitly geared to teaching recruits how to rob the customer regularly and invisibly' as indicating how the fiddle helps solve certain managerial problems.

The officially deviant behaviour in the above cases is very much tied into the implicit contract between the *individual* and the employer. In other cases the illegal activity may be more clearly group-based as happens in the case of dockers (Mars 1974). Here the illegal activity and its control contributes to group solidarity, which may indeed contribute to its oppositional potential. Yet it is also likely, given the particular technology involved, to increase their technical efficiency, and hence the meeting of official goals. The social functions of illegal activity in the workplace have been strongly emphasised by Stuart Henry (1978), who argues that the general trading in pilfered goods which goes on in many workplaces and which constitutes a 'hidden economy' involves deals which 'often have less to do with the material worth of the goods and more to do with fulfilling the expectations and moral obligations of the friendly relationship'. To obtain for a colleague something which 'fell off the back of a lorry' is as much to 'do a favour' for that colleague as it is to make money, we might say.

One form of deviant behaviour with integrative functions which are less obvious than its purely oppositional functions is destructive physical sabotage. Taylor and Walton (1971) argue that such acts should not, however, be seen as meaningless. Their consideration of the meanings which such acts can have leads them to identify three types of physical sabotage: those which represent attempts to reduce tension and frustration (the ship builders who, about to be sacked on completion of a ship, got drunk and smashed the royal suite), those which result from attempts to facilitate or ease the work process ('tapping' nuts into place in aircraft assembly) and those which represent attempts to assert control (the 'collective bargaining by riot' indulged in by the Luddites).

Thus, even literally destructive behaviour can be seen as a part of the process whereby realities are negotiated, interests are defended, and the problems of 'getting through' the day at work are coped with. The most apparently senseless acts of vandalism have a rationale – a rationale which can only be appreciated as long as we note not only the conflicts but also the element of reciprocity between employer and employee expectations which develops in many 'low-trust' employment situations. This reciprocity is illustrated in a tape-recorded account given by a former shop steward in a car industry press shop. Men indulge in acts at work which they would never contemplate outside, it is explained:

> You don't give a fuck. . . . You were never made to feel responsible in any manner – so consequently I think that people tended to think that if we're going to be treated like children we'll fucking act like children. (quoted by Brown 1977).

To understand sociologically deviant behaviour at work, we clearly need to locate it in the social structure and culture of the setting in which it occurs. Earl Quinney (1963) makes this point when he shows how the level of prescription violations committed by retail pharmacists depends on the way the individual deals with a particular 'role conflict' built into the occupation: that between an orientation to professional values on the one hand and business values on the other. In effect, the extent to which those activities which are labelled 'deviant' are ultimately oppositional in society at large is questionable. Ditton (1977), for instance, argues that 'fiddling' shares many features with business and legitimate commerce itself and, suggests that, like selling, it epitomises the 'capitalist spirit'. In the jargon of the deviance theorists, much workplace deviance is sub-cultural rather than contra-cultural: it reflects dominant values and norms as much as or more than it opposes them.

Many of the manifestations of conflict at work which we have considered here occur among lower status workers. But, in many of these activities, supervisors and managers are necessarily implicated. Conflict and co-operation are two sides of the same coin and, at all levels, the breaking of official rules designed to help achieve official goals may, paradoxically, be necessary to meet these goals. In the previous chapter we saw how supervisors operate an 'indulgency pattern' whereby rule-breaking is connived at to achieve employee co-operation (p. 198) and we noted how, in Blau's study (1963), procedures were broken or modified, to get the job done (p. 201).

Writers who have used the insights of ethnomethodology in studying organisations have questioned the common assumption that rules *determine* behaviour. It is argued, instead, that individuals frequently use rules as *resources* or as means to be employed in dealing with whatever situations arise and have to be coped with. Thus, Bittner (1973) shows how the policeman operating on skid-row does not simply enforce the law – even when he invokes it. Instead he will 'merely use it as a resource to solve certain pressing practical problems in keeping the peace'. Zimmerman (1973) has shown how reception personnel in a public assistance organisation similarly *draw on* official rules and procedures to explain or justify the way they chose to cope with the situational exigencies of their jobs and Sudnow (1973) indicates something similar with regard to Public Defenders.

An important insight is gained by noting how people at work recognise what Zimmerman (*op. cit.*) calls 'the practicalities of rule use' in getting their job done. In such ways people cope with the conflicts and contradictions underlying the way work is organised. This is very effectively illustrated in Peter Manning's (1977) discussion of police work. The contradiction here is between the 'myth' of police work which sees it as controlling crime and the reality in which they maintain order (often without invoking the law) and help out people in trouble. In the end the street-based policeman has to be left with the relatively highly discretionary task of applying general rules to particular situations. Here the individual working policeman finds the source of his relative freedom from control by superiors. The 'fractional bargaining' indulged in by industrial supervisors (Kuhn 1961) and the condoning of prisoner rule-breaking by warders (Morris and Morris 1973) can be seen in a similar light.

Given the strong cultural value put upon independence, autonomy and self-expression, problems are as likely to arise for many of those in work which involves taking instructions from customers or clients as they are for people who take orders from bosses. The strategies used by prostitutes to maintain their self-respect in such situations were noted earlier (p. 173) and something similar can be seen across the range of service occupations. The more potentially demeaning the service given might be to the service worker, the more, I suggest, is there the tendency for contempt for the client to become an element of the particular work culture. Hence we get a variety of depersonalising titles used for the client: the mark, john, patsy, trick or punter. In all of these is an implication of naïveté on the part of the client and hence an implied superiority on the part of the worker, one which compensates for his or her superficial subservience.

Labelling of clients is not simply a mechanism used by service workers to maintain their self-respect in the face of implied servant status. The refining of the labelling process and the development of typologies of clients can play a useful technical role and help the individual cope with the exigencies of the job. The taxi-cab driver, for instance, finds that his livelihood depends on how accurately he can 'size up' the ability of potential customers to pay. Hence, as Fred Davis (1959) observes, he may utilise a typology of customers which ranges from the generously-tipping 'sport' through the 'blowhard', the 'businessman' and the 'live ones' to the 'stiffs' who give no tips and are passionately disliked. Correspondingly, Spradley and Mann (1975) describe the complex typology of customers used by cocktail waitresses (jocks, animals, regulars, bitches, annies, zoos, pigs, johnnies, etc.) and note how, in particular, the most potentially antagonistic relationship which exists within the bar, that between waitresses and female customers, is reflected in the way 'bitches' almost become a synonym for 'women'.

Every service occupation has its own types of 'awkward customer' and develops strategies to deal with them, whether it be the handing out of large quantities of low value coins in the change of the shop assistant's over-choosy customer, or the adoption of ludicrously jargon-ridden language by the car-mechanic dealing with a know-all motorist. Sanctions play an important role in the achieving of client control; an integral element of service work, as Joel Richman (1969) observes in noting how busmen tend to *train* their passengers into 'the correct attitude'.

The mobilisation of interests

The typical employee in an industrial capitalist society rarely has the capacity to defend himself or herself against attempts made by the employer to alter the balance of the implicit contract in the employer's favour – let alone improve the conditions of rewards of work, but a concerted challenge coupled with the threat of a general withdrawal of effort can create such a possibility. We therefore see a general tendency within the world of work for groups to form around common interests and for collective action to be taken to defend or further those interests.

The formation of groups or coalitions of interest is seen as a general and key social process in the theoretical scheme underlying this study. It is suggested that groups form and mobilise themselves when they perceive a common *objective* (or potential) interest which, as awareness of their common position increases, becomes a *subjective* or consciously recognised interest. In the discussion of occupational strategies and cultures in chapter 5 we saw how such mobilisation may occur around a common *occupational* interest and particular attention was paid to the professionalisation process. Here we are particularly concerned with situations where the common interest primarily arises, although not always exclusively, from the individuals' statuses as employees.

Groups of employees located at all levels tend to form groups to defend or further their interests. In addition to the tendency of groups to make claims to professional status, even when they are primarily administrators (Watson 1976), there are processes such as those whereby managers form themselves into defensive cliques or assertive cabals, depending on how they perceive their career interests within the organisation (see above p. 210). However, it is at the lower levels, where autonomy and discretion is lower, that defensive groups are most necessary. It is here that we have traditionally seen the strategy of unionisation.

Trade unions can be seen as necessary defensive mechanisms which developed among employees in industrialising societies as the typical employment relationship changed from the traditional one based on a *status contract*, a relatively diffuse master-servant relationship with an implication of longer term mutual commitment, to one based on a *purposive contract* where, as Fox (1974) puts it, 'the emphasis is on a transitory arrangement for limited and specific performances'. Given the low-trust type of economic exchange associated with this form of contract, collective defence of the employees' position becomes necessary. It would be wrong, however, to view the history of trade unionism simply in terms of necessary and inevitable reactions of a purely calculative kind. Trade unionism, particularly in Britain, has always been associated with the idea of a *labour movement*, something which has provided an ideology over and above the legitimation of sectional interests. Yet, on the other hand, we have to balance our recognition of this wider and often socialist ethos and initiative with a recognition of the point made by J. A. Banks (1974), that 'innovation in the social, as in the material world, takes its point of departure from the nature of the circumstances with which men have to cope'. To put this another way: to mobilise people to act collectively a fairly clear and direct link has to be established in their minds between the proposed action. And the specific circumstances of their lives which may be changed by that action, and the specific circumstances to which group leaders and spokesmen typically have to look are connected with the implicit contract with the employer. To appeal to generalised ideal interests in the absence of a clear link between these and specific local advantage is unlikely to be effective given the essentially calculative ethos of the industrial capitalist workplace. There is a basic contradiction characterising many trade unions which leads to a need to somehow combine an essentially capitalistic function – negotiating a price for labour – with socialist principles and ideals.

The *trade* unions, as their increasingly anachronistic name implies, have their origins among manual workers. With the growing rationalisation of work organisations and the spread of low-discretion direct-control work tasks among white-collar groups (see above p. 177) unionism has spread to groups higher and higher up the organisational and occupational hierarchy. As John Eldridge (1975) has observed, it is the increasing application of what Baldamus (1961) calls 'administrative instruments of effort intensification' on the part of employers that leads to a shift from status to performance criteria and hence the militancy of groups like teachers and doctors. Increasing stress on the cash nexus and the erosion of the 'moral obligations which are traditionally embedded in the idea of vocation' (Eldridge 1975) is reflected in the spread of what Goldthorpe and Lockwood (1969) term 'instrumental collectivism'.

As a result of these various changes the size of general trade union membership has increased. By the end of 1978 the total number of trade union members in Britain was 12,707,000, an increase of almost a quarter over the previous ten years (HMSO 1979). We need to treat trade union membership figures with care, noting the distinction made by Blackburn (1967) between a union's becoming *complete* (referring to the proportion of potential members who join) and its becoming *unionate*, that is becoming independent of employers, regarding collective bargaining and protection of members as its main function, being willing to use all forms of industrial action and affiliating itself to the Trades Union Congress and the Labour Party. Nevertheless we can reasonably interpret the behaviour of an increasing proportion of relatively high-status groups as reflecting a growing willingness to mobilise on a 'unionate' basis. There is a growing reluctance to trust the employer-sponsored staff association as a medium of representation.

The increasing use of traditionally working-class means of interest mobilisation cannot be seen as representing an unequivocal enthusiasm for solidaristic action among middle-class groups. Roberts *et al.* (1972), for instance, characterised the subjectively relatively-deprived and career-blocked technicians whom they studied as 'reluctant militants'. It is difficult to see such groups becoming *unambiguously* proletarianised, as the Carchedi analysis (pp. 161–3) suggests. There is a strong ambivalence in the attitudes of many trade union members, nowhere better illustrated than in the case of the police in Britain who, as Robert Reiner (1978) has shown, are pushed towards defensive trade unionism on the one hand yet, on the other hand, frequently find themselves coming into antagonism and conflict with organised labour in the course of their duties.

The spread of trade unionism is associated in Britain with a trend towards a decreasing number of trade unions of increasing size. The rationalising trend and growing concentration among employing organisations is reflected in similar trends among trade unions and the corresponding trend for rationalised co-ordination and planning at the national level has seen the Trades Union Congress increasingly representing the trade union membership as a whole at this level. However, initiatives taken by bodies on this scale and at this level are always in danger of becoming isolated from the needs of members in the workplace. This point brings our attention to a tension which has long existed within the trade union movement: that between the need for large-scale representation of members across a wide constituency and the need for the defence of interests of individuals and groups in specific domestic work settings.

It was in the face of a growing tension between the need for general and domestic representation which saw the growth of the first shop steward movement during World War I. This movement was motivated in part by radical and syndicalist ideals (Hinton 1973) but the more contemporary importance of the workplace representative (known in different settings as shop stewards, office representatives, fathers of chapel, corresponding members, for example) has a more pragmatic basis. The spread of payment-by-results schemes, the high demand for labour, the inappropriateness of the district (rather than plant-based) organisation of union branches, and the decline of employer associations all contributed to the tendency for the workplace itself to become the point at which the implicit contract was to be protected or improved. As Goodman and Whittington (1973) show, managements themselves contributed in great part to the growing importance of the shop steward. This is not only because of managerial deficiencies of procrastination and inconsistency of policy within and between plants but because of the value to a management of there being an individual to speak for a group of employees on day-to-day work control issues.

The importance of the shop steward to managements, and the dependence on management policy for the extent and form of their organisation (Brown *et al.* 1978) strongly contradicts the popular image of the shop steward as a rabble-rouser, troublemaker and general folk devil. The stereotyped 'I'm alright Jack' figure of the cinema and television comedy sketch functions as a kind of mythical proletarian scapegoat in certain quarters of British society where the assumed popularity of the 'everybody out' cry is claimed to be a root cause of industrial decline or stagnation. Few stereotypes have been so extensively contradicted by research evidence, however.

The most useful way to look at the role of the steward is to regard him as a group 'spokesman', in the sense of my theoretical scheme. This implies far more than his being a 'mouthpiece', however. It sees him playing the part of articulating the common *objective* interests of the group, thereby creating subjective interests and willingness to mobilise. As research has shown, this equally readily may mean encouraging members to desist from immediate and spontaneous action as it might the opposite (Donovan 1968, Cousins 1972). In fact, as Batstone *et al.* (1977) show, it is the 'leader' type of steward who is more successful than the 'populist'. His stronger links with other stewards and the respect which he obtains from the management not only enables the more effective defence of employee interests in the face of managerial control and the improvement in wages but also aids management by ensuring a greater predictability of shopfloor behaviour and fewer strikes.

The effectiveness of group mobilisation in the workplace cannot, however, be seen as entirely dependent on the leadership skills of shop stewards. The technology used in a particular situation and the skills of the workers associated with it clearly create important *conditions* which are relevant to the potential for mobilisation (Sayles 1958). To become aware of the range of relevant factors we may apply to workgroups the insights of the strategic contingency theory of organisational power discussed earlier (p. 212). Batstone *et al.* (1978) have taken such an approach and locate four 'sources' of power: the extent to which workers have skills which cannot easily be replaced; the extent to which the position occupied is crucial to the production process; the immediacy with which a group can disrupt the company; and, finally, the extent to which a group can create or cope with uncertainty in the production process.

The logic of the above analysis is one which reveals pressures which encourage groups to concentrate on sectional interests specific to themselves. Indeed the willingness of managements to act differently in the face of the different power potentials of groups of workers can be seen as consonant with their own interest in keeping a divided workforce (see Nichols and Armstrong 1976). Remaining divided along craft, skill, racial, sexual or any other lines can seriously weaken workforces faced with the increasing tendency towards concentration of capital and the expansion of multi-national corporations and conglomerates. As Brown and Terry (1978) point out, the threat this concentration poses for shop steward organisations is a profound one and explains the attention which is being turned towards *combine committees* in which 'stewards representing a number of workplaces in the same company come together, sometimes regularly, sometimes fitfully, to try to influence management at the more strategic company level, rather than the workplace level'.

To return to the level of the workplace itself, and bearing in mind the ways in which the capacity for effective mobilisation varies from situation to situation, we can observe a variety of different strategies followed by employees to protect their relative autonomy *vis à vis* management and generally to defend their implicit contract with the employer. These are job control strategies or, more pejoratively, restrictive practices. A particularly significant activity here, given the constant pressure on employers to rationalise their methods and improve their efficiency, is the tendency towards *resisting change*.

Resistance to change on the part of lower status employees is frequently regarded as a kind of neurotic behaviour or an irrational conservatism. In practice, it can be seen as highly rational. This only becomes clear once we recognise that any change in work organisation, payment scheme, technology or whatever, contains a potential threat to the implicit contract between employer and employee. Unless the employee can clearly see that there is not going to be a disparity in the favour of the employer (and a consequent loss to the employee), the safest thing to do is to resist that change. The charge of irrationality often arises, however, because managers tend to see resistance occurring to changes which they believe will benefit the employee as well as the employer. It is important to recognise that many changes of this kind are made, but it is equally important to recognise that in the low-trust atmosphere which characterises so much of contemporary industrial relations, it is most unlikely that employees will 'take the management's word for it'. When employees have any kind of countervailing power whatsoever they are likely to draw on it and insist on negotiating over any managerially-initiated change which may threaten their current implicit contract.

The argument here can be illustrated by a study which I did of a major organisational change in the engineering industry (Watson 1972). The management of the company designed and began to build a new factory into which it intended to move over a thousand employees. Planning and design was carried out without consulting the workforce and the official management position was that the change was a minor geographical one and that employee objections were unlikely, since the only implication for the workforce was an improvement in working conditions. But as awareness of the intended move increased so the resistance of the workforce to it grew. Complaints were made about the likelihood of increased bus fares to the new site, the threat to health involved in working in a windowless factory, the arrogance of management's deciding what was best for the workforce and the potential undermining of certain craft distinctions by the locating of the whole workforce under one roof. The issue which emerged as the main talking point and the item over which strike action was threatened was the management intention to encourage employees to use the newly purchased vending machines for tea and coffee by making illegal the 'mashing' of tea on the shopfloor.

The tea-making issue was initially regarded by the management as arising from shopfloor irrationality and, had a strike in fact occurred, one can well imagine, on the evidence of similar cases, how the press would have handled it! Yet the shopfloor perceived the management's intention to interfere with their established break-time practices as a very serious infringement of their autonomy. In my terms, the implicit contract was seriously threatened by the management's apparent intention to increase the sphere in which it exerted control over employee behaviour. As many employees explicitly stated, this was a matter of principle. Ultimately this issue was conceded by the company and a number of other fairly costly concessions had to be made in the course of negotiations before union co-operation with the introduction of changes was secured. The whole shopfloor strategy was based on a sensible, rational and wisely sceptical approach to defending the existing implicit contracts of employees. Yet to many observers, especially those within management, this essential rationality was far from clear.

One form of job control strategy which has received a great deal of attention over the years has been the practice of work-groups paid on an incentive scheme to restrict their output to a level which they find acceptable. F. W. Taylor called this 'systematic soldiering' (p. 37) and saw it as an abuse which scientific management would remove. The Human Relations investigators, noting such behaviour in the Bank Wiring Room, did not stress the rationality of the fixing of a norm of a 'fair day's work' and the defence of this norm by the sanctioning of 'ratebuster' and 'chiseller' behaviour (going above and below the norm, respectively) but interpreted the phenomenon in terms of an assumed social need and the necessary defence of a psychologically supportive group social system. More recent studies of the way incentive schemes are 'fiddled', especially those of Roy (1952, 1953, 1954) and Lupton (1963) have laid emphasis on the rationality behind them, however. Tom Lupton argued that the fiddles which he observed ('systematic manipulation of the incentive scheme') were an effective form of worker control over the job environment. The fiddle not only gives a measure of control over the relationship between effort and reward but protects the workers against the effects of management shortcomings, defends them against rate cutting and helps stabilise earnings. The widely followed practices of 'cross-booking' and 'banking' of work helps hide high bonuses when these are earned and enables workers to carry over and spread earnings.

An extensive range of practices in which employees retain control in the face of managerial prerogatives exist and are found in different forms in many industries and occupations. The limitation of entry to a job through an apprenticeship system, the control of promotion through a seniority rule, the insistence on certain manning levels and demarcation arrangements are just a few of these. Although such practices may severely reduce the efficiency of operating units, from a managerial viewpoint, it is important to recognise, as Alan Aldridge (1976) argues, that not only do managements frequently connive at and condone such institutions but may well at times see distinct advantages in their continuation.

To match the practices which attempt to maintain a continuous defence of or partial control over the implicit contract are a range of *sanctions* which can be applied when the underlying employer-employee conflict becomes such that a working parity is lost and has to be restored. The strike or complete withdrawal of labour is the basic sanction on which all possibilities of employee defence are necessarily and ultimately dependent. It is not, however, the strike itself which plays a major part in the actual conduct of industrial relations: it is the awareness on *both sides* of the ever present threat of the strike. Generally speaking, the strike is a sanction of the last resort and, as the detailed studies of strike behaviour like those of Batstone *et al.* (1978) and Lane and Roberts (1971) show, apparently spontaneous action is usually the outcome of some long standing grievance, or set of grievances. The study of the large strike at Pilkington's by the latter authors, for instance, shows how the strike which began with a company error in wage payment calculation was a culmination of a series of grievances – in this case with both the employer and the official trade union. To understand strikes it is always vital to distinguish between their *occasion* and their *underlying causes*.

Strikes play a significant part in the folk mythology of Britain's relatively poor economic performance. Their real significance becomes more difficult to see when Britain's strike record is compared with that of other countries. Between 1973 and 1977, for example, although nine countries lost fewer working days through strikes than Britain, another nine lost more, these including Canada, the United States, Australia, India and Italy (HMSO 1979). However, strike statistics must be interpreted with care, since wide variations exist both between nations and within them over what is defined as a strike, how its significance is quantified and – especially important – whether or not a given action is deemed worthy of recording or reporting as a strike. This is not to say that comparative studies cannot be made and studies like those of Geoffrey Ingham (1974) valuably link the level of strike occurrence to the national infrastructure. Ingham relates the lower level of strikes in Scandinavian countries to the greater possibility which is created for the formalised and centralised regulation of conflict by their greater degree of industrial concentration, their lesser degree of technical and organisational complexity and their greater degree of product specialisation. When we compare strike levels, we must remember that we are comparing the ways in which conflict manifests itself and not necessarily the degree of conflict as such.

Despite popular myths which see government welfare payments as encouraging strike behaviour, it is important to recognise that, as John Gennard (1978) establishes in the course of putting forward evidence which establishes the relative insignificance of such payments, there are considerable costs to both striker and trade union in the event of a strike. It is not surprising therefore that a range of other sanctions are used as alternatives to complete withdrawal of labour. These include the go-slow, the work to rule, the refusal to do overtime, the blocking of subcontracted work and the 'ca' canny'. Geoff Brown (1977) argues that much of this activity can be called *sabotage*, in what he claims is the correct meaning of this term, derived from expressions like *travailler comme un sabot* – to work slowly, clumsily and over-deliberately. The principle of reciprocating a poor level of reward with a poor quality of work performance is often traced back to strategies devised in the Glasgow docks in the late nineteenth century when, with an almost gleeful irony, union leaders were able to justify their actions on the basis of what they had read in economics textbooks, explaining that they were simply applying 'the common-sense commercial rule which provides a commodity in accordance with the price' (*ibid.*).

The variety of sanctions applied by employees in their workplaces is almost infinite, ranging from a refusal to speak to certain supervisors to, in one case reported to me, the maintaining of a high level of shrill whistling throughout the working day of a drawing office. A tactic which became widely publicised in the 1970s was the sit-in or the work-in. As John Greenwood (1977) argues, it is all too easy to exaggerate the significance of work-ins and to forget their small scale and limited objectives. Greenwood's review of such activities leads him to characterise these as a 'tactical response to a problem in hand', that of saving jobs, and concludes that they have 'nothing in principle and little in practice to do with attempts to establish workers' control or workers' management'.

Ultimately all the forms of activity which we have considered and which protect and further the interests of those involved at the lower levels in work organisations and occupations have to be related back to the basic social, economic and political structures in which they occur. The radical frame of reference which has been advocated here as most useful for the analysis of industrial conflict suggests that there are irresolvable contradictions existing between various aspects of these structures. Industrial capitalism is seen as unstable. This does not necessarily mean that it is ultimately doomed. These contradictions can be seen as creating the *dynamics* of industrial capitalist societies rather than the conditions of their destruction. The directions these dynamics may take and the involvement in them of government, employer, management, trade union and employee are the concern of the next and final chapter.

Chapter 8

Individual, work and society: choice and possibility

Introduction

Sociology studies the relationships which exist between people, the patterns of social organisation within which people live and the trends and contradictory tendencies which provide the ever shifting context of individuals' lives. The social patterns and the processes with which sociology concerns itself are both an outcome of the efforts of individuals and social groups and a constraint upon the projects which they pursue. If sociology can help people inform themselves about existing patterns and the possibilities and potential which exists for changing them, then it can be seen as a resource to enable human beings to more consciously and rationally control those social institutions and structures which can otherwise seem to control them. Yet sociology itself is a social product. It is part of the social world which it is intended to study. If it has any potential as an aid to the human control of the social world it is always in danger of becoming a resource to be used by particular interest groups to help in their attempted control of others. To the extent to which sociology has a relevance to human projects, then, it also has some basic ethical dilemmas to face. Whenever we ask what role it *can* have in society, we must also ask what role it *should* have.

A role for sociology

The view of sociology which has been taken in this book is one which saw it emerging as part of a particular human enterprise: the attempt by certain nineteenth and early twentieth-century social thinkers to draw on a broadly scientific mode of analysis in order to understand the social implications of a fast developing industrial capitalist form of social organisation in western societies. Such analyses, it was suggested, depended on the assumption that there are always a range of alternative ways in which human beings can arrange their social lives.

I have suggested that one characteristic which differentiates humans from other animals is a capacity to conceive of alternative modes of living. In accord with this, social thought was seen as part of an ongoing process whereby human beings seek some 'authentic' form of social living – some type of *community* in which their values can be fulfilled and their ideals achieved. Utopian conceptions play a part here, whether they be ones primarily informed by political thought, economic analysis or religious inspiration. But ideas about how people's lives might be arranged are not developed in some autonomous social zone staffed by free-floating and disinterested intellectuals and social thinkers. The dialectical process by which social change occurs, it has been argued throughout this book, involves a constant interplay of ideas and material interests. This fundamental theoretical insight is of great political significance because it invites us, when we engage in sociological analysis, to view sceptically all conceptions of the world which are put before us and all suggestions of how things might be. We must look critically at all blueprints for a better form of 'community' whether they be managerial proposals which claim to be 'participative', or trade union proposals which claim to be 'democratic' and we must question equally political and economic programmes which claim to meet human needs more effectively by increased use of market mechanisms and ones which claim to allow more readily the fulfilling of human potential by application of socialist principles. All these things involve conceptions of how the social world is and how it might be. So also, whether we like it or not, do the models and theories of social science.

For social science to be 'kept in its place' as a human resource to inform choice, it needs to remain subject or subservient to a wider democratic process of social thinking. Sociology, as with the other social sciences, can only ever be a *tool* to be used in the social and political decision-making process, but sociology, we must recognise, has the potential to become a tool available only to particular interest groups. If we wish to avoid this, and it is a basic desire of the present author, we need to consider just what part sociology is to play in society as a whole and, following from this, how it is to help in the decisions to be made about the future organisation of work institutions.

To simplify the discussion here I wish to suggest that there are three possible ways in which sociology might develop in society. These arguments apply to sociology generally and to its application to the work and industry sphere in particular. The three ways are, first, as a technocratic 'servant of power', second, as a privatised and purely academic pursuit and, third, as a resource to inform political thought and democratic decision-making.

In the first conception of the sociologist's role, the sociologist is employed as an expert to advise governments, employers or other interests. This is the type of role which Loren Baritz (1960) saw being taken up by many American industrial social scientists who became employees of corporations, 'doing what they were told to do and doing it well – and therefore endangering those other personal, group, class and institutional interests which were opposed to the further domination by the modern corporation of the mood and direction of American life'. Sociological knowledge and insight will inevitably have a relevance to practical problem-solving in large organisations and one would be naïve and indeed wrong to deny the right of any group to make use of that knowledge. What can be objected to, however, is the exclusive development of industrial sociology as a manipulative instrument for the pursuit of sectional interests.

The second possible role for sociology is quite distinct from the manipulative one of the previous conception. Here the products of sociological research and theorising become the exclusive concerns of the members of the academic occupation which produces them. I believe that there is a real danger of sociology becoming encapsulated in its own world of scholarly production, polemic and career rivalry, thereby reducing its potential for informing social action outside the academy (see Watson 1979). Arthur Brittan (1977) has written here of the danger of *privatisation* in which sociologists come to know the world only through their 'texts' and where texts, monographs and research reports tend to become substitutes for experience. In this way the opportunities are reduced for sociologists to say anything which is significant – or comprehensible – to participants in the world of 'everyday' concerns outside the academic sociology department.

The third approach, and the one favoured here, takes up the conception of the basic sociological enterprise referred to earlier: that in which a broadly scientific mode of analysis was devised at a particular point in history to try to understand the social implications of a developing industrial capitalist type of society. Having argued in previous chapters that the contemporary advanced societies are still both 'industrial' and 'capitalist', I would suggest that we can draw on and develop the ideas, concepts and theories of the founding theorists to gain insights into the problems and potentials of such a social order. Such a sociology, with its necessarily sophisticated methodologies and theoretical subtleties, is not something immediately accessible or reducible to simple laws and formulae which sociological writers can straightforwardly transmit to their readers. For this reason, and also because of one's desire for sociology not to be the sole preserve of the expert (whether 'privatised' or a 'servant of power'), I suggest that its most appropriate point of entry into the public sphere is by its wide dissemination through formal and informal *educational* institutions. In this way sociological thinking is seen as a general resource in whose development the individual is involved, as a student, and which is subsequently drawn upon in that individual's life in his or her political, work career, domestic and economic activities. This is not only to call for the teaching of sociology in both purely academic and more applied sectors of the education and training world but to look for the increased drawing on social science thinking and research in the various communications media. This would involve a move away from the kind of distortion currently seen in much media treatment of industrial relations activity, for instance (Glasgow University Media Group 1977, Beharrell and Philo, 1977). In the widest sense, we can say, sociology is to be used as something to inform political thought.

The conception of political thought being used here is one which concerns itself with both ends *and* means in a far more centrally value-oriented manner than can or should the social scientific analyses which I am arguing can feed or inform it. It is a conception not dissimilar from that proposed by Raymond Aron (1979), who suggests that political thought be seen as 'essentially an attempt to elucidate, from the study of societies, the goals one can aspire to and the means most likely to reach them'. This is not to imply that the sociological analysis which I am making the subsidiary activity here is a neutral, value-free or wholly objective activity, it is to accept the argument put forward earlier (p. 27) that a certain kind of objectivity can be striven for by the producers of sociological analyses revealing to their audiences, as far as is possible, the assumptions, methods and sentiments informing their work. It is, then, in the forum of democratic political debate that the choices to be made about government, economy, work practices, leisure facilities and all the rest are made. Analyses of current structures, trends, conflicts, contradictions and potentials inform this debate; a debate not just to be pursued in the arena of formal government politics but in the discussions of managers, trade unionists, professional groups, consumer organisations, etc. In a sense, the sociologist's business is, in the words of Tom Burns (1962), 'to conduct a critical debate . . . with the public about its equipment of social institutions'.

There is an *ideal* of democracy behind the present argument. It is an ideal which sees democracy as involving rational and *informed* choice. It is also an ideal to be aspired to rather than a currently easily realisable possibility because it implies some equality of access to education and academic sources which is at present far from the case. However, to reject the model being advocated because it hopes for too much would be to deny that such ideal states are useful indicators of a direction in which we might move rather than serving as ultimate destinations at which we can be confident of arriving.

I am suggesting that it is in the arena of informed and sociologically educated public debate that many of the choices which have emerged in the course of previous chapters should be discussed. Should economic growth continue to be a central goal of public policy? Do we wish work and leisure, workplace and home to remain largely separate spheres in our lives? Do we prefer a society of small work organis-ations or of large corporations? Do we believe that work organisations are better controlled by salaried agents of their owners or by those who work within them? Do we wish the occupational principle to develop to balance the administrative principle of work organisation? Do we wish to preserve current modes of rewarding work effort and do we wish to increase or reduce the differentials which exist between different job rewards? These are all basic questions about the future of work and industry and the list could be vastly extended. They are questions whose answers are dependent on fundamental *value* choices and decisions to be made about social *goals*.

The relevance of sociological analyses to questions like those suggested here is fourfold. First, it can inform us about the point from which we start; helping us understand the situation as it stands. For example, I would suggest that if we tried to answer these questions and looked for a way forward on the assumption that contemporary society is 'classless' – as some people do argue – or that there has been an effective separation of owning and controlling interests in the business sphere – as many argue – then our proceedings would be hampered from the start by sociological misconception. There is an important sociological role of initial clarification and assistance with social critique here, then.

Second, sociological analysis can indicate to us the costs and difficulties of pursuing particular goals. It might point to the considerable threats to social stability which might result from a decision to choose a no-growth economy, for instance. Third, and related to the second area, is the function of examining the compatibility of a number of goals which people might wish to pursue simultaneously. The compatibility of helping to reduce material poverty (at home and abroad) and, at the same time, redesigning work tasks to increase 'job satisfaction' might be examined, for instance. Fourth, sociology can inform decisions which might be made on the means to be used in the meeting of chosen goals. Existing sociological knowledge and understanding could guide us on the extent to which the appointment of worker directors might or might not increase employee identification with corporate policies or on the extent to which reduction of social security payments to strikers' families would or would not lower the general level of strike activity – to take as examples two fairly specific policy matters (see Brannen *et al.* 1976 and Gennard 1978).

The view of sociology put forward here to meet ends like these is not one of a straightforward body of knowledge to be consulted as required. As well as its findings and various substantive analyses, it offers to its 'consumers' various theoretical frameworks, models and concepts to be used in their own thinking and problem solving. The theoretical scheme developed in this book is offered as one possible apparatus. It draws on various strands of the sociological tradition which can assist in the purposes suggested here for sociology. The framework was, in fact, developed with such purposes in mind and, partly because of this, assumes a relatively open set of possibilities. This is in two respects: first in the fairly open conception of human nature (which stresses the extent to which man is what he makes of himself) and, second, in the stress on the importance of human agency, effort and interests in the process of social change (as opposed to any kind of abstract determining force).

Tensions, trends and possibilities

However open a view of history and human nature we try to take, sociology has, nevertheless, by its very nature, to pay close attention to the constraints and limitations on human choice and initiative, not least because one social group's freedom may be another group's lack of freedom and one group's advantage is inevitably dependent on another group's disadvantage. To deal with the interplay between initiative and constraint here much emphasis has been put upon concepts of power, conflict and contradiction. The trends which are discerned in history are seen in terms of the way certain groups pursue interests, are challenged by others, and find the means devised to meet their ends often functioning in a way which fails to meet or even subverts those ends. Thus, 1 have related the process of rationalisation in western societies to the efforts of certain social groups in a world of scarce and desired goods, and I have gone on to observe the range of ways in which this trend has involved consequences which have often been counterproductive or threatening to those interests.

The industrial, technical and bureaucratic developments which have taken place in industrial capitalist societies have been seen as having given social advantage to those whose prime initiatives brought them about whilst achieving continuing legitimacy of their relative advantage through the achievement of a general economic growth. This growth both allowed most social groups to improve their condition and enabled concessions to be made in political, educational and welfare spheres, but the paradox of consequences is always at work and contradictory tendencies work themselves through. Technological developments threaten employment levels and reduce for many the opportunities for intrinsic job satisfaction; bureaucratic and managerial methods of co-ordination undermine the employee commitment necessary for their success; the lack of clear principles underlying the distribution of rewards threatens social cohesion and exacerbates inflation in the economy, and many of the factors which motivate behaviour conducive to economic growth lose effectiveness. On top of all this are questions about major changes in the world economy which constrain every single nation in its policies and domestic programmes and there are problems of pollution and depletion of natural resources also constraining choices.

I suggest that sociological analysis can inform our understanding of existing trends and further possibilities, and future developments are dependent in part upon the extent to which such analyses are used. To give some indication of the issues which are on the agenda for discussion, I shall now very briefly sketch out a number of existing views of the future of industrial capitalist societies – these being a mixture of prognostications and prescriptions – and suggest that they are open to evaluation in light of values brought to bear in their examination and the insights, perspectives and information presented in the previous chapters of this book and in the literature of the sociology of work and industry generally.

In looking for some solution to the pathological tendencies which he saw in the industrialising world, Emile Durkheim (1933) suggested the possibility of occupational associations providing regulative and integrative institutions to mediate between individuals and society as a whole. Various contemporary writers have followed in this tradition and have seen a tendency towards professionalisation of occupations in this light. An example of this kind of view is seen in the work of Paul Halmos (1970), who wrote of a trend towards a 'personal service society', one characterised by a new social ethic said to be more altruistic and humane than that of traditional capitalist society and which has been encouraged by the influence of social science thinking and the ideals of tender-minded professionalism. My own empirical study of one of the occupations which Halmos looks at questions the validity of this argument (1977a, 1977b), but fully to evaluate it one would need to look at the thesis in the light of the overall argument presented here in earlier chapters whereby the administrative (or formal organisational) principle is seen as currently dominant (p. 183), with the criteria for work design and organisation deriving from capitalist priorities (p. 193) and with opportunities for relative occupational autonomy being dependent on the relevance (and unsubstitutability) of any given area of expertise in terms of these priorities (pp. 166–7). In looking at the possible costs of moving to an occupational basis for work organisation – were it feasible – we would need to take into account the argument that the current enthusiasm for 'professional' groupings within British management has been closely associated with the low status attached to work closely involved with manufacturing itself – with a consequent deleterious effect on relative productive performance (Mant 1977, Fores and Glover 1978).

Durkheim not only looked to occupational associations for possibilities of improved social solidarity in an increasingly calculative and market-oriented society. He also saw a role for the state in providing regulation. A growing role for the state has indeed been a trend and can be interpreted as one of the necessary ways in which certain of the contradictions of an industrial capitalist society have been managed. One image of the future which emphasises the state role and sees it working alongside other large formal organisations is that of a developing 'corporate state'. The type of society envisaged here is perhaps close to that which Max Weber feared when he recognised that the rationalising trend of western societies could come to threaten individual liberties, initiatives and opportunities for self-expression. The corporate state is the liberal nightmare. In the kind of corporatism envisaged by writers like Pahl and Winkler (1974b, see also Winkler, 1976, 1977) there is a managed economy replacing the play of free market forces and, as Krishan Kumar (1978) puts it, 'firms and organisations, including trade-union organisations, are "co-opted" or "incorporated" into a unified system supervised on behalf of the community by the state'. To evaluate the significance of this trend and indeed the desirability of its continuation one would need, among other things, to look at the British experience of incomes policies and social contracts with trade unions and note the difficulty which has occurred in the state's attempts to control and the economic behaviour of particular employing companies trade unions' *memberships*. To analyse the issue here it would be helpful to choose between the rival plural and radical models of industrial relations activity set out in chapter 7. The trend towards significant state involvement can be interpreted as a trend towards pluralism or, alternatively, as Colin Crouch (1977) has argued, as a developing type of *domination* in which we can see a 'bargained corporatism', a kind of 'half-way house between outright corporatism and liberal collectivism'.

A future society too dependent on centralised management by either state or public and private corporations would still be likely to face problems of challenge and of achieving only grudging compliance from individuals and groups dissatisfied with the kind of autonomy, intrinsic reward and opportunity for self-expression and individuality which the culture of western societies has, in its typically contradictory manner (p. 103), set up as desirable. Certain thinkers – economists and politicians rather than sociologists predominantly – have seen these, among other goals, being more readily achieved in a society in which the market mechanism is given a greater part to play. Among the variety of problems which arise here is the questionable virtue of relying on free market mechanisms and competition as an economic motivator in a societal form in which those running large and often monopolistic corporations tend to follow a logic of rationalising and attempting to reduce uncertainty (p. 200). In addition to this we would need to raise questions here about how a market economy could cope with the employment implications of currently developing technologies which utilise microprocessors and which may transform many labour intensive areas of employment (on the logic of a capitalist economy whereby technology is generally used whenever it is cheaper than human labour, p. 137).

Yet another alternative future which is envisaged is that in which there is an increasing emphasis on and development of small-scale work enterprises (Schumacher 1973) and the use of simpler so-called 'alternative technologies' (Dickson 1974). One of the main questions that the sociologist, looking at the societal aspects of such a trend, would tend to ask here would be that about the implications of a possible departure from a policy of economic growth implied in this type of image, and the implications for social and political stability in a type of society which, I suggested earlier, has been so dependent in the past for the legitimacy of its institutions and distribution of resources on a growing economy (p. 99).

New values and motivations would be necessary conditions or inevitable consequences of many of the various alternative forms of community considered here. One type of proposal which, in a wide range of different forms, looks towards changes in values, commitments and rewards in the workplace (and consequently outside it) is that for a move towards greater industrial democracy.

It is becoming widely argued that some new ways of involving people in their work will have to be found. David Jenkins (1974), in an international survey of developing forms of 'democratic' work organisation, writes of it as an idea whose 'time has come', arguing that 'neither employees nor work organisations can stand the counterproductive management practices that have come to be accepted as necessary and unavoidable'. The legitimacy of managerial authority is slowly eroding and being increasingly met with both formal challenge and the more typical grudging mode of compliance, as traditional criteria of social superiority become less reliable and as the technical necessity of existing and growing organisational hierarchies becomes less arguable (see pp. 202–3). However, the types of solution offered to these problems differ widely.

We can usefully follow Brannen *et al.* (1976) here and note three basic approaches to increased 'participation'. These authors describe three philosophies of participation and these correspond to the three approaches to industrial conflict discussed in our previous chapter – once again indicating the important connection which exists between the theoretical framework which is used and the possibilities for change which are envisaged. Within a unitary philosophy can be included all those attempts discussed in chapter 6 (p. 227) to reorganise work on lines whereby increased scope is provided for the satisfaction of worker needs at the same time as the efficiency of the enterprise is better catered for. Especially important here are the attempts to modify organisations on the socio-technical lines advocated by the Tavistock Institute (see Brown 1967, Davis and Taylor 1972, and Davis and Cherns 1975). A more pluralist philosophy of participation, however, is that associated with Hugh Clegg, in which trade unions sufficiently strong to oppose managements are accepted by managements as a loyal opposition with whom they are willing to compromise and come to terms in the interests of harmony and unity (see Clegg 1960 and, for discussion and critique, Blumberg 1968 and Poole 1978).

If a more radical view of social and work relations is taken we tend to find it associated with arguments for 'worker control', 'self management' and 'worker co-operatives'. The proposals here may be 'gradualist', as with the ideas of the Institute for Workers' Control (see Coates and Topham 1970, for example), or they may be revolutionary. Richard Hyman (1974), for instance, questions the validity of attempting to reject current structures of domination without attending 'systematically to the need to transcend capitalism *as a system*'. The development of worker co-operatives within an essentially capitalist framework is another possibility, whether these are seen as growing and flourishing within a continuing capitalist context or as eventually transcending it.

Some important necessary conditions for the success of co-operatives have been usefully set out by Robert Oakeshott on the basis of personal experience in Britain and observation of co-operatives abroad (especially the flourishing ones in the Mondragon area of Spain). Here we see an example of how social investigation can give us guidance on what means are necessary for the pursuit of certain goals. Oakeshott (1978) argues for the necessity of the initial thrust for the enterprise coming from the potential workforce itself; for the securing of further commitment by the requirement of a significant capital stake; for the use of a management team whose expertise is at least as good as that available to conventional enterprises and, finally, for a materially supportive surrounding. Enterprises of this kind can be looked at as developing a kind of participative capitalism or as a way of achieving many of the ideals of socialism – without accepting the centralised control of a command economy. Alan Fox (1978), for instance, has discussed the possibility of a 'system of self-managed enterprises within a market economy duly structured and "corrected" by government action' developing as an extension of the 'grass-roots democracy and group self-determination' currently found in shop-floor worker organisation and as a defence against the current 'drift towards corporatist domination'.

Throughout discussions of alternative future social forms, in imaginative literature as well as in sociological and political thought, we tend to see a tension between recognition of the advantage of large-scale units of organisation and recognition of the human costs — social and psychological – of living and working in a world of large corporations and bureaucratic structures. It is often felt that it is only when individuals are integrated into relatively small units that democratic participation becomes a possibility and psychologically satisfying social involvement is facilitated. There is a long tradition of believing that the 'authentic' human community is a kind of family 'writ large'. An interesting question to ask here is whether it would be possible for a society to be developed in which the advantages of large-scale production were combined with the benefits of widespread involvement in smaller enterprises and associations. Interesting suggestions along these lines have been made by Jonathan Gershuny (1978) in the course of a critique of theories of post-industrialism. Before considering this economist's own suggestions for a future type of economic organisation it is worth looking at his analysis of current trends.

Gershuny is strongly critical of some of the central assertions made by post-industrial theorists like Daniel Bell (see above pp. 154–5). He particularly questions the assertion that a move from secondary sector employment (manufacturing) to tertiary sector employment (services) indicates a basic move from an interest in goods to an interest in services in the consumption sphere. Much of the apparent increase in service employment (increases in numbers of managers, technologists and other professionals) is, in fact, associated with an increase in activities aimed at improving the efficiency of systems of material production. This is not to say that people are not looking for increased services, however. Gershuny's essential argument is that service requirements will be met by *increased production by manufacturing industry*. For example, we do not take washing to a laundry, so creating laundry service employment, but purchase washing machines, thus putting demand on the manufacturing sector. What we have is a developing *self-service economy*, and technological developments may be such that those service occupations proper whose increased numbers have been part of the growth of the tertiary employment sector – education and health occupations – may in the future begin to be replaced by technically supplied services used more directly by the consumer (televised and videotaped educational services, for example).

With the increasing possibilities of automation in the manufacturing sphere it is possible to imagine a future self-service economy in which, as Gershuny puts it,

> an educated élite minority is employed in intrinsically rewarding
> technical tasks connected with the process of material production,
> and the majority is employed only in the undemanding
> manipulation of automated machinery for the satisfaction of their
> own needs, perhaps materially well provided for, but starved of
> rewarding occupation.

In this scenario, the majority of people are 'mere machines for consumption' – a situation reminiscent of the one in Kurt Vonnegut's novel *Player Piano*. According to taste, we have here an image of either Utopia or nightmare. Among other doubts about whether it would work, we would need to raise questions about the strain which such a situation would put upon the home and the family in what would be an essentially 'privatised' existence for the majority (see above p. 109).

Rather than resisting the trend towards a self-service economy by short term and meliorative subsidy of underemployment in manufacturing industry or by subsidising further employment in the tertiary sector, Gershuny suggests that we go along with the trend and develop a *dual economy*. Economic efficiency would continue to be pursued in the *formal* sector of the economy whilst those not needing or wanting to work in this sector would operate in a *informal sector* where recreation, education, housework and other production activities are pursued, making use of materials and productive capital produced in the formal sector. In this way we would see, not the move from the economic to the social sphere of life, as Bell envisages, but a 'closer harmonisation of the social and economic realms'.

The type of possible future set out above is one which would have to be *chosen* and is one which would require a fundamental reconsideration of the place of work, employment and leisure in our system of values (see Anthony 1977). The economic growth envisaged in the model would make it possible for inequalities of the type currently existing to survive – with modifications. It might not be necessary to remove them in any essential way. Whether this were to happen or, instead, socialist and egalitarian principles were to be adopted would be a matter for the informed kind of political debate called for earlier.

The envisaged future at which we have just looked is just one illustration of the way thinking informed by social science might help in the making of social choices. Whatever kind of future comes about, whether by design or by muddling through, it will be subject to paradoxical and unintended consequences in the social sphere. Tensions, conflicts and contradictions will be present in any social order which is not totally monolithic, totalitarian and capable of excising all human individuality, variety, and interest in conceiving of social alternatives.

Sociological dreams and everyday practice

Much of the discussion in this final chapter is at a rather grandiose level: more to do with dreams than practical realities it might be said. It is also fragmentary and inconclusive. The inconclusive nature of these reflections on the future of industrial capitalist societies is inevitable given the view of sociology which I have taken. The future is in the hands of the potential consumers of sociology – whether they choose or do not choose to utilise sociological thinking and evidence in making whatever choices are possible.

There is a danger in all this of implying that sociology's only relevance is to reflection on the futures of whole societies and to grand political, economic and social designs, but this is not my intention. If political thought, as I suggested earlier, is basically to do with reflection on the goals which can be aspired to and the means by which they can be reached, then it is as applicable to issues at the level of job and organisational design, occupational and workplace strategy, bargaining processes and a whole range of other everyday issues in the sphere of work and industry as it is to informing large-scale social change.

I believe that the study of the sociology of work and industry is relevant to the lives of individuals not just as citizens of societies but as workers, managers, producers, consumers, organisers, negotiators and proprietors. Despite the seeming complexity of much of sociology's conceptual apparatus and the need to recognise the ethical and methodological limitations of its scope, I believe that it does have a relevance for practitioners.

Sociologists are, however, in continual need of being challenged not to confine their activities to the stratosphere of pure theory or to an exclusive concern with whatever millennium is to their own taste. Paul Willis (1977) points out that practitioners continually face the problem of 'Monday morning'. Too much concern with the millennium can leave us with nothing to say about what can be done on Monday morning. If this happens, 'everything is yielded to a purist structuralist immobilising reductionist tautology: nothing can be done until the basic structures of society are changed but the structures prevent us making any changes'.

Many of the concepts, insights and findings reported and developed in this book can be helpful to the individual in his or her everyday life, it is claimed. What characterises all of this knowledge and all of these ideas, as they have been presented, as *sociological* is that they have all been related back to the way society as a whole is organised. It is here that sociology offers its most valuable and essential insight. This is the insight that no social action, at however mundane a level, is without its implications for the wider social structures and processes of the society of which it is a part. These structures and processes, with all their related inequalities and power distributions, are seen as the source of both constraints and opportunities which individuals meet in conducting their lives. The better and more widely these structures and processes are understood and the better the connections between specific actions and arrangements and these basic structures and processes are appreciated, then the greater is the opportunity for the achievement of democratic control over work, industry and every other kind of social institution.

Bibliography

Abell, P. (1975), *Organisations as Bargaining and Influence Systems*, London: Heinemann.

Aberle, D. F. and Naegele, K. D. (1961), 'Middle-class fathers' occupational role and attitudes towards children' in N. W. Bell and E. F. Vogel (eds), *A Modern Introduction to the Family*, London: Routledge & Kegan Paul.

Abrams, P. (ed.) (1978), *Work, Urbanism and Inequality*, London: Weidenfeld & Nicolson.

Albrow, M. (1968), 'The study of organisations: objectivity or bias?' in J. Gould (ed.), *Penguin Social Sciences Survey*, Harmondsworth: Penguin.

Albrow, M. (1970), *Bureaucracy*, London: Macmillan.

Aldrich, H. E. (1972), 'Technology and organisational structure', *Administrative Science Quarterly*, vol. 17.

Aldridge, A. (1976), *Power, Authority and Restrictive Practices*, Oxford: Blackwell.

Allen, V. L. (1971), *The Sociology of Industrial Relations*, London: Longman.

Anderson, C. H. (1974), *The Political Economy of Social Class*, Englewood Cliffs, NJ: Prentice-Hall.

Anthony, P. D. (1977), *The Ideology of Work*, London: Tavistock.

Argyris, C. (1964), *Integrating the Individual and the Organisation*, New York: Wiley.

Argyris, C. (1972), *The Applicability of Organisational Sociology*, Cambridge University Press.

Argyris, C. (1973), 'Personality and organisation theory revisited', *Administrative Science Quarterly*, vol. 18.

Aron, R. (1967), *Eighteen Lectures on Industrial Society*, London: Weidenfeld & Nicolson.

Aron, R. (1979), *Politics and History: Selected Essays*, London: Collier-Macmillan.

Ashton, D. N. and Field, D. (1976), *Young Workers from School to Work*, London: Heinemann.

Baechler, J. (1975), *The Origins of Capitalism*, Oxford: Blackwell.

Bain, G. S. (1970), *The Growth of White Collar Unionism*, Oxford: Clarendon Press.

Bain, G. S., Coates, D. and Ellis, V. (1973), *Social Stratification and Trade Unionism*, London: Heinemann.

Baldamus, W. (1951), 'Types of work and motivation', *British Journal of Sociology*, vol. 2.

Baldamus, W. (1961), *Efficiency and Effort*, London: Tavistock.

Banks, J. A. (1970), *Marxist Sociology in Action*, London: Faber.

Banks, J. A. (1974), *Trade Unionism*, London: Collier-Macmillan.

Banks, O. (1976), *The Sociology of Education*, London: Batsford.

Baritz, L. (1960), *The Servants of Power*, New York: Wiley.

Barker, D. L. and Allen, S. (eds) (1976), *Dependence and Exploitation in Work and Marriage*, London: Longman.

Barnard, C. I. (1956), *The Functions of the Executive*, Harvard University Press.

Barron, R. D. and Norris, G. M. (1976), 'Sexual divisions and the dual labour market', in Barker and Allen (eds) (1976).

Batstone, E., Boraston, I. and Frenkel, S. (1977), *Shop Stewards in Action*, Oxford: Blackwell.

Batstone, E., Boraston, I. and Frenkel, S. (1978), *The Social Organisation of Strikes*, Oxford: Blackwell.

Batstone, E. and Davies, P. L. (1976), *Industrial Democracy, the European Experience*, London: HMSO.

Bechhofer, F. (1973), 'The relation between technology and shop-floor behaviour', in Edge and Wolfe (eds), *Meaning and Control*, London: Tavistock.

Bechhofer, F., Elliot, B., Rushworth, M. and Bland, R. (1974), 'The petits bourgeois in the class structure', in Parkin (ed.) (1974).

Becker, H. S. (1952), 'The career of the Chicago public school teacher', *American Journal of Sociology*, vol. 57.

Becker, H. S. (1960), 'Notes on the concept of commitment', *American Journal of Sociology*, vol. 66.

Becker, H. S. (1971), 'The nature of a profession' in *Sociological Work: Method and Substance*, London: Allen Lane.

Becker, H. S. and Carper, J. (1956), 'The elements of identification with an occupation', *American Sociological Review*, vol. 21.

Becker, H. S. and Geer, B. (1958), 'The fate of idealism in a medical school', *American Sociological Review*, vol. 23.

Becker, H. S., Geer, B., Hughes, E. C. and Strauss, A. L. (1961), *Boys in White*, University of Chicago Press.

Becker, H. S., Geer, B., Reisman, D. and Weiss, R. (eds) (1968), *Institutions and the Person*, Chicago: Aldine.

Beharrell, P. and Philo, G. (eds) (1977), *Trade Unions and the Media*, London: Macmillan.

Behrend, H. (1957), 'The Effort Bargain', *International Labor Relations Review*, vol. 10.

Bell, D. (1974), *The Coming of Post-Industrial Society*, London: Heinemann.

Bell, D. (1976), *The Cultural Contradictions of Capitalism*, London: Heinemann.

Bendix, R. (1963), *Work and Authority in Industry*, New York: Harper & Row.

Bendix, R. (1965), 'Max Weber's sociology today', *International Social Science Journal*, vol. 17.

Bensman, J. and Lilienfeld, R. (1973), *Craft Consciousness*, New York: Wiley.

Berger, P. L. (ed.) (1964), *The Human Shape of Work*, New York: Macmillan.

Berger, P. L. (1966), *Invitation to Sociology*, Harmondsworth: Penguin.

Berger, P. L. (1973), *The Social Reality of Religions*, Harmondsworth: Penguin.

Berger, P. L. and Luckmann, T. (1971), *The Social Construction of Reality*, Harmondsworth: Penguin.

Beynon, H. (1973), *Working for Ford*, Harmondsworth: Penguin.

Beynon, H. (1978), 'The real reason why Leyland axed Speke', *New Society*, 7 September.

Beynon, H. and Blackburn, R. M. (1972), *Perceptions of Work*, Cambridge University Press.

Bittner, E. (1973), 'The police on skid-row' in Salaman and Thompson (eds) (1973).

Blackburn, R. M. (1967), *Union Character and Social Class*, London: Batsford.

Blau, P. M. (1963), *The Dynamics of Bureaucracy*, University of Chicago Press.

Blau, P. M. (1974), *On the Nature of Organisations*, New York: Wiley.

Blau, P. M. (ed.) (1976), *Approaches to the Study of Social Structure*, London: Open Books.

Blau, P. M. and Duncan, O. D. (1967), *The American Occupational Structure*, New York: Wiley.

Blau, P. M. and Scott, W. R. (1963), *Formal Organisations*, London: Routledge & Kegan Paul.

Blau, P. M. and Schoenherr, A. (1971), *The Structure of Organisations*, New York: Basic Books.

Blauner, R. (1960), 'Work satisfaction and industrial trends' in W. Galenson and S. H. Lipset (eds), *Labor and Trade Unions*, New York: Wiley.

Blauner, R. (1964), *Alienation and Freedom*, Chicago University Press.

Blum, F. H. (1968), *Work and Community*, London: Routledge & Kegan Paul.

Blumberg, P. (1968), *Industrial Democracy: the sociology of participation*, London: Constable.

Boraston, I., Clegg, H. and Rimmer, M. (1975), *Workplace and Union*, London: Heinemann.

Bottomore, T. and Nisbet, R. (eds) (1979), *A History of Sociological Analysis*, London: Heinemann.

Bourdieu, P. and Boltanski, L. (1978), 'Changes in social structure and changes in the demand for education' in Giner and Archer (eds) (1978).

Bourdieu, P. and Passeron, C. J. (1977), *Reproduction in Education, Society and Culture*, London: Sage.

Bowen, P. (1976), *Social Control in Industrial Organisations*, London: Routledge & Kegan Paul.

Bowey, A. (1976), *The Sociology of Organisations*, London: Hodder & Stoughton.

Bowles, S. and Gintis, H. (1976), *Schooling in Capitalist America*, London: Routledge & Kegan Paul.

Boyd, D. (1973), *Elites and their Education*, London: National Foundation for Educational Research.

Bradney, P. (1973), 'The Joking Relationship in Industry' in D. Weir (ed.) (1973).

Brannen, P. (ed.) (1975), *Entering the World of Work*, London: HMSO.

Brannen, P., Batstone, E., Fatchett, D. and White, P. (1976), *The Worker Directors*, London: Hutchinson.

Braude, L. (1975), *Work and Workers*, New York: Praeger.

Braverman, H. (1974), *Labor and Monopoly Capital*, New York: Monthly Review Press.

Brittan, A. (1977), *The Privatised World*, London: Routledge & Kegan Paul.

Brown, D. and Harrison, M. J. (1978), *A Sociology of Industrialisation*, London: Macmillan.

Brown, G. (1977), *Sabotage*, Nottingham: Spokesman Books.

Brown, R. K. (1967), 'Research and consultancy in industrial enterprises', *Sociology*, vol. 1.

Brown, R. K. (1974), 'The attitudes to work, expectations and social perspectives of shipbuilding apprentices' in T. Leggatt (ed.), *Sociological Theory and Survey Research*, London: Sage.

Brown, R. K. (1976), 'Women as employees: some comments on research in industrial sociology' in Barker and Allen (eds) (1976).

Brown, R. K. (1978a), 'Work', in Abrams (ed.) (1978).

Brown, R. K. (1978b), 'From Donovan to where? Interpretations of industrial relations in Britain since 1968', *British Journal of Sociology*, vol. 29.

Brown, R. K. and Brannen, P. (1970), 'Social relations and social perspectives amongst shipbuilding workers', *Sociology*, vol. 4.

Brown, R. K., Brannen, P., Cousins, J. and Samphier, M. (1973), 'Leisure in work' in Smith *et al.* (eds) (1977).

Brown, W. (1973), *Piecework Bargaining*, London: Heinemann.

Brown, W., Ebsworth, R. and Terry, M. (1978), 'Factors shaping shop steward organisation in Britain', *British Journal of Industrial Relations*, vol. 16.

Brown, W. and Terry, M. (1978), 'The future of collective bargaining', *New Society*, 23 March.

Bryan, J. H. (1965), 'Apprenticeships in prostitution', *Social Problems*, vol. 12.

Bryant, C. G. A. (1976), *Sociology in Action*, London: Allen & Unwin.

Bulmer, M. (ed.) (1975), *Working Class Images of Society*, London: Routledge & Kegan Paul.

Burnham, J. (1945), *The Managerial Revolution*, Harmondsworth: Penguin.

Burns, T. (1955), 'The reference of conduct in small groups', *Human Relations*, vol. 8.

Burns, T. (1961), 'Micropolitics', *Administrative Science Quarterly*, vol. 6.

Burns, T. (1962), 'The sociology of industry' in Welford *et al.* (eds), *Society: Problems and Methods of Study*, London: Routledge & Kegan Paul.

Burns, T. (ed.) (1969), *Industrial Man*, Harmondsworth: Penguin.

Burns, T. (1977), *The BBC: Public Institution and Private World*, London: Macmillan.

Burns, T. and Stalker, G. M. (1961), *The Management of Innovation*, London: Pergamon.

Burrow, J. W. (1966), *Evolution and Society*, Cambridge University Press.

Campanis, P. (1970), 'Normlessness in management' in J. Douglas (ed.), *Deviance and Respectability*, New York: Basic Books.

Cannon, I. C. (1967), 'Ideology and occupational community', *Sociology*, vol. 1.

Caplow, T. (1954), *The Sociology of Work*, New York: McGraw Hill.

Carchedi, G. (1975), 'On the economic identification of the new middle class', *Economy and Society*, vol. 4.

Carey, A. (1967), 'The Hawthorne Studies: a radical criticism', *American Sociological Review*, vol. 32.

Carter, M. P. (1966), *Into Work*, Harmondsworth: Penguin.

Cherns, A. B. (1979), *Using the Social Sciences*, London: Routledge & Kegan Paul.

Child, J. (1969a), *British Management Thought*, London: Allen & Unwin.

Child, J. (1969b), *The Business Enterprise in Modern Industrial Society*, London: Collier-Macmillan.

Child, J. (1970), 'More myths of management organisation', *Journal of Management Studies*, vol. 7.

Child, J. (1972), 'Organisational structure, environment and performance', *Sociology*, vol. 6.

Child, J. (ed.) (1973), *Man and Organisation*, London: Allen & Unwin.

Child, J. (1975), 'The industrial supervisor' in Esland *et al.* (eds) (1975).

Child, J. (1977), *Organisation: a guide to problem and practice*, London: Harper.

Child, J. and Macmillan, B. (1973), 'Managers and their leisure' in Smith *et al.* (eds) (1977).

Chinoy, E. (1955), *Automobile Workers and the American Dream*, New York: Doubleday.

Clark, P. A. (1972), *Action Research and Organisational Change*, London: Harper.

Clarke, D. G. (1966), *The Industrial Manager*, London: Business Publications.

Clarke, R. O., Fatchett, D. J. and Roberts, B. C. (1972), *Workers' Participation in Management in Britain*, London: Heinemann.

Clarke, T. and Clements, L. (eds) (1977), *Trade Unions under Capitalism*, London: Fontana.

Clegg, H. A. (1960), *A New Approach to Industrial Democracy*, Oxford: Blackwell.

Clegg, H. A. (1976), *The System of Industrial Relations in Great Britain*, Oxford: Blackwell.

Clegg, S. R. (1975), *Power, Rule and Domination*, London: Routledge & Kegan Paul.

Clegg, S. R. (1979), *The Theory of Power and Organisations*, London: Routledge & Kegan Paul.

Clegg, S. R. and Dunkerley, D. (eds) (1977), *Critical Issues in Organisations*, London: Routledge & Kegan Paul.

Clements, R. V. (1958), *Managers: a study of their careers in industry*, London: Allen & Unwin.

Coates, C. H. and Pellegrin, R. J. (1962), 'Executives and supervisors' in B. H. Stoodley (ed.), *Society and Self*, New York: Free Press.

Coates, K. and Topham, T. (eds) (1970), *Workers' Control*, London: Panther.

Cotgrove, S. and Box, S. (1970), *Science, Industry and Society*, London: Allen & Unwin.

Cotgrove, S., Dunham, J. and Vamplew, C. (1971), *The Nylon Spinners*, London: Allen & Unwin.

Cousins, J. M. (1972), 'The non-militant shop steward', *New Society*, 3 February.

Crompton, R. (1976), 'Approaches to the study of white collar unionism', *Sociology*, vol. 10.

Crompton, R. and Gubbay, J. (1977), *Economy and Class Structure*, London: Macmillan.

Crouch, C. (1977), *Class Conflict and the Industrial Relations Crisis*, London: Heinemann.

Crozier, M. (1964), *The Bureaucratic Phenomenon*, London: Tavistock.

Crozier, M. (1971), *The World of the Office Worker*, Chicago University Press.

Cunnison, S. (1966), *Wages and Work Allocation*, London: Tavistock.

Cyert, R. M. and March, J. G. (1963), *A Behavioral Theory of the Firm*, Englewood Cliffs, NJ: Prentice-Hall.

Dahrendorf, R. (1959), *Class and Class Conflict in Industrial Society*, London: Routledge & Kegan Paul.

Dalton, M. (1948), 'The Industrial Ratebuster', *Applied Anthropology*, vol. 7.

Dalton, M. (1950), 'Conflicts between line and staff managerial officers', *American Sociological Review*, vol. 15.

Dalton, M. (1951), 'Informal factors in career achievement', *American Journal of Sociology*, vol. 56.

Dalton, M. (1959), *Men Who Manage*, New York: Wiley.

Daniel, W. W. (1973), 'Understanding employee behaviour in its context' in Child (ed.) (1973).

Daniels, A. K. (1975), 'Professionalism in formal organisations' in McKinlay (ed.) (1975).

Davidoff, L. (1976), 'The rationalisation of housework' in Barker and Allen (eds) (1976).

Davis, F. (1959), 'The cabdriver and his fare', *American Journal of Sociology*, vol. 65.

Davis, K. and Moore, W. E. (1945), 'Some principles of stratification', *American Sociological Review*, vol. 10.

Davis, L. E. (1972), 'The design of jobs' in Davis and Taylor (eds) (1972).

Davis, L. E., Canter, R. R. and Hoffman, J. (1972), 'Current job design criteria' in L. E. Davis and J. C. Taylor (eds) (!972).

Davis, L. E. and Cherns, A. B. (eds) (1975), *The Quality of Working Life*, New York: Free Press.

Davis, L. E. and Taylor, J. C. (eds) (1972), *Design of Jobs*, Harmondsworth: Penguin.

Dawe, A. (1970), 'The two sociologies', *British Journal of Sociology*, vol. 21.

Dawe, A. (1971), 'The relevance of values', in Sahay (ed.) (1971).

Dawe, A. (1973), 'The role of experience in the construction of social theories', *Sociological Review*, vol. 21.

Dennis, N., Henriques, F. and Slaughter, C. (1969), *Coal is our Life*, London: Tavistock.

Dibble, V. K. (1962), 'Occupations and ideologies', *American Journal of Sociology*, vol. 68.

Dickson, D. (1974), *Alternative Technology*, London: Fontana.

Ditton, J. (1972), 'Absent at work', *New Society*, 21 December.

Ditton, J. (1974), 'The fiddling salesman', *New Society*, 28 November.

Ditton, J. (1977), *Part-time Crime*, London: Macmillan.

Doeringer, P. B. and Piore, M. J. (1971), *Internal Labor Markets and Manpower Analysis*, Lexington, Mass.: D. C. Heath.

Domhoff, G. W. (1967), *Who Rules America?*, Englewood Cliffs, NJ: Prentice-Hall.

Donovan, Lord (1968), *Report of the Royal Commission on Trade Unions and Employers' Associations*, London: HMSO.

Dore, R. (1973), *British Factory–Japanese Factory*, London: Allen & Unwin.

Douglas, J. D. (1970), *The Relevance of Sociology*, New York: Appleton-Century-Crofts.

Dubin, R. (1956), 'Industrial Workers' Worlds', *Social Problems*, vol. 3.

Dubin, R. (1970), 'Management in Britain: impression of a visiting professor', *Journal of Management Studies*, vol. 7.

Dubin, R. (ed.)(1976), *Handbook of Work, Organisation and Society*, Chicago: Rand McNally.

Dubin, R., Champoux, J. E. and Porter, L. W. (1976), 'Central life interests and organisational commitment of blue-collar and clerical workers', *Administrative Science Quarterly*, vol. 20.

Dumazedier, J. (1974), *The Sociology of Leisure*, Amsterdam: Elsevier.

Dunkerley, D. (1975a), *Occupations and Society*, London: Routledge & Kegan Paul.

Dunkerley, D. (1975b), *The Foreman*, London: Routledge & Kegan Paul.

Durkheim, E. (1933), *The Division of Labour in Society*, Chicago: Free Press.

Edelstein, J. D. and Warner, M. (1975), *Comparative Union Democracy*, London: Allen & Unwin.

Edgell, S. (1970), 'Spiralists: their careers and family lives', *British Journal of Sociology*, vol. 21.

Eisenstadt, S. N. (1973), *Tradition, Change and Modernity*, New York: Wiley.

Eldridge, J. E. T. (1968), *Industrial Disputes*, London: Routledge & Kegan Paul.

Eldridge, J. E. T. (1971a), *Sociology and Industrial Life*, London: Michael Joseph.

Eldridge, J. E. T. (1971b), 'Weber's approach to the study of industrial workers' in Sahay (ed.) (1971).

Eldridge, J. E. T. (1975), 'Industrial relations and industrial capitalism' in Esland *et al.* (eds) (1975).

Elger, A. J. (1975), 'Industrial organisations: a processual approach' in McKinlay (ed.) (1975).

Elliot, P. (1972), *The Sociology of the Professions*, London: Macmillan.

Elliot, P. (1973), 'Professional ideology and social situation', *Sociological Review*, vol. 21.

Ellis, T. and Child, J. (1973), 'Placing stereotypes of the manager into perspective', *Journal of Management Studies*, vol. 10.

Ellul, J. (1964), *The Technological Society*, New York: Vintage Books.

Emery, F. E. (ed.) (1969), *Systems Thinking*, Harmondsworth: Penguin.

Emery, F. E. and Trist, E. L. (1969), 'Sociotechnical systems' in Emery (ed.) (1969).

Engel, G. V. (1970), 'Professional autonomy and bureaucratic organisation', *Administrative Science Quarterly*, vol. 15.

Esland, G. and Salaman, G. (1975), 'Towards a sociology of work' in Esland *et al.* (eds) (1975).

Esland, G., Salaman, G. and Speakman, M. (eds) (1975), *People and Work*, Edinburgh: Holmes McDougall.

Etzioni, A. (ed.) (1970), *A Sociological Reader on Complex Organisations*, New York: Free Press.

Etzioni, A. (1975), *A Comparative Analysis of Complex Organisations*, New York: Free Press.

Fatchett, D. and Whittingham, W. M. (1976), 'Trends and development in industrial relations theory', *Industrial Relations Journal*, vol. 7.

Faunce, W. A. (ed.) (1967), *Readings in Industrial Sociology*, New York: Appleton-Century-Crofts.

Faunce, W. A. (1968), *Problems of an Industrial Society*, New York: McGraw-Hill.

Faunce, W. A. and Form, W. H. (1969), *Comparative Perspectives on Industrial Sociology*, Boston: Little, Brown.

Fay, B. (1975), *Social Theory and Political Practice*, London: Allen & Unwin.

Fayol, H. (1949), *General and Industrial Management*, London: Pitman.

Flanders, A. (1964), *The Fawley Productivity Agreements*, London: Faber.

Flanders, A. (1970), *Management and Unions*, London: Faber.

Flanders, A., Pomeranz, R. and Woodward, J. (1968), *Experiment in Industrial Democracy: a study of the John Lewis Partnership*, London: Faber.

Fletcher, C. (1973), 'The end of management' in Child (ed.) (1973).

Fogarty, M. P. (1971), *Sex, Career and Family*, London: Allen & Unwin.

Fores, M. and Glover, I. (1978), *Manufacturing and Management*, London: HMSO.

Form, W. H. and Miller, D. C. (1960), *Industry, Labor and Community*, New York: Harper & Row.

Foster, J. (1974), *Class Struggle and the Industrial Revolution*, London: Weidenfeld & Nicolson.

Fox, A. (1966), *Industrial Sociology and Industrial Relations*, Research Paper 3, Royal Commission on Trade Unions and Employers' Associations, London: HMSO.

Fox, A. (1971), *A Sociology of Work in Industry*, London: Collier-Macmillan.

Fox, A. (1973), 'Industrial relations: a social critique of pluralist ideology' in Child (ed.) (1973).

Fox, A. (1974), *Beyond Contract, work, power and trust relations*, London: Faber.

Fox, A. (1978), *Socialism and Shopfloor Power*, London: Fabian Research Pamphlets.

Fox, A. and Flanders, A. (1969), 'The reform of collective bargaining: from Donovan to Durkheim', *British Journal of Industrial Relations*, vol. 7.

Frank, A. G. (1971), *Sociology of Development and the Underdevelopment of Sociology*, London: Pluto Press.

Freidson, E. (1970), *Profession of Medicine*, New York: Dodd Mead.

Freidson, E. (1973), 'Professionalisation and the organisation of middle-class labour in post-industrial society', *Sociological Review Monograph* 20.

Freund, J. (1972), *The Sociology of Max Weber*, Harmondsworth: Penguin.

Friedman, A. L. (1977), *Industry and Labour*, London: Macmillan.

Friedman, G. (1955), *Industrial Society*, Chicago: Free Press.

Friedman, G. (1961), *The Anatomy of Work*, London: Heinemann.

Friedmann, E. A. and Havighurst, R. J. (1954), *The Meaning of Work and Retirement*, University of Chicago Press.

Galbraith, J. K. (1972), *The New Industrial State*, Harmondsworth: Penguin.

Gallie, D. (1978), *In search of the new working class*, Cambridge University Press.

Gardiner, J. (1976), 'Political economy of domestic labour in capitalist society' in Barker and Allen (eds) (1976).

Garnsey, E. (1975), 'Occupational structure in industrialised societies', *Sociology*, vol. 9.

Geer, B. *et al.* (1968), 'Learning the ropes' in J. Deutscher and J. Thompson (eds), *Among the People*, New York: Basic Books.

Gennard, J. (1978), *Financing Strikes*, London: Macmillan.

Gershuny, J. I. (1978), *After Industrial Society*, London: Macmillan.

Gerstl, J. E. and Hutton, S. P. (1966), *Engineers: the anatomy of a profession*, London: Tavistock.

Giddens, A. (1971), *Capitalism and Modern Social Theory*, Cambridge University Press.

Giddens, A. (1973), *The Class Structure of the Advanced Societies*, London: Hutchinson.

Giddens, A. (1976), *New Rules of Sociological Method*, London: Hutchinson.

Giddens, A. and Stanworth, P. (1978), 'Elites and Privilege' in Abrams (ed.) (1978).

Giner, S. and Archer, M. (eds) (1978), *Contemporary Europe*, London: Routledge & Kegan Paul.

Ginzberg, E. J. *et al.* (1951), *Occupational Choice*, New York: Columbia University Press.

Glaser, B. G. (ed.) (1968), *Organisational Careers*, Chicago: Aldine.

Glaser, B. G. and Strauss, A. L. (1967), *The Discovery of Grand Theory*, Chicago: Aldine.

Glasgow University Media Group (1977), *Bad News*, vol. I, London: Routledge & Kegan Paul.

Glover, I. A. (1974), 'Industrial sociology and industrial democracy', *Sociological Analysis and Theory*, vol. 4.

Glyn, A. and Sutcliffe, R. B., *British Capitalism, Workers and the Profit Squeeze*, Harmondsworth: Penguin.

Goffman, E. (1968), *Asylums*, Harmondsworth: Penguin.

Goldner, F. H. (1970), 'The division of labor: process and power' in Zald (ed.) (1970).

Goldner, F. H. and Ritti, R. R. (1970), 'Professionalisation as career immobility' in Grusky and Miller (eds) (1970).

Goldthorpe, J. H. (1971), 'Theories of Industrial Society', *European Journal of Sociology*, vol. 12.

Goldthorpe, J. H. (1974), 'Social Inequality and Social Integration in Modern Britain' in D. Wedderburn (ed.), *Poverty, Inequality and Class Structure*, Cambridge University Press.

Goldthorpe, J. H. (1977), 'Industrial relations in Great Britain: a critique of reformism' in Clarke and Clements (eds) (1977).

Goldthorpe, J. H. and Llewellyn, C. (1977), 'Class mobility in modern Britain', *Sociology*, vol. 11.

Goldthorpe, J. H., Lockwood, D., Bechhofer, F. and Platt, J. (1968), *The Affluent Worker: industrial attitudes and behaviour*, Cambridge University Press.

Goldthorpe, J. H., Lockwood, D., Bechhofer, F. and Platt, J. (1969), *The Affluent Worker in the Class Structure*, Cambridge University Press.

Goode, W. J. (1957), 'Community within a community: the professions', *American Sociological Review*, vol. 22.

Goodman, J. F. B. and Whittington, T. G. (1973), *Shop Stewards*, London: Pan.

Goodrich, C. (1975), *The Frontier of Control*, London: Pluto Press.

Gorz, A. (ed.) (1976), *The Division of Labour*, London: Harvester.

Gouldner, A. W. (1957), 'Cosmopolitans and locals', *Administrative Science Quarterly*, vol. 2.

Gouldner, A. W. (1964), *Patterns of Industrial Bureaucracy*, New York: Free Press.

Gouldner, A. W. (1971), *The Coming Crisis of Western Sociology*, London: Heinemann.

Gouldner, A. W. (1976), *The Dialectic of Ideology and Technology*, London: Macmillan.

Granick, D. (1961), *The Red Executive*, New York: Doubleday.

Graves, B. (1970), 'Particularism, exchange and organisational efficiency', *Social Forces*, vol. 49.

Greenwood, J. (1977), *Worker Sit-ins and Job Protection*, Farnborough: Gower Press.

Gross, E. (1959), 'The occupational variable as a research category', *American Sociological Review*, vol. 24.

Gross, E. (1965), *Industry and Social Life*, Duboque, Iowa: Brown.

Grusky, O. and Miller, G. A. (eds) (1970), *The Sociology of Organisations*, New York: Free Press.

Guest, R. H. (1962), *Organisational Change*, Homewood, Ill.: Dorsey Press.

Haber, S. (1964), *Efficiency and Uplift*, Chicago University Press.

Habermas, J. (1971), *Toward a Rational Society*, London: Heinemann.

Hage, J. and Aiken, M. (1970), *Social Change in Complex Organisations*, New York: Random House.

Hall, R. H. (1975), *Occupations and the Social Structure*, Englewood Cliffs, NJ: Prentice-Hall.

Hall, R. H. (ed.) (1972), *The Formal Organisation*, New York: Basic Books.

Hall, R. H. (1977), *Organisations: Structure and Process*, Englewood Cliffs, NJ: Prentice-Hall.

Halmos, P. (1970), *The Personal Service Society*, London: Constable.

Halmos, P. (ed.) (1973), 'Professionalisation and Social Change', *Sociological Review Monograph* 20.

Halsey, A. H., Floud, J. and Anderson, C. (eds) (1961), *Education, Economy and Social Class*, New York: Free Press.

Hamilton, R. (1978), *The Liberation of Women*, London: Allen & Unwin.

Hammond, J. L. and Hammond, B. (1966), *The Rise of Modern Industry*, London: Methuen.

Handy, L. J. (1968), 'Absenteeism in the British coal-mining industry', *British Journal of Industrial Relations*, vol. 6.

Haraszti, M. (1977), *A Worker in a Workers' State*, Harmondsworth: Penguin.

Harbison, F. H. and Myers, C. A. (1959), *Management in the Industrial World*, New York: McGraw-Hill.

Harvey, E. B. (1975), *Industrial Society*, Homewood, Ill.: Dorsey Press.

Hatt, P. K. (1950), 'Occupations and social stratification', *American Journal of Sociology*, vol. 55.

Henry, S. (1978), *The Hidden Economy*, London: Martin Robertson.

Herbst, P. G. (1974), *Socio-technical Design*, London: Tavistock.

Herzberg, F. (1966), *Work and the Nature of Man*, New York: Crowell.

Hickson, D. J., Pugh, D. S. and Pheysey, D. C. (1969), 'Operations technology and organisational structure: an empirical reappraisal', *Administrative Science Quarterly*, vol. 14.

Hickson, D. J. *et al.* (1971), 'A strategic contingencies theory of intraorganisational power', *Administrative Science Quarterly*, vol. 16.

Hill, C. (1974), *Change and Continuity in Seventeenth Century England*, London: Weidenfeld & Nicolson.

Hill, M. J., Harrison, R. M., Sergeant, A. V. and Talbot, V. (1973), *Men Out of Work*, Cambridge University Press.

Hill, S. (1976), *The Dockers: class and tradition in London*, London: Heinemann.

Hill, S. and Thurley, K. (1974), 'Sociology and industrial relations', *British Journal of Industrial Relations*, vol. 12.

Hinton, J. (1973), *The First Shop Stewards' Movement*, London: Allen & Unwin.

Hirsch, F. (1977), *Social Limits to Growth*, London: Routledge & Kegan Paul.

HMSO (1968), *Workplace Industrial Relations*, London.

HMSO (1977), *Third Report on the Standing Reference*, Royal Commission on the Distribution of Income and Wealth, London.

HMSO (1979), *The Employment Gazette*, vol. 87, no. 1, London.

Hobsbawm, E. J. (1969), *Industry and Empire*, Harmondsworth: Penguin.

Hollowell, P. G. (1968), *The Lorry Driver*, London: Routledge & Kegan Paul.

Hopper, E. and Pearce, A. (1973), 'Relative deprivation, occupational status, and occupational "situs"' in Warner (ed.) (1973).

Horton, J. (1964), 'The dehumanisation of anomie and alienation', *British Journal of Sociology*, vol. 15.

Hughes, E. C. (1958), *Men and their Work*, New York: Free Press.

Hunt, A. (1975), *Management Attitudes and Practices Towards Women at Work*, London: HMSO.

Hyman, R. (1974), 'Workers' Control and Revolutionary Theory' in *Socialist Register*, London: Merlin Press.

Hyman, R. (1977a), *Strikes*, rev. edn, London: Fontana.

Hyman, R. (1977b), 'Occupational structure, collective organisation and industrial militancy' in Crouch, C. and Pizzorno, A. (eds), *The Resurgence of Class Conflict since 1968*, vol. II, London: Macmillan.

Hyman, R. and Brough, I. (1975), *Social Values and Industrial Relations*, Oxford: Blackwell.

Hyman, R. and Fryer, R. H. (1975), 'Trade unions and political economy' in McKinlay (ed.) (1975).

Ingham, G. K. (1970), *Size of Industrial Organisation and Worker Behaviour*, Cambridge University Press.

Ingham, G. K. (1974), *Strikes and Industrial Conflict*, London: Macmillan.

Israel, H. (1966), 'Some religious factors in the emergence of industrial society in England', *American Sociological Review*, vol. 31.

Jackson, J. A. (ed.) (1970), *Professions and Professionalisation*, Cambridge University Press.

James, L. (1973), 'On the game', *New Society*, 24 May.

Jenkins, D. (1974), *Job Power*, London: Heinemann.

Johnson, T. J. (1972), *Professions and Power*, London: Macmillan.

Johnson, T. J. (1977), 'The professions in the class structure' in Scase (ed.) (1977).

Kahn, R. L. *et al.* (1964), *Organisational Stress*, New York: Wiley.

Kakar, S. (1970), *Frederick Taylor: A Study in Personality and Innovation*, MIT Press.

Kaplan, M. and Bosserman, P. (eds) (1971), *Technology, Human Values and Leisure*, New York: Abingdon.

Katz, D. and Kahn, R. L. (1967), *The Social Psychology of Organisations*, London: Batsford.

Katz, F. E. (1968), *Autonomy and Organisation*, New York: Random House.

Kempner, T., Macmillan, K. and Hawkins, K. (1976), *Business and Society*, Harmondsworth: Penguin.

Kerr, C., Dunlop, J. T., Harbison, F. and Myers, C. A. (1973), *Industrialism and Industrial Man*, Harmondsworth: Penguin.

Kerr, C. and Siegal, A. J. (1954), 'The inter-industry propensity to strike' in Kornhauser *et al.* (eds), *Industrial Conflict*, New York: McGraw-Hill.

Klein, L. (1976), *A Social Scientist in Industry*, London: Gower Press.

Klein, V. (1965), *Britain's Married Women Workers*, London: Routledge & Kegan Paul.

Knights, D. (1975), 'A classification for occupations', *British Journal of*

Sociology, vol. 26.

Kohn, M. (1969), *Class and Conformity*, Homewood, Ill.: Dorsey Press.

Kohn, M. (1971), 'Bureaucratic man: a portrait and an interpretation', *American Sociological Review*, vol. 36.

Krause, E. A. (1971), *The Sociology of Occupations*, Boston: Little, Brown.

Kuhn, J. W. (1961), *Bargaining in Grievance Settlement*, Columbia University Press.

Kumar, K. (1978), *Prophecy and Progress*, Harmondsworth: Penguin.

Landsberger, H. A. (1958), *Hawthorne Revisited*, Cornell University Press.

Landsberger, H. A. (1961), 'The horizontal dimension in bureaucracy', *Administrative Science Quarterly*, vol. 6.

Lane, D. (1976), *The Socialist Industrial State*, London: Allen & Unwin.

Lane, D. and O'Dell, F. (1978), *The Soviet Industrial Worker*, London: Martin Robertson.

Lane, T. and Roberts, K. (1971), *Strike at Pilkingtons*, London: Fontana.

Langer, E. (1970), 'The women of the telephone company', *New York Review of Books*, 12 March and 26 March.

Larson, M. S. (1977), *The Rise of Professionalism*, University of California Press.

Lawrence, P. R. and Lorsch, J. W. (1967), *Organisation and Environment*, Boston: Harvard University Press.

Likert, R. (1961), *New Patterns of Management*, New York: McGraw-Hill.

Likert, R. (1967), *The Human Organisation*, New York: McGraw-Hill.

Lipset, S. M. (1976), 'Social structure and social change' in Blau (ed.) (1976).

Lipset, S. M., Trow, M. and Coleman, J. (1956), *Union Democracy*, Chicago: Free Press.

Littler, C. (1978), 'Understanding Taylorism', *British Journal of Sociology*, vol. 29.

Lockwood, D. (1958), *The Blackcoated Worker*, London: Allen & Unwin.

Lockwood, D. (1960), 'The "new working class"', *European Journal of Sociology*, vol. 1.

Loewith, K. (1970), 'Weber's interpretation of the bourgeois-capitalistic world in terms of the guiding principle of "rationalisation"' in D. Wrong (ed.), *Max Weber*, Englewood Cliffs, NJ: Prentice-Hall.

Lukes, S. (1967), 'Alienation and Anomie' in P. Laslett and W. G. Runciman (eds), *Philosophy, Politics and Society*, third series, Oxford: Blackwell.

Lumley, R. (1973), *White Collar Unionism in Britain*, London: Methuen.

Lummis, T. (1977), 'The occupational community of the East Anglian fishermen', *British Journal of Sociology*, vol. 28.

Lupton, T. (1963), *On the Shopfloor*, Oxford: Pergamon.

Lupton, T. (1971), *Management and the Social Sciences*, Harmondsworth: Penguin.

Lupton, T. (1976), 'Shopfloor behaviour' in Dubin (ed.) (1976).

McCarthy, W. E. J. (1967), *The Role of Shop Stewards in British Industrial Relations*, Royal Commission on Trade Unions and Employers' Associations, Research Paper no. 1, London, HMSO.

McCarthy, W. E. J. (ed.) (1972), *Trade Unions*, Harmondsworth: Penguin.

McCarthy, W. E. J. and Parker, S. R. (1968), *Shop Stewards and Workshop Relations*, Royal Commission on Trade Unions and Employers' Associations, Research Paper no. 10, London: HMSO.

McGregor, D. (1960), *The Human Side of Enterprise*, New York: McGraw-Hill.

Mackenzie, G. (1973), *The Aristocracy of Labour*, Cambridge University Press.

Mackenzie, G. (1974), 'The "affluent worker study": an evaluation and critique' in Parkin (ed.) (1974).

Mackenzie, G. (1975), 'World images and the world of work' in Esland *et al.* (eds) (1975).

Mackie, L. and Pattullo, P. (1977), *Women at Work*, London: Tavistock.

McKinlay, J. B. (ed.) (1975), *Processing People*, London: Holt, Rinehart & Winston.

McNeil, K. (1978), 'Understanding organisational power', *Administrative Science Quarterly*, vol. 23.

Madge, C. (1963), *The Origins of Scientific Sociology*, London: Tavistock.

Mallet, S. (1975), *The New Working Class*, Nottingham: Spokesman Books.

Mann, M. (1973), *Workers on the Move*, Cambridge University Press.

Manning, P. K. (1977), *Police Work: the social organisation of policing*, MIT Press.

Mant, A. (1977), *The Rise and Fall of the British Manager*, London: Macmillan.

Marceau, J., Thomas, A. B. and Whitley, R. (1977), 'Business and the state: managerial education and business elites in France and Great Britain' in Littlejohn, G. *et al.* (eds), *Power and the State*, London: Croom Helm.

Marcson, S. (1970), *Automation, Alienation and Anomie*, New York: Harper.

Marcuse, H. (1965), 'Industrialization and capitalism', *New Left Review*, no. 30.

Marcuse, H. (1968), *One Dimensional Man*, London: Sphere.

Marglin, S. (1971), *What do Bosses do?*, Harvard Institute of Economic Research discussion paper, no. 222 (also in Gorz (ed.) (1976)).

Mars, G. (1973), 'Chance, punters and the fiddle' in Warner (ed.) (1973).

Mars, G. (1974), 'Dock pilferage', in P. Rock and M. McIntosh (eds), *Deviance and Control*, London: Tavistock.

Martin, R. (1968), 'Union democracy: an explanatory framework'. *Sociology*, vol. 2.

Martin, R. (1977), *The Sociology of Power*, London: Routledge & Kegan Paul.

Martin, R. and Fryer, R. H. (1973), *Redundancy and Paternalist Capitalism*, London: Allen & Unwin.

Maslow, A. (1954), *Motivation and Personality*, New York: Harper & Row.

Mayo, E. (1933), *The Human Problems of an Industrial Civilisation*, New York: Macmillan.

Mayo, E. (1949), *The Social Problems of an Industrial Civilisation*, London: Routledge & Kegan Paul.

Meakin, D. (1976), *Man and Work: literature and culture in industrial society*, London: Methuen.

Meara, H. (1974), 'Honor in dirty work', *Sociology of Work and Occupations*, vol. 1.

Meissner, M. (1969), *Technology and the Worker*, New York: Chandler Publishing.

Meissner, M. (1971), 'The long arm of the job', *Industrial Relations*, vol. 2.

Meissner, M. (1976), 'The language of work' in Dubin (ed.) (1976).

Meltzer, B. N., Petras, J. W. and Reynolds, L. T. (1975), *Symbolic Interactionism*, London: Routledge & Kegan Paul.

Merton, R. K. (1957), 'Bureaucratic structure and personality' in *Social Theory and Social Structure*, New York: Free Press.

Mesthene, E. G. (1970), *Technological Change*, Harvard University Press.

Middleton, C. (1974), 'Sexual inequality and stratification theory' in Parkin (ed.) (1974).

Miliband, R. (1969), *The State in Capitalist Society*, London: Weidenfeld & Nicolson.

Miller, D. C. and Form, W. H. (1964), *Industrial Sociology*, New York: Harper & Row.

Miller, D. and Swanson, G. (1958), *The Changing American Parent*, New York: Wiley.

Miller, E. and Rice, A. K. (1967), *Systems of Organisation*, London: Tavistock.

Millerson, G. (1964), *The Qualifying Associations*, London: Routledge & Kegan Paul.

Mills, C. W. (1953), *White Collar*, New York: Oxford University Press.

Mills, C. W. (1970), *The Sociological Imagination*, Harmondsworth: Penguin.

Mintzberg, H. (1973), *The Nature of Managerial Work*, New York: Harper.

Mishra, R. (1973), 'Welfare and industrial man', *Sociological Review*, vol. 21.

Mommsen, W. J. (1974), *The Age of Bureaucracy*, Oxford: Blackwell.

Montagna, P. D. (1977), *Occupations and Society*, New York: Wiley.

Moore, R. (1971), 'History, economics and religion: a review of "the Max Weber thesis" thesis' in Sahay (ed.) (1971).

Moore, R. (1974), *Pitmen, Preachers and Politics*, Cambridge University Press.

Moore, R. (1975), 'Religion as a source of variation in working class images of society' in Bulmer (ed.) (1975).

Moore, W. E. (1965), *The Impact of Industry*, Englewood Cliffs, NJ: Prentice-Hall.

Moore, W. E. (1970), *The Professions: roles and rules*, New York: Sage.

Morris, R. T. and Murphy, R. J. (1959), 'The situs dimension in occupational structure', *American Sociological Review*, vol. 24.

Morris, T. and Morris, P. (1973), 'The prison officer' in Weir (ed.) (1973).

Morse, N. C. and Weiss, R. S. (1955), 'The function and meaning of work and the job', *American Sociological Review*, vol. 20.

Mott, J. (1973), 'Miners, weavers and pigeon racing' in Smith *et al.* (eds) (1973).

Mouzelis, N. (1975), *Organisation and Bureaucracy*, London: Routledge & Kegan Paul.

Mumford, E. (1972), *Job Satisfaction*, London: Longman.

Musgrave, P. W. (1967), 'Towards a sociological theory of occupational choice', *Sociological Review*, vol. 15.

Myrdal, A. and Klein, V. (1968), *Women's Two Roles*, London: Routledge & Kegan Paul.

Newby, H. (1979), *The Deferential Worker*, Harmondsworth: Penguin.

Nichols, T. (1969), *Ownership, Control and Ideology*, London: Allen & Unwin.

Nichols, T. (1975), 'The sociology of accidents and the social production of industrial accidents' in Esland *et al.* (eds) (1975).

Nichols, T. and Armstrong, P. (1976), *Workers Divided*, London: Fontana.

Nichols, T. and Beynon, H. (1977), *Living with Capitalism*, London: Routledge & Kegan Paul.

Nicholson, N. (1976), 'The role of the shop steward', *Industrial Relations Journal*, vol. 7.

Nisbet, R. (1969), *Social Change and History*, Oxford University Press.

Nisbet, R. (1970), *The Sociological Tradition*, London: Heinemann.

Nisbet, R. (1976), *The Social Philosophers*, London: Paladin.

Noble, T. (1975), *Modern Britain*, London: Batsford.

Nosow, S. and Form, W. H. (eds) (1962), *Man, Work and Society*, New York: Basic Books.

Oakeshott, R. (1978), *The Case for Workers' Co-operatives*, London: Routledge & Kegan Paul.

Oakley, A. (1974), *Housewife*, London: Allen Lane.

Oakley, A. (1975), *The Sociology of Housework*, London: Martin Robertson.

Offe, C. (1976), *Industry and Inequality*, London: Edward Arnold.

Oppenheimer, M. (1973), 'The proletarianisation of the professional', *Sociological Review Monograph*, 20.

Orzack, L. (1959), 'Work as a central life interest of professionals', *Social Problems*, vol. 6.

Pahl, J. M. and Pahl, R. E. (1972), *Managers and their Wives*, Harmondsworth: Penguin.

Pahl, R. E. and Winkler, J. T. (1974a), 'The economic elite' in P. Stanworth and A. Giddens (eds), *Elites and Power in British Society*, Cambridge University Press.

Pahl, R. E. and Winkler, J. T. (1974b), 'The coming corporatism', *New Society*, 10 October.

Parker, S. R. (1971), *The Future of Work and Leisure*, London: Paladin.

Parker, S. R. (1976), *The Sociology of Leisure*, London: Allen & Unwin.

Parker, S. R., Brown, R. K., Child, J. and Smith, M. A. (1977), *The Sociology of Industry*, London: Allen & Unwin.

Parker, S. R. and Smith, M. A. (1976), 'Work and Leisure' in Dubin (ed.) (1976).

Parkin, F. (1972a), *Class, Inequality and Political Order*, London: Paladin.

Parkin, F. (1972b), 'System contradiction and political transformation', *European Journal of Sociology*, vol. 13.

Parkin, F. (ed.) (1974), *The Social Analysis of Class Structure*, London: Tavistock.

Parry, N. and Parry, J. (1977), 'Social closure and collective mobility' in Scase (ed.) (1977).

Parsons, T. and Smelser, N. (1956), *Economy and Society*, London: Routledge & Kegan Paul.

Pavalko, R. (1971), *The Sociology of Occupations and Professions*, Itasca, Ill.: Peacock.

Pavalko, R. (ed.) (1972), *Sociological Perspectives on Occupations*, Itasca, Ill.: Peacock.

Payne, G. (1977), 'Occupational transition in advanced industrial societies', *Sociological Review*, vol. 25.

Perrow, C. (1970a), 'Departmental power' in Zald (ed.) (1970).

Perrow, C. (1970b), *Organisational Analysis*, London: Tavistock.

Perrow, C. (1972), *Complex Organisations*, Glenview, Ill.: Scott, Foresman.

Pettigrew, A. (1973), *The Politics of Organisational Decisionmaking*, London: Tavistock.

Pettigrew, A. (1975), 'Occupational specialisation as a emergent process' in Esland *et al.* (eds) (1975).

Pichierri, A. (1978), 'Diffusion and crisis of scientific management in European industry' in S. Giner and H. S. Archer (eds) (1978).

Piore, J. M. (1972), 'Notes for a theory of labor market stratification', *Working Paper no. 95*, Department of Economics, MIT.

Piven, F. F. and Cloward, R. A. (1974), *Regulating the Poor*, London: Tavistock.

Polanyi, K. (1945), *Origins of our Time*, London: Gollancz.

Pollard, S. (1968), *The Genesis of Modern Management*, Harmondsworth: Penguin.

Polsky, N. I. (1971), *Hustlers, Beats and Others*, Harmondsworth: Penguin.

Poole, M. J. F. (1974), 'Towards a sociology of shop stewards', *Sociological Review*, vol. 22.

Poole, M. J. F. (1978), *Workers' Participation in Industry*, London: Routledge & Kegan Paul.

Popper, K. (1957), *The Poverty of Historicism*, London: Routledge & Kegan Paul.

Prandy, K. (1965), *Professional Employees*, London: Faber.

Pribicevic, B. (1959), *The Shop Stewards' Movement and Workers' Control*, Oxford: Blackwell.

Pugh, D. S. and Hickson, D. J. (1976), *Organisational Structure and its Context*, London: Saxon House.

Quinney, E. R. (1963), 'Occupational structure and criminal behaviour', *Social Problems*, vol. 11.

Radcliffe-Brown, A. R. (1965), *Structure and Function in Primitive Society*, New York: Free Press.

Ramsey, H. (1977), 'Cycles of control: worker participation in sociological and historical perspective', *Sociology*, vol. 11.

Rapoport, R. and Rapoport, R. (1976), *Dual Career Families Re-examined*, London: Martin Robertson.

Reiner, R. (1978), *The Blue-coated Worker*, Cambridge University Press.

Rex, J. (1974), *Sociology and the Demystification of the Modern World*, London: Routledge & Kegan Paul.

Reynolds, S. (1979), 'The march to stop more jobs being sold down the river', *Guardian*, 22 March.

Rhenman, E. (1968), *Industrial Democracy and Industrial Management*, London: Tavistock.

Rice, A. K. (1958), *Productivity and Social Organisation*, London: Tavistock.

Rice, A. K. (1963), *The Enterprise and its Environment*, London: Tavistock.

Richman, J. (1969), 'Busmen v. the public', *New Society*, 14 August.

Rimlinger, G. V. (1971), *Welfare Policy and Industrialisation in Europe, America and Russia*, New York: Wiley.

Rimmer, M. (1972), *Race and Industrial Conflict*, London: Heinemann.

Ritzer, G. (1972), *Man and his Work*, New York: Appleton-Century-Crofts.

Ritzer, G. and Trice, H. M. (1969), *An Occupation in Conflict*, Cornell University Press.

Roberts, B. C., Loveridge, R., Gennard, J. and Eason, J. V. (1972), *Reluctant Militants*, London: Heinemann.

Roberts, K. (1968), 'The entry into employment', *Sociological Review*, vol. 16.

Roberts, K. (1975), 'The developmental theory of occupational choice: a critique and alternative' in Esland *et al.* (eds) (1975).

Roberts, K., Cook, F. G., Clark, S. C. and Semeonoff, E. (1977), *The Fragmentary Class Structure*, London: Heinemann.

Roethlisberger, F. J. (1945), 'The foreman: master and victim of double talk', *Harvard Business Review*, vol. 23.

Roethlisberger, F. J. and Dickson, W. J. (1939), *Management and the Worker*, Harvard University Press.

Rogers, D. and Berg, I. E. (1961), 'Occupation and Ideology', *Human Organisation*, vol. 20.

Rose, M. (1975), *Industrial Behaviour*, London: Allen Lane.

Rosenberg, M. (1957), *Occupations and Values*, Chicago: Free Press.

Ross, G. (1974), 'The second coming of Daniel Bell', *Socialist Register*, London: Merlin Press.

Rostow, W. W. (1960), *The Stages of Economic Growth*, Cambridge University Press.

Roy, D. (1952), 'Quota restriction and goldbricking in a machine shop', *American Journal of Sociology*, vol. 57.

Roy, D. (1953), 'Work satisfaction and the social reward in quota achievement', *American Sociological Review*, vol. 18.

Roy, D. (1954), 'Efficiency and "the fix"', *American Journal of Sociology*, vol. 60.

Rubenstein, D. (1978), 'Love and Work', *Sociological Review*, vol. 26.

Sadler, P. (1968), *Social Research on Automation*, London: Heinemann.

Sahay, A. (1971), *Max Weber and Modern Sociology*, London: Routledge & Kegan Paul.

Salaman, G. (1974), *Community and Occupation*, Cambridge University Press.

Salaman, G. (1978), 'Towards a sociology of organisational structure', *Sociological Review*, vol. 20.

Salaman, G. and Thompson, K. (eds) (1973), *People and Organisations*, London: Longman.

Salaman, G. and Thompson, K. (1978), 'Class culture and the persistence of an elite', *Sociological Review*, vol. 26.

Salutin, M. (1971), 'Stripper morality', *Transaction*, vol. 8.

Saville, J. (1975), 'The Welfare State: An historical approach' in Butterworth and Holman (eds), *Social Welfare in Modern Britain*, London: Fontana.

Sayles, L. R. (1958), *Behaviour of Industrial Workgroups*, New York: Wiley.

Scase, R. (ed.) (1977), *Industrial Society: Cleavage and Control*, London: Allen & Unwin.

Schacht, R. (1970), *Alienation*, London: Allen & Unwin.

Schmidt, G. (1976), 'Max Weber and modern industrial sociology', *Sociological Analysis and Theory*, vol. 6.

Schneider, E. V. (1969), *Industrial Sociology*, New York: McGraw-Hill.

Schroyer, T. (1970), 'Toward a critical theory for advanced industrial society', in H. P. Dreitzel (ed.), *Recent Sociology*, no. 2, New York: Macmillan.

Schumacher, E. F. (1973), *Small is Beautiful*, London: Blond & Briggs.

Scott, W. H., Halsey, A. H., Lupton, T. and Banks, J. A. (1956), *Technical Change and Industrial Relations*, Liverpool University Press.

Scott, W. H., McGivering, I. C., Mumford, E. and Kirkby, J. M. (1963), *Coal and Conflict*, Liverpool University Press.

Selznick, P. (1966), *T.V.A. and the Grassroots*, New York: Harper & Row.

Sennett, R. and Cobb, J. (1977), *The Hidden Injuries of Class*, Cambridge University Press.

Sharpe, S. (1976), *Just Like a Girl*, Harmondsworth: Penguin.

Silverman, D. (1970), *The Theory of Organisations*, London: Heinemann.

Silverman, D. and Jones, J. (1976), *Organisational Work*, London: Collier-Macmillan.

Skipper, J. and McCaghy, C. (1970), 'Stripteasers', *Social Problems*, vol. 17.

Smelser, N. J. (1959), *Social Change in the Industrial Revolution*, London: Routledge & Kegan Paul.

Smelser, N. J. (1963), *The Sociology of Economic Life*, Englewood Cliffs, NJ: Prentice-Hall.

Smelser, N. J. (ed.) (1965), *Readings in Economic Sociology*, Englewood Cliffs, NJ: Prentice-Hall.

Smith, A. (1970), *The Wealth of Nations*, Harmondsworth: Penguin.

Smith, D. J. (1977), *Racial Disadvantage in Britain*, Harmondsworth: Penguin.

Smith, M. A., Parker, S. and Smith, C. S. (eds) (1977), *Leisure and Society in Britain*, London: Allen Lane.

Sofer, C. (1970), *Men in Mid-Career*, Cambridge University Press.

Sofer, C. (1972), *Organisations in Theory and Practice*, London: Heinemann.

Solomon, D. N. (1968), 'Sociological perspectives on occupations' in Becker *et al.* (eds) (1968).

Spradley, J. P. and Mann, B. J. (1975), *The Cocktail Waitress*, New York: Wiley.

Stewart, R. (1967), *Managers and their Jobs*, London: Macmillan.

Stewart, P. and Cantor, M. (1974), *Varieties of Work Experience*, New York: Wiley.

Strauss, G. (1962), 'Tactics of lateral relationships: the purchasing agent', *Administrative Science Quarterly*, vol. 7.

Sudnow, D. (1973), 'Normal Crimes' in Salaman and Thompson (eds) (1973).

Super, D. E. (1957), *The Psychology of Careers*, New York: Harper & Row.

Sutton, F. X., Harris, S. E., Kaysen, C. and Tobin, J. (1962), *The American Business Creed*, Harvard University Press.

Sykes, A. J. M. (1966), 'Joking relationships in an industrial setting', *American Anthropologist*, vol. 68.

Sykes, A. J. M. (1969), 'Navvies: their work attitudes', *Sociology*, vol. 3.

Tausky, C. (1970), *Work Organisations*, Itasca, Ill.: Peacock.

Taylor, F. W. (1911), *The Principles of Scientific Management*, New York: Harper & Row.

Taylor, I. and Walton, P. (1971), 'Industrial sabotage: motives and meanings' in S. Cohen (ed.), *Images of Deviance*, Harmondsworth: Penguin.

Taylor, L. (1968), *Occupational Sociology*, New York: Oxford University Press.

Terkel, S. (1977), *Working*, Harmondsworth: Penguin.

Thompson, E. P. (1967), 'Time, work-discipline and industrial capitalism', *Past and Present*, vol. 38.

Thompson, E. P. (1968), *The Making of the English Working Class*, Harmondsworth: Penguin.

Thompson, J. D. (1967), *Organisations in Action*, New York: McGraw-Hill.

Thorn, D. C. (1971), 'Work and its definitions', *Sociological Review*, vol. 19.

Thurley, K. and Hamblin, A. C. (1963), *The Supervisor and his Job*, London: HMSO.

Thurley, K. and Wirdenius, M. (1973), *Supervision: a reappraisal*, London: Heinemann.

Timperley, S. R. (1974), *Personnel Planning and Occupational Choice*, London: Allen & Unwin.

Touraine, A. (1971), *The Post-Industrial Society*, New York: Random House.

Treiman, D. J. (1975), *Occupational Prestige in Contemporary Perspective*, New York: Academic Press.

Trist, E. L., Higgin, G. W., Murray, H. and Pollock, A. B. (1963), *Organisational Choice*, London: Tavistock.

Tunstall, J. (1962), *The Fisherman*, MacGibbon & Kee.

Turner, A. and Lawrence, P. (1966), *Industrial Jobs and the Worker*, Harvard University Press.

Turner, B. A. (1971), *Exploring the Industrial Subculture*, London: Macmillan.

Turner, B. A. (1975), *Industrialism*, London: Longman.

Turner, H. A. (1969), *Is Britain Really Strike Prone?*, Cambridge University Press.

Turner, H. A., Clack, C. and Roberts, G. (1967), *Labour Relations in the Motor Industry*, London: Allen & Unwin.

Turner, H. A., Roberts, G. and Roberts, D. (1977), *Management Characteristics and Labour Conflict*, Cambridge University Press.

Udy, S. H. (1970), *Work in Traditional and Modern Societies*, Englewood Cliffs, NJ: Prentice-Hall.

Urry, J. and Wakeford, J. (eds) (1973), *Power in Britain*, London: Heinemann.

Urwick, L. (1956), *The Pattern of Management*, London: Pitman.

Vanek, J. (ed.) (1975), *Self Management*, Harmondsworth: Penguin.

Vollmer, H. M. and Mills, D. L. (eds) (1966), *Professionalisation*, Englewood Cliffs, NJ: Prentice-Hall.

Vroom, V. H. (1964), *Work and Motivation*, New York: Wiley.

Vroom, V. H. and Deci, E. L. (eds) (1970), *Management and Motivation*, Harmondsworth: Penguin.

Wainwright, H. (1978), 'Women and the division of Labour' in Abrams (ed.) (1978).

Walker, C. R. and Guest, R. H. (1952), *The Man on the Assembly Line*, Harvard University Press.

Walker, C. R., Guest, R. H. and Turner, A. N. (1956), *The Foreman on the Assembly Line*, Harvard University Press.

Warmington, A., Lupton, T. and Gribbin, C. (1977), *Organisational Behaviour and Performance*, London: Macmillan.

Warner, M. (ed.) (1973), *Sociology of the Workplace*, London: Allen & Unwin.

Warner, M. (1978), *Organisational Choice and Constraint*, London: Saxon House.

Warner, W. L. and Low, J. O. (1947), *The Social System of the Modern Factory*, Yale University Press.

Warwick, D. (1974), *Bureaucracy*, London: Longman.

Watson, T. J. (1972), 'Some Sociological Aspects of Organisational Change', Unpublished MSc. thesis, Loughborough University of Technology.

Watson, T. J. (1976), 'The professionalisation process: a critical note', *Sociological Review*, vol. 24.

Watson, T. J. (1977a), *The Personnel Managers: a study in the sociology of work and employment*, London: Routledge & Kegan Paul.

Watson, T. J. (1977b), 'The people processors', *New Society*, 27 October.

Watson, T. J. (1979), 'Industrial sociology: theory, research and teaching – some problems and proposals', *Journal of Management Studies*, vol. 16.

Watson, W. (1964), 'Social mobility and social class in industrial communities', in M. Gluckman and E. Devon (eds), *Closed Systems and Open Minds*, Edinburgh: Oliver & Boyd.

Weber, M. (1927), *General Economic History*, New York: Free Press.

Weber, M. (1965), *The Protestant Ethic and the Spirit of Capitalism*, London: Allen & Unwin.

Weber, M. (1968), *Economy and Society*, New York: Bedminster Press.

Wedderburn, D. and Craig, C. (1974), 'Relative deprivation in work' in D. Wedderburn (ed.), *Poverty, Inequality and Class Structure*, Cambridge University Press.

Wedderburn, D. and Crompton, R. (1972), *Workers' Attitudes and Technology*, Cambridge University Press.

Weir, D. (ed.) (1973), *Men and Work in Modern Britain*, London: Fontana.

Weir, M. (ed.) (1976), *Job Satisfaction*, London: Fontana.

Westergaard, J. and Resler, H. (1975), *Class in a Capitalist Society*, London: Heinemann.

Whelan, C. T. (1976), 'Orientation to work: some theoretical and methodological problems', *British Journal of Industrial Relations*, vol. 14.

Whitehead, T. N. (1938), *The Industrial Worker*, New York: Oxford University Press.

Whyte, W. F. (1955), *Money and Motivation*, New York: Harper.

Whyte, W. H. (1961), *The Organisation Man*, Harmondsworth: Penguin.

Wilensky, H. L. (1960), 'Work careers and social integration', *International Social Science Journal*, vol. 12.

Wilensky, H. L. and Lebaux, C. N. (1965), *Industrial Society and Social Welfare*, New York: Free Press.

Williams, R. (1965), *The Long Revolution*, Harmondsworth: Penguin.

Williams, R. (1976), *Keywords*, London: Fontana.

Williams, W. M. (ed.) (1974), *Occupational Choice*, London: Allen & Unwin.

Willis, P. E. (1977), *Learning to Labour*, London: Saxon House.

Wilson, D. F. (1972), *Dockers*, London: Fontana.

Winkler, J. T. (1974), 'The ghost at the bargaining table', *British Journal of Industrial Relations*, vol. 12.

Winkler, J. T. (1976), 'Corporatism', *European Journal of Sociology*, vol. 17.

Winkler, J. T. (1977), 'The corporatist economy: theory and administration' in Scase (ed.) (1977).

Woodward, J. (1958), *Management and Technology*, London: HMSO.

Woodward, J. (1965), *Industrial Organisation*, Oxford University Press.

Woodward, J. (ed.) (1970), *Industrial Organisation: Behaviour and Control*, Oxford University Press.

Worsley, P. (1964), 'The distribution of power in industrial society', *Sociological Review Monograph* no. 8.

Worsley, P. (ed.) (1977), *Introducing Sociology*, Harmondsworth: Penguin.

Wray, D. (1949), 'Marginal men of industry: the foremen', *American Journal of Sociology*, vol. 54.

Young, M. and Willmott, P. (1973), *The Symmetrical Family*, London: Routledge & Kegan Paul.

Zald, M. (ed.) (1970), *Power in Organisations*, Vanderbilt University Press.

Zald, M. (1971), *Occupations and Organisations in American Society*, Chicago: Markham.

Zeitlin, M. (1974), 'Corporate ownership and control', *American Journal of Sociology*, vol. 79.

Zimmerman, D. H. (1973), 'The practicalities of rule use' in Salaman and Thompson (eds) (1973).

Zwerman, W. (1970), *New Perspectives in Organisation Theory*, Westport, Conn.: Greenwood.

Index